American Political Women

AMERICAN POLITICAL WOMEN

Contemporary and Historical Profiles

Esther Stineman

1980
Libraries Unlimited, Inc. • Littleton, Colorado

Copyright © 1980 Esther Stineman
All Rights Reserved
Printed in the United States of America

No part of this publication may be reproduced, stored in a retrieval system, or transmitted, in any form or by any means, electronic, mechanical, photocopying, recording, or otherwise, without the prior written permission of the publisher.

LIBRARIES UNLIMITED, INC.
P.O. Box 263
Littleton, Colorado 80160

Library of Congress Cataloging in Publication Data

Stineman, Esther, 1947-
    American political women.

    Bibliography: p. 161
    Includes index.
    1. Women in politics--United States--Biography.
I. Title.
HQ1236.S74   320.973'092'2 [B]   80-24478
ISBN 0-87287-238-6

Libraries Unlimited books are bound with Type II nonwoven material that meets and exceeds National Association of State Textbook Administrators' Type II nonwoven material specifications Class A through E.

Preface

The publication of *American Political Women* is reassuring for two reasons. The relatively few women who have risen to national political power have been real stars, and they deserve recognition. Frances Perkins, for example, completely overshadows every other Secretary of Labor this country has ever had. Jeannette Rankin is the quintessential American pacifist, feisty and acerbic to the end. Bella Abzug is the activist's activist. Stineman's work covers these visible and vocal political women, as well as those less publicized women who have served in various government positions. Think of the talent that's out there waiting to be harnessed!

Secondly, although the number of women members of Congress has not changed much over the past few years, the composition *has* changed. We used to be all widows or accidents. (I am an accident. I was first allowed to run because the incumbent was thought to be unbeatable—he wasn't.) But more and more our hardy band is being made up of women who came up through the ranks: party work, local office, then Congress. *American Political Women* reflects the impact these women have had on government and society. The sharp jump in the number of women holding local offices bodes well for a quantum leap in the number of women in the House and the Senate. Hopefully, the next edition of *American Political Women* will be a multi-volume work.

Pat Schroeder
Congresswoman, Colorado

Acknowledgments

I thank the following people and institutions for providing books, papers, citations, letters, and other materials that have substantially helped to move this project forward: Frederick Aandahl, of the Office of the Historian, U.S. Department of State; State of Alabama, Department of Archives and History, Montgomery; Alaska Historical Library, Juneau; Arkansas History Commission, Little Rock; Nancy C. Benson of New Mexico and *El Palacio*, the *Quarterly Journal* of the Museum of New Mexico; Congresswoman Lindy Boggs, Louisiana; Rose Elizabeth Bird, Chief Justice, The Supreme Court of California; Congresswoman Beverly Byron, Maryland; California State Library, Sacramento; Phyllis L. Cleveland, Reference Branch, the U.S. Department of Agriculture, Science and Education Administration; Colorado Historical Society, Denver; Congresswomen's Caucus, Congress of the United States; Connecticut Historical Society, Hartford; Historical Society of Delaware, Wilmington; Lieutenant Governor Nancy Dick and her staff, especially Pat Schlatter; March Fong Eu, Secretary of State, California; Joyce Duncan Falk, Director, American Bibliographical Center; Frances Farenthold, President of Wells College; Congresswoman Millicent Fenwick, New Jersey, and her office; Congresswoman Geraldine Ferraro, New York; Elizabeth Frick and her User Services Staff, University of Colorado Library, Colorado Springs; Lieutenant Governor Evelyn Gandy, Mississippi; Department of Archives and History, Atlanta, GA; Barbara J. Good, Director of International Programs, U.S. Department of State; Governor Ella Grasso, Connecticut; Barbara Haber, Curator of Books at the Arthur and Elizabeth Schlesinger Library, Radcliffe College; Hawaiian Historical Society, Honolulu; Congresswoman Margaret Heckler, Massachusetts, and her staff; Congresswoman Marjorie Holt, Maryland; Illinois State Historical Library, Springfield; Indiana Division of Indiana State Library, Indianapolis; Interdepartmental Task Force on Women, Washington, DC; Iowa State Historical Department, Des Moines; Kansas State Historical Society, Topeka; Senator Nancy Kassebaum, Kansas; Division of Archives and Records Management for Kentucky, Frankfort; Lieutenant Governor Madeleine Kunin, Vermont; Jan Littlefield, of Libraries Unlimited; Catherine Loeb, Assistant to the Librarian-at-Large for Women's Studies, University of Wisconsin System; Paul J. Hardy, Secretary of State, Louisiana, Baton Rouge; Women's Archives, University of South Western Louisiana; the Staff of former Ambassador Clare Boothe Luce; Museum and Library of Maryland History, The Maryland Historical Society, Baltimore; Massachusetts Historical Society, Boston; Bentley Historical Library, The University of Michigan, Ann Arbor; Congresswoman Barbara Mikulski, Maryland; Minnesota Historical Society, St. Paul; Mississippi Department of Archives and History, Jackson; Missouri Historical Society, St. Louis; Nebraska State Historical Society, Lincoln; Nevada State Historical Society, Reno; New Jersey Reference Division, viii / Acknowledgments

Newark; New Jersey Historical Commission, Trenton; New Mexico State Records and Archives, Santa Fe; Museum of New Mexico, Santa Fe; New York State Library, Cultural Education Center, Albany; Newark Public Library, Lending and Reference Department, Newark; State of North Carolina, Department of Cultural Resources, Raleigh; State Historical Society of North Dakota, Bismarck; Ohio Historical Society, Ohio Historical Center, Columbus; Oregon Historical Society, Portland; Library of the University of Oregon in Eugene, especially Librarian Phillip Zorich; Pennsylvania Historical Society and Commission, Harrisburg; Governor Dixy Lee Ray, Washington State; Rhode Island Historical Society, Providence; Rutgers, The State University of New Jersey, Archibald Stevens Alexander Library, Special Collections Department, New Brunswick; Congresswoman Patricia Schroeder, Colorado, and her staff, especially Robert Lettin; Congresswoman Olympia Snowe, Maine; Congresswoman Gladys Noon Spellman, Maryland, and her staff; The Sophia Smith Collection, Women's History Archive, Smith College, Northhampton, MA; South Carolina Department of Archives and History, Columbia; Lieutenant Governor Nancy Stevenson, South Carolina, Columbia; Tennessee State Library and Archives, Nashville; University of Tennessee Library, Knoxville; Texas State Library, Austin; Duane Thomas of Penrose Public Library, Colorado Springs; Barbara F. Thomson, Federal Women's Program Manager, Office of EEO, Washington, DC; State of Utah, Division of State History, Salt Lake City; U.S. Office of the Treasurer; U.S. Department of State; Vermont Historical Society, Montpelier; Washington State Historical Society, Tacoma; Sarah Weddington, The White House; Anne Wexler, The White House; former Ambassador Jean Wilkowski; State of Wisconsin Legislative Reference Bureau, Madison; Wyoming State Archives and Historical Department, Cheyenne.

Special thanks must go to Patricia Lanigan Franco, researcher, who tracked many periodical references to political women, provided citations and bibliographic references that might otherwise have escaped my attention, and assisted with the indexing. Thanks to Elaine Schantz for typing the manuscript. Susan Holte, editor at Libraries Unlimited, meticulously copyedited the manuscript, and suggested many ways in which the original manuscript might be improved. This volume owes its existence to Professor Charles Hinkle of the University of Colorado, who believed in the legitimacy of the project from the outset, offered stimulating editorial comments throughout the writing and research process, and provided office space and other amenities to see the project through to completion. A project such as this one draws strength from many supportive professionals, but final responsibility for errors of fact and judgment lies solely with the author, who has interpreted the lives of these political women.

Table of Contents

Preface v
Acknowledgments vii
Introduction xi

Bella Abzug 1
Eugenie Moore Anderson 4
Anne Legendre Armstrong 7
Shirley Temple Black 9
Corinne C. (Lindy) Boggs 12
Frances Payne Bolton 15
Marilyn Lloyd Bouquard 18
Yvonne Braithwaite Burke 19
Jane Burke Byrne 22
Beverly Butcher Byron 25
Shirley Anita Chisholm 28
Cardiss Robertson Collins 31
Nancy Dick 33
Helen Gahagan Douglas 36
Frances Tarlton (Sissy) Farenthold 39
Dianne Feinstein 42
Millicent Hammond Fenwick 44
Geraldine A. Ferraro 47
Ella Grasso 50
Edith Starrett Green 53
Martha Wright Griffiths 55
Julia Butler Hansen 59
Patricia Roberts Harris 61
Margaret O'Shaughnessy Heckler 65
Carla Anderson Hills 68
Oveta Culp Hobby 71
Marjorie S. Holt 73
Elizabeth Holtzman 76
Shirley Mount Hufstedler 80
Muriel Buck Humphrey 82
Barbara Jordan 83
Florence Prag Kahn 86
Nancy Landon Kassebaum 88
Martha Keys 91
Coya Knutson 93
Juanita Kreps 95
Mary Anne Krupsak 98

Madeleine May Kunin ... 101
Clare Boothe Luce ... 102
Helen Stevenson Meyner ... 107
Barbara Ann Mikulski ... 109
Patsy Takemoto Mink ... 111
Maurine Brown Neuberger ... 114
Mary Rose Oakar ... 117
Frances Perkins ... 118
Esther Eggertsen Peterson ... 121
(Eliza) Jane Pratt ... 125
Jeannette Rankin ... 126
Dixy Lee Ray ... 129
Patricia Scott Schroeder ... 133
Margaret Chase Smith ... 137
Virginia Dodd Smith ... 141
Olympia Snowe ... 143
Gladys Noon Spellman ... 145
Nancy Stevenson ... 147
Leonor Kretzer Sullivan ... 148
Lurleen Burns Wallace ... 151
Sarah Ragle Weddington ... 154
Jessica (Judy) McCullough Weis ... 156
Anne Wexler ... 158

Bibliography
    Political Women: The Literature ... 161
    Major Reference Materials on Political Women ... 163
    Historical Treatments: American Politics and Suffrage ... 167
    Contemporary Women in Politics, Current Voting
        Studies, and Political Issues Relating to Women ... 170
    ERA, Contemporary Feminism, Social and Political Theory ... 179
    Political Science on Women: Critiques of the Literature ... 182
    Selected 1970s Dissertations ... 184
    General Indexes and Abstracting Services ... 185
    Resource List on Women in Politics ... 186
    Serial Publications ... 188

Appendix I—Women of the Congress 1917-1980 ... 191
Appendix II—Women Ambassadors of the United States
    Currently Serving (Spring 1980) ... 198
Appendix III—Women Chiefs of Mission (COM) 1933-1980 ... 199
Appendix IV—Women Currently Serving as Federal Judges ... 202
Appendix V—Women Currently Serving in Government in
    Key Departmental, Agency, and White House Positions
    (Spring 1980) ... 204

Index ... 221

Introduction

Nothing in politics is as certain as change itself, whether the political position be elective or appointive, in the Senate, or the House, in the Cabinet, the Diplomatic Corps, or the White House. During recent years in national, state, and local government, the more visible political participation of women in public office has brought about the publication of a number of biographical reference sources designed to track the dynamic scene of women's political accomplishments. Some have provided short portraits of past and present members of Congress (Chamberlin's *A Minority of Members*, 1973; Engelbarts' *Women in the United States Congress*, 1974; and Tolchin's *Women in Congress*, 1976), or of women who have contributed to foreign affairs in ministerial or ambassadorial capacities (Calkin's *Women in American Foreign Affairs*, 1977). Still others have been massive undertakings seeking to name political office holders at every level and to analyze the statistical trends that account for women's absence or presence in politics (*Women in Public Office*, Eagleton Institute of Rutgers University, 1976 and 1978). "Who's who" materials have always been available, rendering in skeletal outlines the careers of political women; but no single reference source on American political women has existed to date that traces the career patterns of past and present prominent participants in high-level politics, in their various capacities and roles.

The 60 portraits presented here, accompanied by individual bibliographies, are of congresswomen, ambassadors, special presidential assistants, governors, lieutenant governors, mayors, and sometimes a combination of these offices, filling a biographical gap in the literature of American political women. The sketches emphasize contemporary women serving in major positions during the late 1970s and early 1980s, taking up where previous reference sources have, of necessity, left off, and providing biographical and bibliographic information about many women previously unlocatable except through correspondence with them and their offices, combined with research at historical societies and archives. Particular attention is given here to legislative or other specific program accomplishments, views held by these women concerning the women's movement, and their individual career preparation and development. Appendix material lists the names of women not represented in the sketches who have served or are now serving in the policy-making areas of government.

Among the group of profiles in this volume are "firsts" of all descriptions: first woman to hold the rank of ambassador; first woman mayor of a major U.S. city; first congresswoman; first woman in the Cabinet; first woman elected governor; first woman to serve both in the Cabinet and as an ambassador; the first black woman in the House of Representatives; the first black woman to serve in the Cabinet; the first woman to have a baby while serving in Congress. Although the "firsts" are significant leaps forward and worthy of record, it is perhaps the less exceptional achievements of less exceptional women that will establish real progress for women in public life.

Twenty-one women in 1980 hold a miniscule share (about 3.5% across the board) of the highest ranking elective and appointed political positions in the land, out of a possible 600 or so high-ranking positions. Of these, 17 are congresswomen (16 in the House, 1 in the Senate); 2 are governors; 2 are secretaries in President Carter's Cabinet. This book outlines the careers of this contemporary elite of 21, and places them in the company of other past and present American women who have served as ambassadors, lieutenant governors, presidential assistants, and mayors of major American cities. Another significant area, presidentially appointed federal judges, shows 28 women, or around 6% of all U.S. district court and U.S. circuit court judges. These women are identified in the appendix section, along with other women serving in government, politics, and the foreign service, though individual career profiles of women in the federal judiciary do not appear here.

Each woman chosen for inclusion helps to define the pattern of women who have served since 1917 in the American political context. The diversity among these women—of backgrounds, political contributions, and political savvy—serves at once to suggest their similarities and their differences, and to forecast political possibilities for women as we move into the 1980s. Certainly the American political woman has been with us since the eighteenth century, working politically, as Anne Hutchinson and Abigail Adams did, within the family circle. But she has emerged a political entity in partisan politics only in the twentieth century with Jeannette Rankin and the fallout from suffrage. Pacifist Rankin began a tradition of congressional service that has limped slowly along through mid-century until gaining momentum in the early 1970s, along with women's greater awareness of self and society and their increasingly public responsibilities. Their numbers, though certainly not large in political office, appear to be growing, especially at the local levels.

The congressional women selected for inclusion here are not necessarily the brightest nor the best women who have served. Quite simply they represent the dissimilar as well as the typical paths women have taken to get to Congress. Jessica Weis, Republican clubwoman, is here, as is Clare Boothe Luce, the prototype of the "extraordinary" woman whose achievements leaped across the worlds of theatre, media, art, fashion, and politics. Because women have so often come to politics through the death of a spouse, it seemed important to choose a cross-section of such women, euphemistically termed "the widows' caucus." Maurine Neuberger, a former senator from Oregon, is a woman who successfully assumed her husband's seat but blanched when it came to the difficulty of financing the inevitable reelection campaign (now estimated to cost a minimum of $1 million for the Senate). Former senator Muriel Humphrey discharged her widow's obligation with no thought to continuing on, though she had been in the public eye most of her adult life as Hubert Humphrey's wife. In contrast, perennial winner Margaret Chase Smith found a winning formula so appropriate for her particular constituency that only advanced age could defeat her. While the career of 1950s San Francisco congresswoman Florence Prag Kahn illustrates the importance of speaking out, the career of feminist congresswoman Bella Abzug hints at the advisability of occasionally adopting a more subdued political voice. Patsy Mink and Yvonne Braithwaite Burke's promising congressional careers, nipped in the bud by their personal decisions to move on to more ambitious posts, serve as terse reminders that in some cases women may have more to lose when they dare to take risks. In contrast, former representative Barbara Jordan's enigmatic service in and retirement from Congress chronicles a rapid rise to power and notoriety, terminated by personal preference for a less hectic life.

Marriage appears to have affected the careers of political women in various, sometimes drastic, ways; a widow, Frances Bolton enjoyed a long and legendary legislative career, while Coya Knutson, plagued by scandal brought on by her husband's slanderous charges, prematurely exited from the political scene. Representative Martha Griffiths, the woman who birthed and nurtured the Equal Rights Amendment before she retired, pioneered a new era of women's political history, one of women's coalitions and strategy sessions; Congresswoman Julia Butler Hansen, on the other hand, contented herself with intimidating even her male colleagues with the power of her seniority, even as she carefully reminded them that being a woman in Congress carried no special privilege, penalty, or obligations. Leonor Sullivan made the most of her political arabesque; she started as an administrative aide to a congressman, and eventually became a congresswoman herself; Eliza Jane Pratt tried the same maneuver, but fell flat — not because she did not know the dance and the timing, but because she failed to project an image that political leaders in her district would buy. Martha Keys' congressional career demonstrates how volatile the combination of a public life and a public romance can be in the political arena, even for the most competent and committed woman.

As interesting and various as the careers of former congresswomen appear to be retrospectively, they pale next to those of the five women chosen in this century to assume Cabinet posts: Perkins, Hobby, Hills, Kreps, and Hufstedler's appointments to the Cabinet profile the power these women have capably wielded as well as their political vulnerability due to their unique visibility in government. Less vulnerable because less visible, the careers of assistants to the president — Weddington, Wexler, and Peterson, for example — project a muted portrait of political clout, though their decisions and advice often affect the underseam of power where national policy is shaped and made ready for public consumption.

Women who have taken on political appointments as ambassadors and wear the mantle of presidential favoritism in a foreign land operate far away from the nexus of presidential power, and usually return after their service ends to influential positions in corporate structures rather than to political lives. Shirley Temple Black, Anne Armstrong, and Eugenie Anderson are examples of this breed of political women. The career of Patricia Harris, who moved laterally and longitudinally from diplomacy to the highest levels of domestic policy-setting defies this traditional pattern of a diplomatic career. Indeed, her brilliance and her blackness have moved her outside the familiar orbits of almost all contemporary political women.

The office of lieutenant governor, so typically considered secondary to the main event — the governor himself — is becoming more accessible to American women who pay their dues in state legislatures, though woe to the woman who bucks the first in command: witness former lieutenant governor of New York, Mary Anne Krupsak. Nancy Dick of Colorado, Nancy Stevenson of South Carolina, and Madeleine Kunin of Vermont — contemporary lieutenant governors all — provide interesting studies of married, relatively nonpolitical women who have achieved the highest state office ever held by a woman in their respective states. Their management styles in the lieutenant's office generally lean toward a consumer approach to government, a departure from the traditional male interpretation of the lieutenant's role.

Deceased governor Lurleen Wallace stands alone in the history of American political women, a unique profile of political pathos. Some have described her role as that of a puppet in her husband's quest for political power, rather than a political women in her own right. More positive and stable gubernatorial successes mark the careers of current female governors Ray of Washington State and Grasso of Connecticut.

Only in the 1970s have women found major municipalities amenable to their leadership. Mayor Dianne Feinstein came to power in San Francisco through the violent death of a controversial mayor, and Mayor Jane Byrne took over Chicago in the wake of political unheaval after the notorious Mayor Daley was no longer alive to pick his successor.

The career of one woman in this biographical and bibliographic collection—that of Sissy Farenthold, the first woman U.S. vice presidential nominee to be taken seriously—falls outside the scope of women who have served or are currently serving in the highest echelons of government. Farenthold's career, a patchwork of public positions that have taken her from Texas to New York, demonstrates perhaps most impressively of all, the power for change that becomes possible when an effective woman moves from the political sphere to academe with the aim of transforming institutions into training grounds for future political women.

Although few women have held high-level public office, even into the 1980s, information about women office holders and women's political participation is of increasing interest to political scientists, to students, and to those women wishing to seek office themselves who look to the careers of past and present women in politics as their blueprints. The biographical and bibliographic materials of *American Political Women*, taken at one level, provide ready factual reference information on a number of selected women while establishing the distinct personalities that exist behind the political names. Additional reference material on political women, in their varied high-level government roles, appears here in the form of a bibliography and several appendixes, intended as pathfinders to the current state-of-the-art on American women in politics.

The information found within these pages was compiled by use of standard bibliographical sources, computer searches, archives and manuscript collections, congressional reports, newspapers, press files, and newsletters, speeches, and writings prepared by the individuals included in this work. Much of the data was supplied or verified by women's organizations, the Congresswomen's Caucus, or staff members of women office holders. Many of the women currently serving were in correspondence with the author during the preparation of the sketches; others were interviewed. The information appearing in *American Political Women* is current as of June 1980.

Bella Abzug
July 24, 1920-

B. New York City; D. Emmanuel and Esther Savitsky; M. Martin Abzug, 1944; Served in U.S. House of Representatives as Democrat—New York, January 21, 1971 to January 3, 1977, 92nd through 94th Congress.

In her autobiography, *Bella! Ms. Abzug Goes to Washington* (1972), Abzug introduces herself: "I've been described as a tough and noisy woman, a prizefighter, a man-hater, you name it. They call me Battling Bella, Mother Courage, and a Jewish mother with more complaints than Portnoy. There are those who say I'm impatient, impetuous, uppity, rude, profane, brash and overbearing. Whether I'm any of those things, or all of them, you can decide for yourself. But whatever I am—and this ought to be made very clear at the outset—I am a very serious woman." She might have added "and a woman whose words and actions receive considerable attention wherever I go." Bella Abzug's flamboyant style, of dress and rhetoric, has forced people to notice (some say the effect has been to drown out) the issues she has championed from the beginning of her public life—issues involving the poor, minorities, and women.

After her graduation from Columbia Law School in 1947 where she was an editor of the *Columbia Law Review*, Abzug represented labor interests in New York City. Her other major legal passion in this early period was civil rights litigation. During the McCarthy purges of the 1950s she defended the civil rights of individuals indicted for leftist activities. Her work on behalf of minorities had considerable influence upon the Civil Rights Act of 1954 and the Voting Rights Act of 1965, and her social activism in the 1950s metamorphosed into anti-war activism in the sixties, when she became involved in the founding of Women Strike for Peace. During the sixties there was no issue embraced by the New Left—disarmament, the nuclear test ban, the Vietnam War—in which Abzug was not center-stage, demonstrating, forming coalitions, actively working through the system in visible positions of power. She was well known to New York Democrats as a prime mover in the "Dump Johnson" camp, and as president of the Democratic Alternative she supported Eugene McCarthy in his 1968 campaign. Lindsay welcomed her aboard his mayoral campaign in 1969, and when he won she had a place on the mayor's advisory committee.

From there Abzug made the logical leap to national politics by announcing her candidacy for the congressional seat from the ethnically and economically complex 19th Congressional District. In doing so, she asked the constituents of the district (Chinatown, the lower east side, the upper west side, Little Italy, and Greenwich Village) to choose between her and the low-profile incumbent, Leonard Farbskin, who had quietly controlled this seat for 14 years. Her campaign slogan read "This woman belongs in the House," and her campaign pledges covered the liberal terrain—from ending the Vietnam War to equal rights for women. Handily winning the primary, she moved into the showdown with her Republican opponent, broadcaster Barry Farber, with a battalion of liberal supporters and women's groups behind her. The issues were the most burning of the decade, and New Yorkers warmed to the colorful campaign. Abzug racked up 47,000 votes to Farber's 38,000, a respectable send-off to Washington, which awaited excitedly this remarkable woman with her extraordinary hats and her decisively liberal agenda.

The House had never seen a first day like Abzug's. On day one she proposed the withdrawal of all troops from Southeast Asia by July 4, 1971. While hundreds of women from Women Strike for Peace stood on the steps of the Capitol cheering "Give 'em hell, Bella," Congresswoman Shirley Chisholm administered a special oath of office. On the same day, Abzug made an abortive attempt to be placed on the powerful House Armed Services Committee, an unprecedented request by a newcomer to the House.

During the 91st Congress, Congresswoman Abzug concentrated on the war issue, though even House doves often did not support her direct methods for settling the conflict; consequently, her resolution for withdrawal of U.S. troops from Vietnam by summer 1971 failed. From that tack, she moved to a call for the abolition of the draft and the initiation of informal hearings on United States war crimes in Vietnam. During the 92nd Congress, Abzug began to unveil a national priority list on behalf of women, one which worked towards meeting the needs of poor, unemployed, underemployed, minority, and widowed women. She testified on behalf of the Equal Rights Amendment in the House and spoke throughout the country for the proposed constitutional amendment which passed the House in 1971.

Abzug wrote the public law which funded the National Women's Conference in Houston in 1977, and, not surprisingly, President Carter appointed her presiding officer of the National Commission on the Observance of International Women's Year in 1977. The three bills she introduced to outlaw discrimination against women in financial and credit transactions were enacted into law. Child-care centers, health care programs for mothers and children, displaced homemaker job training and counseling, shelters for battered women, affirmative action implementation, equitable Social Security benefits, Medicaid funding for abortions—these were the feminist issues Abzug's legislation addressed in Congress and for which she lobbied during her brief and stormy stint as President Carter's appointee to the co-chair of his National Advisory Council on Women (1978-1979). When Abzug protested administration decisions to cut spending on behalf of women's needs in favor of increased defense and military budgets, Carter fired her for "lack of good cooperation."

Although many identify Abzug solely with legislation on behalf of women, her record during her three terms in the House speaks well of her effectiveness in writing and passing legislation in other areas for the benefit of her urban New York City constituency: urban transportation, harbor clean-up, assistance for the elderly and the handicapped, and federal aid to New York City in recognition of its extraordinary expenses in housing the United Nations. She won national support for Soviet Jewry by using the congressional forum to publicize the human rights violations suffered by this group.

Although Abzug's political star has hardly burned out, her career miscarried in 1976 when she passed up a sure fourth term in the House in favor of running for the Senate; Daniel Patrick Moynihan inched past her in that race.

She ran unsuccessfully for mayor of New York City in 1977, and lost out in a return bid to the House in a 1978 special election. If Abzug's style has been abrasive to some, her achievements for women and for New York City have been notable. In national polls she has consistently surfaced as one of "the most influential" public figures, even though her message is often lost in the hullabaloo of her personality.

Selected Speeches and Writings

In *Woman: An Issue*, Little, Brown (1972), orig. "Women and Politics: The Struggle for Representation," *Massachusetts Review*, Vol. 13, Nos. 1/2; also *Massachusetts Review*, Vol. 15 (Winter 1971-Spring 1972); *Bella! Ms. Abzug Goes to Washington* (1972); "Bella's Eye View of Her Party's Future," *Ms.*, April 1974; "Credit Where It's Overdue," *Civil Liberties Review*, Vol. 1, No. 3 (1974); "U.S. National Women's Agenda," *Ms.*, December 1975.

A more complete listing of Abzug's public speeches may be found in B. Manning, *Index to American Women Speakers* (1980), p. 27.

Bibliography

"Bella's Last Chance," *Economist*, December 31, 1977.

Bennetts, L. "Bella Abzug: Picking Up the Pieces," *New York Times Biography Service*, December 1978.

Burstein, P. "Politics, Like Travel, Was Broadening for Bella Abzug," *People*, November 13, 1978.

Capell, F. A. "The Left: Collectivists in the Congress," *American Opinion*, July 1974.

In Chamberlin, Hope. *A Minority of Members* (1973).

Faber, Doris. *Bella Abzug* (1976).

Hiss, T. "Dilemma in the New 20th Congressional District," *New York Times Magazine*, June 18, 1972.

Keerdoja, E., et al. "Battling Bella Bounces Back," *Newsweek*, June 18, 1979.

Kelber, Mim. "What Bella Knew," *Ms.*, April 1979.

Mano, D. K. "Abzug," *National Review*, March 14, 1975.

Matthews, T., et al. "Bye-bye Bella," *Newsweek*, January 22, 1979.

Nies, Judith. "The Abzug Campaign: A Lesson in Politics," *Ms.*, February 1973.

O'Hara, J. "People," *Macleans*, November 20, 1978.

Osborne, J. "Booting Bella," *New Republic*, January 27, 1979.

Storck, D. "Bella's Won Respect from Congressmen," *Biography News*, January 1975.

Tripp, Maggie, ed. *Woman in the Year 2000* (essay) (1974).

Eugenie Moore Anderson
May 26, 1909-

B. Adair, Iowa; D. Ezekiel Arrowsmith and Flora Belle McMillen Moore; M. John Anderson, 1930; Served as U.S. Ambassador to Denmark, December 22, 1949 to January 19, 1953; Served as U.S. Ambassador to Bulgaria, August 3, 1962 to December 6, 1964.

Political women appointed to ambassadorial posts generally stay at their jobs for a comparatively short period of time, in contrast to women who are career diplomats, not subject to the changing tides of partisan politics and new presidential administrations. Eugenie Moore Anderson, who came of political age under the tutelage of such Minnesota political giants as Hubert Humphrey and Orville Freeman, must be classified as a political woman first and foremost. Truman named her ambassador to Denmark, and Kennedy chose her for the ambassadorial post in Bulgaria, due to her work as a national Democratic committeewoman and endorsements from her Minnesota friends in high places.

Anderson's political story, however, is atypical. She and her husband John, a musician and an artist, respectively, with the independent resources to pursue these interests, were not at all committed to local or national politics during their twenties. Instead, they pursued the quiet life, each following their artistic instincts and studies, enjoying a close family life, and spending considerable time on their farm, High Tower, in Minnesota. Eugenie Anderson was a student at Juilliard from 1930 to 1932. Though Minnesota is noted for its political activism and interesting squabbles within political parties, Eugenie knew little about this aspect of her state until she became politically involved in the early 1940s. It was in the late 1930s, however, when she took a tentative first step and joined the bipartisan National League of Women Voters, sensing that the international political climate of the times made it morally imperative for people to be informed citizens. Nazism and communism were repugnant to her even from her limited knowledge gleaned from reading and traveling. In 1944, when she decided to become involved in partisan politics, she learned about communism firsthand with the formation of the Democratic-Farmer-Labor party (DFL) in Minnesota, whose founding leader was Hubert Horatio Humphrey, a progressive professor from Macalester College in St. Paul and soon to be mayor of Minneapolis.

Anderson ran the campaign of a DFL candidate from her own first Congressional District, and though her man lost, Anderson's enthusiasm for politics at the grass roots level had been kindled. She joined Humphrey and his liberal cadre, including Orville Freeman and Eugene McCarthy, to architect the "new politics" of the Democratic-Farmer-Labor party, which was to bring so many of her colleagues to positions of national prominence. A rift between the Humphrey-led contingent of the DFL and the dissident, Communist element took on the proportions of warfare, though Humphrey and his band fought the Communist factions from within and emerged as the leaders of the DFL, strongly aligned to the Roosevelt New Deal administration. Eugenie

Anderson was in on the strategy sessions of the anti-Communist wing of the DFL and stomped the state to drum up support and delegates for the Truman candidacy in 1948. Anderson, Humphrey, Freeman, and McCarthy, all members of the Americans for Democratic Action, successfully overthrew their opponents, captured the DFL slate for state offices, and engineered Truman's victory in Minnesota over Communist DFL candidate, Henry Wallace. Anderson emerged as a DFL national committeewoman.

During this trying period of hot and heavy local political struggles, John Anderson appears to have been content to take care of the farm and the two small children while Eugenie forged the political alliances that ultimately resulted in her being asked by Truman and Secretary of State Dean Acheson to take on the United States ambassadorship in Denmark. Her appointment was controversial in that no American woman had ever held the rank of ambassador. The nearest a woman had come to an ambassadorial appointment was as head of a mission. Anderson's natural charm and poise, for which she became famous during her ambassadorship, helped her during the interviewing process at the Department of State and at the White House. Shortly after the appointment was made public, she stated: "Of course, I understand ... that when President Truman nominated me as our first woman ambassador, he did so as a symbol of his own belief in the abilities of women in public life. I know that he intended my appointment to signify to all women that he recognizes our growing assumption of mature responsible citizenship, our work for the public good, not simply as women and mothers, but as citizens and as people" (*National Bulletin*, November 21, 1949).

On October 20, 1949, her appointment was made official, and just before Christmas in that same year with her husband and children accompanying her to Denmark, she presented her diplomatic credentials. What followed was a love affair between Denmark and the new American ambassador, due principally to her initiative in learning the language. After six months on the job she was able to deliver a speech in Danish, and to meet and greet the Danes in their own language during the course of her diplomatic duties. Though much has been made of the extensive goodwill appearances and gestures extended by Ambassador Anderson, which were undoubtedly responsible for her unusual popularity in Denmark, she was at the time in the eye of an international tempest due to Denmark's strategic location adjacent to the Soviet Union. Her diplomacy assisted in bringing about the Treaty of Friendship, Commerce and Navigation in 1951, which provided that the island of Greenland be included in the NATO defense circumference, thus making it possible to preserve and maintain the American World War II bases established in Greenland. In signing the treaty with Denmark, Eugenie Anderson became the first woman representing the United States to sign such a pact. The treaty was a historic one for the Danes, too, for theirs was a traditionally neutral country before the war, now in an increasingly sensitive position due to cold war tensions. In January of 1953, with the advent of the Eisenhower administration, the Andersons regretfully left Denmark and returned to their Red Wing, Minnesota home, fluent in Danish and skilled in riding bicycles.

By now Eugenie Anderson, Minnesota's most prominent woman, had been bitten by the political and diplomatic bug, and decided in 1958 to run for a Senate seat from Minnesota. But competition was fierce in her old stomping grounds, and she failed to garner the support she needed to win the primary race against Eugene McCarthy, generally felt to be a charismatic political figure on his way to national fame. It was 1960 before she resumed public life, this time as President Kennedy's choice for ambassador to Bulgaria, one of the more difficult diplomatic assignments to the eastern bloc nations. Her anti-Communist sentiments still smoldering from her brush with the party in her DFL days in Minnesota politics, she accepted the appointment and set out for the stern ideological climate of the Iron Curtain. During the late fifties she had been a member of the Zellerbach Commission, which gave her an excellent grounding in the problems facing Iron Curtain refugees. But even with diplomatic experience behind her, no assignment could have differed more radically from the pleasant years she and her family remembered from Denmark than the difficult Bulgarian assignment of censorship and surveillance.

She learned the language, and sought diplomatic opportunities to speak out, though the public exposure was much less frequent than in her Denmark days. Her most outstanding diplomatic achievement in Bulgaria, the talks to settle World War II claims and other matters which had been pending unresolved during the cold war of the 1950s, resulted in improved relations between the United States and Bulgaria. However, matters were hardly pacific, and in 1964, after several Bulgarian demonstrations at the U.S. Embassy to protest CIA espionage activities, Ambassador Anderson wrote to President Johnson asking that her resignation be accepted. She returned to the States in early December of 1964.

Anderson's diplomatic career was not over, however. In the following years she took on several assignments with the rank of ambassador in the United Nations and in the State Department: U.S. representative to the United Nations General Assembly (1965-1967); the Trusteeship Council in the United Nations (1965-1968); and the Economic Commission for Europe (1966). Perhaps this phase of her work was most distinguished in the area of African diplomacy. She toured Africa in 1966, vocally representing the United States on the racial question in Angola, Rhodesia, and Mozambique; and she contributed substantially to the resolutions prepared for the General Assembly stating a forceful American position on the South African question—namely, that South Africa should no longer control Southwest Africa.

Ambassador Eugenie Anderson's career has been one of ideological paradoxes. Though she came to politics through the ultra-liberal Democratic-Farmer-Labor party, her stance on communism suggests a distinctly conservative position. She vigorously supported the Vietnam War, subscribing to the domino theory in Southeast Asia. When she resigned from the United Nations in 1968, she took a post in the Department of State as a special assistant to the secretary and retained her rank as ambassador. In her later years she retired to Red Wing, Minnesota, but maintained a lively interest in politics and in fine arts, serving as a trustee of the Minneapolis Society of Fine Arts since 1976.

Selected Speeches and Writings

"Basic Decision for the U.S.: Trade or Aid," *U.S. Department of State Bulletin*, October 20, 1952; "Evaluation of European Defense Efforts" (excerpts), *U.S. Department of State Bulletin*, November 26, 1951; "How Our Foreign Policy Is Working," *Vital Speeches*, December 15, 1951; "In the Front Line of Freedom," *U.S. Department of State Bulletin*, October 29, 1951; "Opening Statement at Meeting of Commission on Prisoners of War," September 15, 1952; "Security Efforts of Free World Aided by Danish Contributions," *U.S. Department of State Bulletin*, October 22, 1951.

Papers of Eugenie Moore Anderson related to her political activism in the DFL, her primary campaign for the U.S. Senate in 1958, and her diplomatic career are held by the Minnesota Historical Society, Archive and Manuscripts Division. Miscellaneous papers can be found in the Iowa Women in Politics Collection held by the State Library Commission of Iowa.

Bibliography

In Lamson, Peggy. *Few Are Chosen* (1968).

Lesiser, E. "Denmark's American Sweetheart," *Saturday Evening Post*, May 5, 1951.

In Stuhler, Barbara, and Gretchen Kreuter. *Women of Minnesota* (1977).

"U.S. Ambassadors," *Time*, December 31, 1951.

Anne Legendre Armstrong
December 27, 1927-

B. New Orleans, Louisiana; D. Darmant and Olive Martindale Legendre; M. Tobin Armstrong, 1950; Served as U.S. Ambassador to Great Britain and Northern Ireland, January 29, 1976 to March 3, 1977; Counselor to the President, 1973-1974.

Though combining a family and a political career is becoming less noteworthy a feat, it is still remarkable to trace the outstanding career of any woman who is, at the same time, the mother of five children. Anne Armstrong is such a woman, who through the good graces of a fine education (Vassar, 1949) and money (Texas-style)—not to mention a great deal of ambition and stamina—has become well known in Republican politics, a counselor to the president under Nixon, and Ford's choice for ambassador to England, thus becoming the first woman to serve as an ambassador to a major Western power since Clare Boothe Luce, and the first female ambassador to Great Britain from the United States. She holds directorships in such companies as Braniff International, General Motors, General Foods, and First City Bancorp of Texas. Explaining her visibility on major boards in 1980, she stated, "My tour as ambassador and my continuing interest in foreign affairs have given me first-hand experience of the increasing world interdependence that offers multinational corporations some of their biggest problems and brightest opportunities" (*Harvard Business Review*, March-April 1980, p. 12).

Anne Armstrong has never held an elective office higher than that of a local schoolboard member, though her work on behalf of the Republican party and Republican candidates has often taken on the feverish pitch of running her own political campaign. Everything Anne Armstrong has ever done in the public or private sphere reveals a personality of great energy and commitment: Phi Beta Kappa at Vassar, five children and her participation in all aspects of the Armstrong Ranch, the first woman co-chair of the Republican National Convention in 1972 after serving as a national committeewoman from 1968 on. Reportedly, she rides well and shoots accurately, skills she picked up after her marriage to Texas rancher Tobin Armstrong in 1950, a man who apparently encouraged her interest in ranching, in politics, and in public life. In fact, it was the riding and shooting, accompanied by the political expertise, that most intrigued the English when she arrived at the Court of St. James to present her credentials on St. Patrick's Day, 1976.

Previous to Armstrong's appointment as ambassador, she had worked under President Nixon as a counselor to the president, the first woman to hold such a position. During her time under Nixon, from 1973 to 1974, she established a reputation as a woman fiercely dedicated to women's equal rights under the law, and she organized the first Office of the Women's Program in the White House. Through her efforts during the Nixon administration more than 100 capable women were brought into the highest levels of government, and as the president's specialist in women-related issues she represented the United States at both the World Food Conference in Rome (1974) and the Conference for International Women's Year in Mexico City (1975). Throughout her entire involvement with party politics she has encouraged greater participation of women by working toward their inclusion at the decision-making and delegate levels.

This is not to say that Anne Armstrong supports all aspects of the women's liberation agenda. Radical legislation such as abortion reform did not gain her sympathies. One could say, however, that during her career she has been close to the pulse of the country's leaders in business and government, and has been in an excellent position, therefore, to effect changes for women. Her remarks in an interview about the directorships she assumed after leaving government speak equally well to her philosophy of being a woman in a visible political position. "Women directors have unique opportunities to assist other women both to enter and rise in the corporate world. By maintaining contact with women managers and employees in the corporations they serve, women directors can constantly watch for women who have the capacity to be directors or to hold management positions."

In many ways Anne Armstrong has demonstrated a high degree of courage during her public career. When her appointments to major positions have been announced, controversies have ensued. Within the GOP it was speculated that Nixon had appointed Armstrong to co-chair the Republican National Convention, and later to act as his presidential counselor, merely to placate certain special interests in the GOP. She combatted such criticism when she was counselor to the president by undertaking an array of difficult assignments, dispelling any notion that she lacked the preparation or competence for policy making. Among other duties she became Nixon's specialist on Hispanic Americans, her fluent Spanish lending credibility to her role. She took on active membership roles in the Organization of Government for the Conduct of Foreign Policy, the Council on Wage and Price Stability, and the Domestic Council, and chaired the Federal Property Council, which supervised the administration of federal real estate.

Later, when Ford appointed Armstrong to the ambassadorship to Britain, her nomination was hooted by some as inappropriate and an example of political favoritism. Ignoring these critics, she accepted the appointment and set off for England with her husband—to the delight of the English, who found her Texas background and her attractiveness "romantic." When she was sworn in as ambassador at a White House ceremony, with her family and the Fords in attendance, she invoked Abigail Adams, who had accompanied her husband, the first ambassador to the Court of St. James, to England in the eighteenth century. "Abigail Adams would have been just as excited as Betty Ford and I," she said, referring to her own historic diplomatic mission. Even though the Ford administration terminated Armstrong's diplomatic assignment in Britain, she has retained an active interest in international affairs, lecturing on diplomacy and serving on the board of governors of the Atlantic Institute for International Affairs.

Selected Speeches and Writings

"America's Bicentennial," *Vital Speeches*, March 15, 1974 (given when Armstrong was a presidential counselor and the White House bicentennial coordinator).

Bibliography

In Calkin, Homer L. *Women in the Department of State: Their Role in American Foreign Affairs.* Washington, DC: Department of State #8951, 1978.

Carpenter, L. "Six Women Who Could Be President," *Redbook*, November 1975.

Danfield, B. "She's the President's Adviser," *Biography News*, 1974.

Kinkaid, S. "Says Women Have Priority," *Biography News*, April 1974.

"Progress in the Role of Women Is Steady and It Is Sure," *U.S. News and World Report*, February 4, 1980.

Salmans, S., and J. Witmore. "Auntie Sam," *Newsweek*, January 19, 1976.

In Schwartz, Felice N. " 'Invisible' Resource: Women for Boards," *Harvard Business Review*, March/April 1980.

"Sugar and Steel," *Time*, January 19, 1976.

"Surprise Appointments for Two Women," *U.S. News and World Report*, January 19, 1976.

"Texas Goes to London," *U.S. News and World Report*, January 19, 1976.

Shirley Temple Black
April 23, 1928-

B. Santa Monica, California; D. George Francis and Gertrude Creiger Temple; M. Charles Alden Black, 1950; Served as U.S. Delegate to the United Nations, 1969-1972; U.S. Ambassador to Ghana, December 6, 1974 to July 1976; Chief of Protocol U.S. Department of State, 1976.

The childhood stardom of singer and dancer Shirley Temple is an American legend. During the Depression she lightened the lives of moviegoers who flocked to theatres to see "America's Little Sweetheart" in such films as

Stand Up and Cheer, *Baby, Take a Bow*, and *Bright Eyes*. Reigning as the princess of the box office, her name became a household word during the 1930s when she starred in movies like *Rebecca of Sunnybrook Farm, Wee Willie Winkie, The Little Colonel, Curly Top,* and the *Littlest Rebel.* Always the image of cheeriness and unspoiled innocence, her photograph appeared everywhere, and the story of the child star's daily routine was served up in article after article to a public who never tired of reading about her life on the set, her $10,000-a-week salary, and her tutored education in the studio dressing room, which doubled as her playhouse. Her formal education concluded when she graduated from Los Angeles' Westlake School for Girls in 1945, the same year that she married for the first time, and published her autobiography, *My Young Life.* The late forties appear to have been difficult years for Shirley Temple, with several of her films failing commercially and her first marriage over by 1949. She married again in 1950, this time to Charles A. Black, prominent in San Francisco business and social circles. Through this marriage she entered the more ordered, less ephemeral world of civic affairs and public service.

During the Korean War the Blacks moved to the Washington area, where Charles Black served at the Pentagon, a period that marked the beginning of Shirley Temple Black's involvement with politics and international affairs. When the Blacks returned to California in the late fifties, Shirley turned again to her professional career, this time starring in such staid television programs as "Shirley Temple's Storybook." She appears to have found a comfortable niche in California civic circles, chairing cultural projects such as the San Francisco International Film Festival, while rearing her three children.

Perhaps it was the image Black projected of the child star making a successful adjustment to the "real world" of marriage and motherhood, fairy princess but shrewd businesswoman, too, that appealed to California Republicans. Her life as a woman became the model of conscientious matron, as her screen life had been the quintessence of cherubic girlhood. She crusaded against the evils of pornography in films, and championed volunteer efforts to combat the crippling disease of multiple sclerosis, founding the International Federation of Multiple Sclerosis Societies. By 1967 her momentum in California Republican party activities was such that she confidently announced her candidacy for Congress. She had a time shaking off the many jokes about "The Good Ship Lollipop" and other jibes alluding to her film past, but Black managed to do so with wit and humor, maybe because she had only to look around her to see that the movies had not hurt the political chances of former costars residing in California, Senator George Murphy and Governor Ronald Reagan. Although she made *pro forma* disclaimers that she was not campaigning on her name, California voters were not likely to forget who Shirley Temple Black was. Still, she lost to liberal Republican Paul McCloskey in 1967, even though she racked up an impressive number of votes. Her campaign centered around her charge of President Johnson's ineptness as a president and called for a hawkish solution to Vietnam. Her platform message prescribed more law and order, fewer taxes, and crackdowns on drug abuse and welfare.

Black cheerfully conceded the election to McCloskey, promising to return to public service at a later date as an elected official. For the next two years she channelled her energies into international work on behalf of multiple sclerosis and into fundraising for the Republican party, in particular for Richard Nixon. Though the Nixon appointment of Shirley Temple Black to the United Nations raised eyebrows among Americans who did not know the international side of her career (for many, she lived on in the image of storybook princess or tap-dancing child star), she was welcomed by her colleagues at the 24th Session of the General Assembly in the fall of 1969. As a member of the Social, Humanitarian, and Cultural Committee, Black addressed problems of international cooperation to achieve humanitarian goals—programs for the aged, assistance to refugees, and solutions for the world's ecological problems. Particularly dedicated to working for youth, she spoke extensively around the United States in the late sixties endorsing the vote for 18-year-olds.

Named ambassador to Ghana in December 1974, Shirley Temple Black enjoyed enormous popularity in Africa. After her ambassadorship, she spoke out sharply against U.S. policy abroad, especially on America's altered relations with China. "U.S. diplomatic recognition of China today is ill-timed," she stated in a San Francisco speech in 1975. "It sets the stage for miscalculations by the Soviet Union, produces only marginal incremental values for the U.S., and leaves unanswered ... the old hostilities of the Korean Peninsula." Her speeches in recent years have emphasized the need for American nationalism: "No country has washed more dirty laundry in public than we have."

In 1976, Black rose to the position of the first American woman ever named to the State Department post of chief of protocol.

Selected Speeches and Writings

My Young Life (1945); "Don't Sit Home and Be Afraid," *McCall's*, February 1973; "Will Young People Ever Have Heroes Again?," *Seventeen*, September 1977; Speech Commonwealth Club, San Francisco (May 13, 1977).

A more complete listing of Black's public speeches may be found in B. Manning, *Index to American Women Speakers* (1980), p. 57.

Honors

Special Oscar from Academy of Motion Picture Arts and Sciences, "Outstanding Personality of 1934"; Kiwanis International Award (1967); Cross of Malta (1968); numerous honors by civic groups, states, and colleges, including Fellow of College of Notre Dame (1972).

Bibliography

Black, L. S. "Shirley Temple Black in Africa," *Ladies Home Journal*, October 1975.

In Calkin, Homer. *Women in American Foreign Affairs*. U.S. Department of State, 1977.

Flagler, J. M. "Shirley Temple at the U.N.," *Look*, December 16, 1969.

Graustark, B. "Newsmakers," *Newsweek*, April 24, 1978.

Hess, J. "Shirley Temple Black: Gentle Crusader," *National Wildlife*, January 1974.

McEvoy, J. P. "Little Miss Miracle," *Saturday Evening Post*, July 1978.

McEvoy, J. P. "Shirley Temple Black," *Saturday Evening Post*, July 1977.

Massaquoi, H. J. "Ghana's Love Affair with Shirley Temple Black," *Ebony*, March 1976.

Minott, Rodney G. *Sinking of the Lollipop: Shirley Temple vs. Pete McCloskey* (1968).

"Mrs. Black for Congress," *Time*, September 8, 1967.

In Shipman, David. *Great Movie Stars* (1970).

"Sometimes I Feel Like the Oldest Living American," *New York Times Biographical Service*, December 1976.

"Sworn In," *Newsweek*, August 2, 1976.

Williams, L. "Little Miss Candidate," *Look*, November 14, 1967.

Windler, Robert. *Films of Shirley Temple* (1978).

Corinne C. (Lindy) Boggs
March 13, 1916-

B. Brunswick Plantation, Louisiana; D. Roland and Corinne Morrison Claiborne; M. Thomas Hale Boggs, 1938 (widowed 1973); Served in U.S. House of Representatives as Democrat-Louisiana, March 20, 1973- , 93rd Congress- .

A longtime New Orleans resident, the energetic Lindy Boggs has a penchant for political pageantry, reflecting the colorful, celebratory city of her married life. During her career, first as a political wife and later as the representative of New Orleans' Second District, Lindy Boggs has chaired the inaugural balls of two presidents (Kennedy and Johnson), organized whistle-stop campaigns through the South for the Johnsons, headed up the Congressional Club, presided over the Congressional Wives' Forum, chaired the Joint Committee on Congressional Bicentennial Arrangements, and chaired (the first woman to do so) the greatest Democratic spectacle of all—the 1976 National Convention in New York.

Though she is geographical kin to the former chair of the Armed Services Committee, Representative Edward Hébert, who gave Patricia Schroeder of Colorado such a difficult time in the 93rd and 94th Congresses, Representative Boggs is a forward-thinking supporter of equal opportunities for women. Her city of New Orleans has not, as of 1980, ratified the Equal Rights Amendment, putting it off-bounds to many women's organizations and groups that might otherwise slate conventions there. Nevertheless, Lindy Boggs presses forward with legislation to benefit women, particularly in the area of domestic violence, an increasingly visible national problem in the 1980s. Together with her colleague on the Congresswomen's Caucus, Barbara Mikulski, she introduced and nurtured legislation to fund shelters and counseling services for the victims (mainly women and children) of domestic violence. This bill proposed a network approach that would link existing federal and local efforts to provide coordinated services. She also sponsored a measure to fund the National Center for the Prevention and Control of Rape.

Presently on the Appropriations Committee, Boggs is well known for attracting and appointing other women to the committee, though her vocabulary ("rushing" women for certain House committees) is flecked with terminology one might expect in a sorority house rather than in the hallowed halls of Congress. Her committee assignment on Banking, Currency and Housing and its subcommittees on Housing, and Community Development and Financial Institutions Supervision, Regulation and Insurance has netted a cluster of housing legislation directed at solutions for the housing problems of the elderly and other low- and middle-income groups. The Energy Conservation in Buildings Act, which she cosponsored, provided assistance for low-income homeowners to weatherize their homes, while the Middle Income Housing Act provided lower mortgage rates for families who might not otherwise be able to afford home ownership. In the area of credit for women, Boggs has contributed legislation that forces institutions to extend equal access to credit—a benefit to female consumers and to women's business ventures. Many women have been able to launch a small business due to the Boggs amendment to the Small Business Act, which specifically prohibits discrimination on the basis of sex in the granting of small business loans.

Congresswoman Boggs commands an influential position in the House, perhaps a halo effect resulting from the popularity of her late husband, who died tragically in 1973. She had managed many of her husband's campaigns, was heavily involved in the Democratic presidential campaigns of Johnson and Kennedy, and organized her friend Lady Bird Johnson's trip by train through the South during the Johnson-Humphrey campaign of 1964.

In 1979 Boggs participated in the historic congresswomen's delegation to Thailand and Cambodia, the first humanitarian effort of its kind launched by women in the U.S. Congress, or by women members in any world parliamentary or congressional group. She and her sister congresswomen were able to meet with Cambodian authorities and persuaded them to agree to the distribution of 30,000 tons of food and the release of American-donated medical supplies, clothing, and transportation to alleviate the suffering of the starving Cambodians. Together with Congresswomen Holtzman, Heckler, Fenwick, Mikulski, Schroeder, and Snowe, Boggs visited Cambodian camps on the Thai border, where hundreds of thousands of homeless refugees lay starving, sick, and dying. The women legislators called their mission a "journey of conscience."

Boggs' education at Sophie Newcomb College at Tulane University (B.A., 1935) prepared her for a teaching career. After college she taught history in St. James Parrish in Romeville. She continued her avid interest in history, serving on the board of regents of the Smithsonian Institution in Washington from 1977 to 1978. During the years when her political life was bound up with her husband's congressional ambitions, she focused her talents on his career, their three children, and numerous philanthropic and civic interests, though her devotion to the Democratic party was in evidence early on. From 1939 to 1942 she served as a precinct leader in New Orleans. She eased into the Congress via a special election to fill her husband's seat in 1973; in 1974 she campaigned vigorously to emerge as the winner and the first woman from Louisiana to be elected to Congress. One of her opponents in the race used the argument, "I think a man belongs in Congress, no matter who he might be," logic that did not appeal to the voters in the Second District who had seen Lindy Boggs at work over the years.

Boggs displays considerable perception when dealing with the political realities of life as a woman politician. One tactic she employs in garnering support behind special legislation—for example, her domestic violence bill—is to seek out a male cosponsor. "It's important to have a male cosponsor so that people don't think [it] is only wife-battering that we're concerned about, even though it's mostly women who are affected," she told political observer Susan Tolchin in an interview. She chose Republican Newton Steers of Maryland to cosponsor a bill on domestic violence.

Congresswomen are often sought out by women's groups to champion various causes. Women air force service pilots went to Boggs when they fought to receive veterans' benefits denied to them because of their lack of military status. Boggs and every other congresswoman signed the bill in the 95th Congress that guarantees these women their rights as veterans. Interestingly, one of the bill's strongest advocates was conservative Barry Goldwater from Arizona—another tribute to Boggs' political clout and her ability to transcend both gender and party lines.

Because Boggs' district contains a portion of the large and busy port of New Orleans within its boundaries, the congresswoman has given considerable attention to several maritime bills, including the Maritime Bulk Act, a measure intended to promote the bulk cargo carriage on U.S. registered ships, and the Merchant Marine Act, its companion bill, which will provide funding to assist in the construction of bulk-carrying vessels.

The Jean Lafitte Park, a result of her legislation to fund a national historical park across the Mississippi from New Orleans, stands as one of the congresswoman's major visible accomplishments. Designed to preserve bayou vegetation, the park was a project dear to Hale Boggs when he served in Congress, and Lindy Boggs terms it a "long-time dream of sportsmen, naturalists, fishermen, school children, historians and lovers of our unique Louisiana delta...."

Selected Speeches and Writings

Boggs was responsible for *Women in Congress, 1917-1976*, biographical profiles of congresswomen for the use of the Joint Committee on Arrangements for the Commemoration of the Bicentennial (1976).

Papers, including articles and clippings, are held by Tulane University Archives, New Orleans, LA.

Bibliography

Numerous references to Boggs in *The Advocate* (Baton Rouge, LA).

Radcliffe, Donnie. "Rushing on the Hill," *The Washington Post*, December 6, 1978, p. C4.

Tolchin, Susan J. "Congressional Women Pick Up Where Bella Left Off," *Politicks and Other Human Interests* (n.d.).

Frances Payne Bolton
March 29, 1885-March 9, 1977

B. Cleveland, Ohio; D. Charles William and Mary Perry Payne Bingham; M. Chester Castle Bolton, 1907; Served in U.S. House of Representatives as Republican-Ohio, March 5, 1940 to January 3, 1969, 76th through 90th Congress.

Frances Payne Bolton's defeat in the congressional race of 1968 marked the end of a particular breed of political woman in the Congress. A millionaire philanthropist with a finishing school education, Bolton was the granddaughter of a United States senator (Democrat Henry Payne), the wife of a U.S. congressman (Republican Chester Bolton, who died in 1940), and the mother of a congressman during her own tenure in the House (Oliver Bolton). During her 28-year term, she was called at various times "the richest woman in Congress"; the "only mother of a mother-son congressional team" ever to serve; "the dean of congresswomen," and "the First Lady of the House." Few, however, dared to address her as "Congresswoman," as she deplored the term and made no bones about expressing her ridicule for the word, which she claimed could not be located in the dictionary.

Bolton's DAR background was rooted in Cleveland wealth and power, her pedigree strewn with names like Paine, Payne, Perry, and Bingham. Her husband Chester was a wealthy man, and she inherited a vast fortune from her uncle, Oliver Hazard Payne, the multi-millionaire industrialist. Up to the time of her marriage at age 22, Bolton followed the fashionable and traditional pattern among families of her class and time: debutante parties, sketchy schooling, and travelling abroad. While looking for a worthwhile cause to sponsor during her debutante days, she happened on the idea of working with visiting nurses in Cleveland's slums. Though it was some time before she informed her father of her work with the poor, she recalled in later life that her nursing experiences gave focus to her life and an appreciation of the hardships of the working classes and of the people who tended them. When she was in Congress, her legislation on behalf of nurses reflected this early interest: the Bolton Bill, during the Second World War, supplied 125,000 nurses under the Cadet Nurse Corps, and her Public Law 89-609 in 1966, called the "Equal Rights for Men" bill, authorized that male nurses be commissioned into the Army and Navy Nurse Corps. In her view, male nurses were the victims of discriminatory treatment at the hands of the military. In addition to these two notable pieces of legislation, Bolton's special interest in nurses fueled many other bills providing for improvements in nurses' training, pay, and benefits. She spoke out forcefully against the racial segregation of nurses in the service during World War II, consistent with the vigorous civil rights stance she maintained throughout her career.

After Frances Bingham became Mrs. Bolton, she occupied the traditional young matron role, rearing her two children (one daughter died at birth) and supporting her husband in his political work. She became well known in Washington circles after her husband was elected to Congress in 1928. Because of the enormous wealth she possessed in her own right, Bolton knew a great deal about philanthropy, property, and finance. But during her husband's congressional days she came under some criticism for being more interested in Washington and her own family finances than in local politics. This criticism came home to roost after her husband died suddenly and she campaigned to serve out his term. Though party regulars were hardly enthusiastic about Frances Payne Bolton as the representative from the 22nd District, it was difficult to ignore the fact that the Bolton wealth had provided Cleveland with such political plums as the Republican National Convention in 1936 (a check was simply written out for the amount of $125,000).

Bolton stayed in Washington during 1940, ostensibly to fill in while the Republicans searched out a more likely replacement. But it became clear almost immediately that she enjoyed political life, not as a spouse, but as a member of Congress. In the 1940 special election, she defeated Democrat Anthony Fleger by an almost 2-to-1 margin, becoming the first woman from Ohio to be elected to Congress. Though her conservative reputation over the years has become legend, she supported liberal legislation as well—poverty programs, for example, and the drafting of women in the 1950s. She gained a reputation for efficiency in dealing with her sprawling urban and suburban district, the second largest in the country, mainly because she was able to pay for additional staff members out of her own pocket. Similarly, when she felt the necessity to experience global affairs firsthand—trips to Africa, Russia, Europe, and the Middle East—she did not hesitate to use her checkbook to finance a junket (including plane, photographer, and traveling companion in one famous trip through Africa). Perhaps it was because she did not have the vocabulary of a trained diplomatic observer that Bolton's knowledge of foreign affairs was considered "superficial" by many experts, though President Eisenhower seriously considered her for a diplomatic position related to Africa.

Appointed to the Foreign Affairs Committee in 1941, Bolton rose to a high-ranking position on the committee and chaired subcommittees on the Mid-East and Africa, which had been established on her recommendation. In 1944, during the war, she became the first woman in Congress to travel to the front, as later she scored another triumph as the first individual on the Foreign Affairs Committee to get into the Soviet Union. On her official trips she made a point of visiting hospitals and becoming acquainted with worldwide nursing issues.

Her sympathy with the Arab states regarding the Palestine issue caused her many tense moments in the States and abroad. She condemned the use of tax-free dollars raised by American Jews for the support of Palestine, and raised many eyebrows by her frequent allusions to "those poor Arabs." Even when her international point of view reaped unfavorable press for her, the 22nd District found her a colorful "Congressman":

> Clevelanders were intrigued by a woman who could escape an elephant charge in the Congo, dine with Saudi Arabia's King Ibn Saud and his harem, convince Russian U.N. Ambassador Andrei Vishinsky to use his influence to bring to the United States the teenage sons of a Romanian couple in exile, exchange gifts with the Queen Mother of Ruanda-Urundi, host the American visit of the

Angel of Dienbienphu, and ease taut tempers in the course of an angry committee dispute with the improbable question "Mr. Chairman, wouldn't it be a good idea if we all got up and sang?" (Chamberlin, p. 135)

In 1952, when Oliver P. Bolton was elected to the House of Representatives, mother and son received much press because of their differing views. "Just keep the hell out of my district!" he is reported to have said to her during his campaign for Congress.

Throughout her long career Bolton's philanthropy extended over a wide range of human endeavors. She gave $1.5 million to the school of nursing at Western Reserve University. To preserve the view from Mt. Vernon, she purchased land about to be developed by industrial interests and turned over her acreage to the Department of the Interior, which was committed to matching the donation with purchases of smaller parcels along the Potomac. The result was beautiful Piscataway Park, dedicated in 1968. At 82 Bolton retired to her Lyndhurst estate outside of Cleveland to pursue her many philanthropic activities and trusteeships after being defeated by liberal Charles Vanik in the 1968 congressional contest. It seems likely that her 28-year congressional record will be hard to upstage.

Selected Speeches and Writings

"U.S. Position on Question of Southwest Africa," U.S. Department of State Bulletin, November 9, 1953; "World Impact of U.S. Policy: Fundamental Defenses," *Vital Speeches*, June 1, 1948; *Letters from Africa 1955* (1956); "View of Africa," *Annals American Academy*, July 1956.

The papers of Frances Payne Bolton are held at Western Reserve Historical Society, Cleveland (primarily 1940-1969).

A more complete listing of Bolton's public speeches may be found in B. Manning, *Index to American Women Speakers* (1980), p. 61.

Honors

Many honorary degrees and awards. Frances P. Bolton School of Nursing at Western Reserve University named in her honor. The Snow Medal (1949). Human Relations Award (National Conference of Christians and Jews) (June 6, 1976).

Bibliography

In Chamberlin, Hope. *A Minority of Members* (1973).

"Frances P. Bolton Dies," *Cleveland Press*, March 9, 1977.

In Lamson, Peggy. *Few Are Chosen* (1968).

Loth, David. *A Long Way Forward* (1957).

New York Times (Obituary), March 10, 1977.

Pringle, H. F., and K. Pringle. "He Followed Mom to Congress," *Saturday Evening Post*, August 15, 1953.

U.S. Congress. House. Committee on Foreign Affairs. Subcommittee on the Near East and Africa. *Report of the Special Study Mission to Africa, South and East of the Sahara*. Honorable F. P. Bolton, ranking minority member, 85th Congress, 1st Session, House Report No. 307, 1957.

18 / Frances Payne Bolton

U.S. Congress. House. Committee on Foreign Affairs. Subcommittee on Near East and Africa. *Report of the Special Study Mission to the Near East and Africa.* Honorable F. P. Bolton, ranking minority member, 85th Congress, 2nd Session, House Report No. 2214, 1958.

Women's Services Division. Ohio Bureau of Employment Services. *Ohio Women* (1979).

Marilyn Lloyd Bouquard
January 3, 1929-

B. Fort Smith, Arkansas; D. James and Iva Laird; M. Joseph Bouquard; Served in U.S. House of Representatives as Democrat-Tennessee, January 3, 1975- , 94th Congress- .

Marilyn Lloyd Bouquard shares a similar background with other widows in the Congress (Lindy Boggs, Cardiss Collins, Beverly Byron) who might not have been active in politics but for the untimely deaths of their husbands. Bouquard's first husband, Monty Lloyd, was the Democratic nominee for the House when he died in a plane crash in 1974. Marilyn was approached by the Democratic party leadership to step in and run in his place; she did and won, becoming the first woman to win a popular election in Tennessee. Once in Washington, she refused to join the Congresswomen's Caucus, though in the 96th Congress she threw caution aside and joined; her stand on the ERA Amendment is negative.

Marilyn Lloyd Bouquard is hardly a shrinking Southern violet. Before being elected to Congress, she shared in managing the family business, a radio station and an airplane agricultural service. Though her formal credentials were unimpressive, she had carefully studied local issues because of the business and her husband's political aspirations. The mother of four children, she had held only one elective office before her first term in Washington—as president of a local PTA.

Bouquard espouses the conservative Southern Democratic political style popular in her region and serves her Third Congressional District in a manner that insures continued support. She holds seats on the House Committee on Science and Technology, on Public Works, and the Select Committee on Aging (a committee which is becoming a traditional woman's assignment in the House). Her concern for the aged has centered on her own city of Chattanooga, with its sizeable impoverished, elderly population. During the 96th Congress she became the ranking Democratic member of the Fossil, Nuclear Energy Subcommittee of Science and Technology. The only woman ever to have served on this committee, Bouquard's appointment was particularly appropriate since the Oak Ridge laboratories are in her district.

Staunchly conservative, Bouquard belongs to the United Democrats of Congress, a conservative coalition that frequently votes for higher defense and military spending and opposes many social welfare programs. The congresswoman keeps a low profile and is little known on the national scene. She has remarried since serving in the Congress. Her husband, a civil engineer from Chattanooga, supports her career—a necessity, since they have eight children between them from previous marriages.

No bibliographical information is available other than in standard who's who sources.

Yvonne Braithwaite Burke
October 5, 1932-

B. *Los Angeles, California; D. James T. and Lola Moore Watson; M. William Burke, 1972; Served in U.S. House of Representatives as Democrat-California, January 3, 1973 to 1978, 93rd through 95th Congress.*

Yvonne Braithwaite Burke has been a standout in the California political scene, where she became the first woman to go to Congress from the state in 20 years, and the first black woman from the state ever elected to the House. She distinguished herself during her two terms by shepherding more than 30 bills and major amendments through the Congress, all of which can be characterized as liberal and progressive. Mass transit, educational programs for the mentally retarded, flextime employment for the elderly and for women, and rape prevention suggest the range of issues to which Burke commits herself. Her committee assignments included the House Appropriations Committee and the Housing and Urban Development Agencies Subcommittee, as well as the Department of State, Justice, Commerce, the Judiciary and Related Agencies Subcommittee.

A first-rate legislator, parliamentarian, and debater, Burke came to politics by way of the law (J.D., University of Southern California, 1956). She practiced privately in the late fifties, facing many of the problems of minority attorneys during that era. "Getting a job with a law firm was almost unheard of, and getting a position in the state government was difficult," she was to recall in an interview for the *Christian Science Monitor* (July 1, 1972). As the talented daughter of working-class parents, and the only black at the model school she attended (affiliated with the University of Southern California), Burke was used to dealing with racism in its many insidious forms, though she transcended prejudice during her student days because of her outstanding academic performance and notable extracurricular contributions in the areas of drama and oratory. An exceptionally attractive woman, she modeled for *Ebony* magazine to help pay tuition costs during her undergraduate and law school days at UCLA.

The Los Angeles Watts riots of the 1960s tested her expertise as a civil rights attorney and brought her state and national recognition as well. Her defense of Watts rioters, and later her work as counsel for the McCone Commission (formed to investigate the conditions in Watts), introduced her to prominent groups in California politics. By 1964 she had become sufficiently interested in politics to work for Lyndon Johnson's reelection; in 1966 she entered the brutal local political melee for the California General Assembly. In her fight for the seat from California's 63rd District, she was pitted against a John Bircher who repeatedly reminded voters of her litigation role on behalf of the Watts rioters. Throughout the contest, Burke's campaign was slurred by the opposition's charges, labeling her a Communist, a revolutionary, and a black militant.

Fortunately, her opponent's indictments held little water with the 63rd District voters, who returned her to the Assembly three times and supported her creative legislation on behalf of women and minorities, especially in the areas of education, child care, prison reform, and job rights. Because of her excellent knowledge of California's urban housing problems from her work with the NAACP in Los Angeles during the Watts crisis, she contributed much to the Assembly's Committee on Housing and Urban Development, which she chaired in 1971 and 1972. During this period she picked up support from black political leaders in California, who pressed her to run for the U.S. House from the newly created, predominantly black 37th Congressional District, including Watts and southwest Los Angeles. Emerging as the Democratic nominee in a difficult five-way primary, Burke went on to capture public attention as the first black woman to vice-chair the Democratic National Convention (Miami, 1972). During the televised proceedings, she presided confidently and calmly over unruly delegates, making tough parliamentary calls, handling problems with a happy blend of firmness and humor. Since the party platform paid particular attention to the necessity of including minority members in the convention process, she occupied a uniquely sensitive position.

With Burke's election to Congress in November 1972, a political year which saw the defeat of liberal George McGovern for the presidency, Shirley Chisholm gained another black female colleague in the House. Burke, like all women in the House, became a spokesperson for many political have-not groups throughout the country. As a black woman she attracted the following of even more special-interest minority groups. Recognizing the political reality of being a black woman in politics, she joked after her election, "There is no longer any need for anyone to speak for all black women. I expect Shirley Chisholm is feeling relieved." She served as role model for women choosing to combine competitive careers with marriage and motherhood, especially when she took a maternity leave during her first term in the House, thus becoming the first congresswoman to bear a child while in office.

Specifically an advocate of poverty groups, Burke approved legislation to raise the hourly wage, to expand the food stamp program and to fight increased costs of the stamps, to protect the mortgages of unemployed workers, and to improve school nutrition programs. She lashed out against the priorities of a country that expended billions of dollars on defense and high technology at the expense of social change programs, especially educational programs to improve the quality of education for low-income youngsters in the inner-cities. Burke was responsible for the initial displaced homemaker legislation included in the Comprehensive Education and Training Act (CETA), which provided for the training of middle-aged women who had not worked outside of the home before losing their positions as homemakers through the death of a spouse or divorce. As one of the leading members of the Congresswomen's Caucus, she recognized that minority women were a doubly impoverished group, often unskilled for labor outside the home, uncompensated for work as homemakers, and poorly compensated for their work in the clerical categories where they most frequently clustered. Problems of the elderly were of particular concern to Representative Burke, who consistently voted for programs to benefit senior citizens. On many occasions, she predicted that galloping inflation would hit most brutally the poverty groups of women, the elderly, and minorities.

To insure that minorities and women were not overlooked in the granting of defense contracts, Burke used her position on the House Interior and Insular Affairs Committee to introduce legislation which demanded that the awarding of construction contracts be made on an affirmative action basis for the construction of the Alaskan Pipeline in 1975, resulting in more than $255 million in contracts awarded to women and other minorities. This amendment serves as a prototype for governmental award of private contracts with strict affirmative action guidelines attached. No issue dealing with equality was too insignificant for Burke. When she served on the Select Committee for the House Beauty Shop, for example, she looked into the pay and pension disparity between the beauticians and the barbers.

A hardline environmentalist, Burke approved domestic oil price controls and measures to encourage research and development efforts for alternative energy sources. Predictably, she was against strip mining and endorsed strict automobile emission standards.

When she left the House to run for the office of California attorney general, Burke commented, "In Washington, I was only one out of 43 members of the California delegation. In California I will be one out of one." Liberals and progressive women in the House deeply regretted her retirement from the House, leaving California with no female representation in the Congress, and Congress with significant holes in its leadership for the Congressional Black Caucus and for the Congresswomen's Caucus. Burke suffered a political setback in November 1978, when she was defeated in the race for the attorney general's slot in California. Again on the upswing in 1979, she was named to the powerful Los Angeles Board of Supervisors. One suspects that Burke will return at the first opportunity to the national political scene. Meanwhile, she is hardly out of the action in her appointed position to the University of California Board of Regents.

Selected Speeches and Writings

"Feminine Pioneers," *Westways*, Vol. 68, No. 7, 1976; "Let's Play Taps for an All Male Army," *Saturday Evening Post*, October 1977; "Economic Strength Is What Counts," in Bernice Cummings, *Women Organizing* (1979).

A collection of Burke's papers are held by the Southern California Library for Social Studies and Research. This includes some correspondence, newspaper interviews, her first newsletter from Congress, and a copy of her cosponsored bill aimed at preventing further U.S. entry into Vietnam without the consent of Congress. Other papers related to Burke are listed in Andrea Hinding's *Women's History Resources* (1979).

A more complete listing of Burke's public speeches may be found in B. Manning, *Index to American Women Speakers* (1980), p. 71.

Honors

The Loren Miller Award of the NAACP (for contributions to the California Legal System, 1966); Professional Achievement Award, UCLA (1974); 200 Future Leaders, *Time* (1974); achievement citations from numerous organizations, especially from black professional organizations, including the National Association of Black Women Attorneys, the National Association of Negro Business and Professional Women's Clubs; Chubb Fellow, Yale University (1972); Fellow of the Institute of Politics, The John Kennedy School of Government at Harvard (1971-1972).

Bibliography

"Burke Named to Powerful L.A. Board of Supervisors," *Jet*, July 5, 1979.

Buxton, Chuck. "In Sacramento, They Call the High-Ranking Women in the Brown Administration The 'Old Girls Network'," *California Journal*, January 1980.

In Chamberlin, Hope. *A Minority of Members* (1973).

The Christian Science Monitor (interview), August 1, 1972.

"Congressional Black Caucus on the Issue [of Full Employment], *Essence*, April 1976.

In Cummings, Bernice, and Victoria Schuck. *Women Organizing: An Anthology* (1979).

Elliot, J. M. "Congressional Black Caucus," *Negro History Bulletin*, January 1977.

Marks, Marlene A. "Burke's Law," *New West*, April 24, 1978.

"People," *Time*, May 29, 1978.

"Women in Government," *Ebony*, August 1977.

Yong, A. S. *Sepia*, June 1978.

Jane Burke Byrne
May 24, 1934-

B. Chicago, Illinois; D. William Burke; M. William P. Byrne, 1956 (deceased); and Jay McMullen, 1978; Served as Democrat Mayor of Chicago, April 16, 1979- .

As mayor of one of the largest and most politically complicated cities in the country, Jane Byrne wields considerable regional and national clout outside the city of Chicago. During 1980 her support of Ted Kennedy's candidacy for president and her deliberate and vocal rejection of Carter and his urban policies put her at the eye of the 1980 national Democratic hurricane. At stake during this controversy over the Democratic presidential candidate — Chicago's millions of dollars of urban assistance from Washington. Many of Chicago's political regulars have taken the mayor to task for her political maneuverings, especially with the city's already precarious financial situation hanging in the balance.

Jane Byrne first came to power as the Democratic protégé of Mayor Richard Daley, and later as the gadfly of Michael Bilandic, Daley's successor. While she had served Daley obediently and devotedly since 1964, she needled Bilandic about corruption in the ranks, bloated budgets, and payoffs, capturing headlines on a regular basis during the two years before her election. It was Chicago's brutal winter of 1979, leaving Chicagoans disgruntled with Bilandic's management of snow removal and other city services, that finally carried Byrne into office. Bilandic had fired her from the post of Commissioner of Consumer Sales after she charged him with corruption in hiking taxi fares. She retaliated by beating him soundly in the 1979 Democratic primary.

Byrne's surprise victory put her in direct combat with the city's octopus-like political machine, with which she chose to wrangle, rather than to woo over to her camp. The city's labor unions, members of the Chicago Democratic party, and even some of her own appointees joined ranks against her during her first year, effectively quashing the city's traditional philosophy of "play along, get along." According to Byrne, however, dissension in the ranks was to be expected. "We had a half-dozen years of Band Aid government—of ignoring problems and dipping into [bond interest] escrow accounts to pay bills. It was going to blow up eventually, and it finally did," she stated in January 1980. "I intend to face the problems squarely and call things as I see them. If that upsets some people, so be it."

One of the biggest crises for Byrne has been the crippling financial situation of Chicago's public school system, which serves nearly half a million students. At one point it looked as if schools would simply shut down due to the school system's loss of credit. The city's bond system is said to be in jeopardy. Transit and other public employees' strikes have kept the mayor running from one political fire to another while she endures daily public roasts in the Chicago press. Political analysts from academe tend to look on Byrne benignly, calling her "a transitional figure from government-by-machine to something else."

More positive mayoral programs include the Byrne plan for revamping the existing mass transit system, a $2 billion undertaking that would touch every phase of existing public transportation in the city. Other plans for pruning city employees from the payroll have not met with enthusiasm, though Byrne has exposed large deficits in the millions of dollars not considered in the budgets of previous mayors. As the political heat intensified, Byrne fired several top-ranking employees, including her budget director, and gathered family members around her in high-ranking positions. Her brother serves as an adviser, and her husband, Jay McMullen, former columnist for the *Chicago Tribune*, acts as her press secretary. Meanwhile, analysis of her "quarrelsome" personality continues in the press; without Democratic party backing in the city, it is difficult for the mayor to adopt anything but a defensive posture.

Byrne's personal history at first glance contradicts what one might expect of the first female mayor of Chicago. Her upper-middle-class family came from Chicago's North Side (rather than from the working-class roots of Richard Daley's South Side). She attended fashionable Barat College (B.A., 1955), married immediately after graduation, and became a full-time mother.

After the death of her first husband, she decided upon teaching as a career and substituted in the Chicago public schools from 1961 to 1963 while parenting her young daughter.

Before John Kennedy's election and during his presidency, Byrne participated actively in Democratic politics, coming to Kennedy's attention for her excellent work in his behalf. Not long after the president's assassination, Mayor Daley took a personal interest in her political career, urging her to expand her participation in local politics. After appointing her to a post in the Chicago antipoverty program in 1964, he took on the role of Byrne's political mentor. By 1968 she was a member of Daley's cabinet, receiving regular tutoring sessions from the mayor on the machinations of Chicago-style politics. As one of Daley's inner circle she received a delegate's badge at the Miami Democratic Convention in 1972, and later, appointment to the chair for the Democratic National Committee. By 1975 she was co-chair with Daley of the Cook County Democratic Central Committee, a titular post that clearly demonstrated her favored position.

While Byrne was basking in the mayor's reflected glory, and learning the basics of city leadership, Daley's health was declining. Democratic bosses stood in the wings maneuvering for position in the event of his death. When Daley died in December 1976, Byrne's position on the Cook County Democratic Central Committee was snatched from her, probably an act of retribution from Democrats who disliked her for her favored status with Daley and for her public denouncements of them as "political vultures" during the Daley deathwatch. Because of the volatile nature of Chicago's political atmosphere, besting Bilandic in the mayoral election put Byrne in an uncomfortable position with other ambitious Chicago politicos, notably Daley's own son, Richard Daley, Jr. She has been fighting for party control ever since she took over the city.

Although Byrne undoubtedly faces more tempestuous times at the helm of one of the nation's largest cities, it must be remembered that she has a strong following among women, blacks, and ethnics, who represent the anti-machine coalition in Chicago. These people endorsed her overwhelmingly in her first Democratic primary. Then, too, consumerism has been a major interest of Byrne's from the days when she served as Mayor Daley's first woman commissioner in charge of consumer sales, measures, and weights, and became the champion of the ordinary citizen on price posting, fair meat grading, and other consumer issues. Despite her difficulties, many voters trust Byrne over what the mayor herself has labelled the "cabal of evil men" in Chicago politics.

Selected Speeches and Writings

"How I Got Involved: Mayor Jane Byrne's Own Story of Her Rise in Chicago Politics," *Chicago Magazine*, April 1979.

Bibliography

Numerous references in the *Chicago Tribune*, the *Chicago Magazine*, and Chicago's *The Reader*.

"Byrne Joins Mayor's Club: 170 Blacks, 100 Women," *Jet*, April 19, 1979.

"Calamity Jane Strikes Again," *Time*, December 10, 1979.

Griffin, D. "Scramble to Save Chicago's Coalition," *Fortune*, April 9, 1979.

"In More Cities, It's Her Honor the Mayor," *U.S. News and World Report*, July 16, 1979.

Hansen, Henry. "Jane Byrne Guards Her Flanks," *Chicago*, December 1979.

Klein, Frederick C. "Calamity Jane? Quarrelsome Style of Chicago's Mayor Stirs Political Heat," *Wall Street Journal*, January 30, 1980.

McGrath, Paul. "Has Byrne's Revolution Stalled?," *Chicago*, November 1979.

McGrath, Paul. "Beyond Nepotism: Mayor Byrne Needs a More Competent Staff," *Chicago*, December 1979.

MacPherson, Myra. "Jane Byrne," *Washington Post*, March 11, 1979.

Porter, Mary Cornelia, and Ann B. Matasar. "The Role and Status of Women in the Daley Organization." In Jane Jaquette. *Women in Politics* (1974).

Rakovc, Milton. *We Don't Want Nobody Nobody Sent* (1979).

Shapiro, H. D. "Chicago's Rusty Machine," *New Leader*, March 26, 1979.

Stone, Marvin. "Women in Leadership Roles," *U.S. News and World Report*, May 21, 1979.

Talbott, B. "Machine Woman," *New Republic*, March 17, 1979.

Beverly Butcher Byron
July 27, 1932-

B. Baltimore, Maryland; D. Harry C. and Ruth B. Butcher; M. Goodloe E. Byron, 1952 (widow); Served in U.S. House of Representatives as Democrat-Maryland, January 3, 1979- , 96th Congress- .

Beverly Butcher Byron inherited a long tradition of public service from her late husband's side of the family. Her husband, Goodloe E. Byron, and his father, William D. Byron, represented Maryland's Sixth District, as did mother-in-law Katharine E. Byron, who came to office under circumstances similar to Beverly's. The Byron name, before Maryland voters for decades, allowed Beverly Byron to win the seat easily after her husband died suddenly only four weeks before election day. Even in the primary, her chief rival, Dan Rupli, announced to the press, "If Mrs. Byron announces her candidacy for the seat I think I would withdraw my name. It would be appropriate for me and for all contenders to do the same." The members of the Western Maryland Central Democratic Committee agreed to choose Beverly Byron because "... she and Goodloe have campaigned together for eight years for the Congress and eight years in state elections. She knows the district backwards and forwards...."

A curious sidelight of Beverly Byron's campaign was the press coverage given to her Republican opponent. "The Republican nominee for the job, Mr. Perkins, was released from the Baltimore County Jail yesterday after serving 10 days for assaulting a woman bus driver" ([Baltimore] *Evening Sun*, October 12, 1978). Promising to "follow my husband's footsteps," she garnered almost 90% of the vote from Perkins, described in the press as "the Baltimore pauper and political gadfly who embarrassed the state Republican party with his irreverant campaign." Public sympathy helped considerably as Byron's three-week campaign was launched only a week after Goodloe's death. She retained the entire staff of her husband's Washington and Baltimore offices save for one position, and emphasized before and after the campaign her intention to rely heavily on them for counsel.

Though civic and charitable activities had been her long suit before her entry into Congress (chair of the Maryland Commission on Physical Fitness, board of directors of the American Hiking Society, board of associates for Hood College, the American Red Cross, the Heart Association), she had involved herself more heavily than most political wives in grassroots political organizations, managing all of her husband's campaigns until his death in 1978. She actively participated in Maryland's Young Democrats organization during the 1960s, and served as treasurer in 1962 and 1965. She attended Hood College and lists her career as "civic leader." In several ways her career ironically parallels that of her mother-in-law, Katharine Byron, who served in the House from 1941 to 1943 after her husband, Representative William Byron, died in an air crash. At the time of her husband's death, Katharine Byron was the mother of five young children. Beverly Byron, mother of three, has a teen-aged daughter to whom she alludes often: "... if Mary seems to be suffering, then I won't run again." Katharine Byron didn't make the House for a second term, and devoted her energies instead to the Red Cross war effort.

Beverly Byron's legislative achievements include her freshman victory of passing a floor amendment to end duplicate inspections of small businesses by state and federal OSHA (Occupational Safety and Health Agency) officials, giving her the distinction of being "the first freshman member of the 96th Congress to get a floor amendment passed by a recorded vote in both House and Senate." As a conservative member of the House Armed Services Committee, she takes a position far removed from that of her Democratic congresswoman colleague, Patricia Schroeder, who also serves on Armed Services. In a 1979 report to her constituency, Byron emphasized her commitment to the defense industry. "As a staunch supporter of a strong national defense posture [Armed Services] is allowing me to continue Goodloe's efforts on behalf of the many defense-related programs affecting citizens of central and western Maryland." While Schroeder has outlined the reasons for waste in the country's defense spending, Byron appears pleased to participate in the research and development of military paraphernalia. In a 1979 letter to this writer she noted, "In conjunction with my work on the House Armed Services Committee, I earlier this year became the first U.S. representative to fly in the A-10 fighter aircraft and the first congresswoman to fly the F-15."

Byron also serves on the Installations and Facilities, Military Compensation, Seapower, and Strategic and Critical Materials subcommittees of Armed Services. As a member of the Select Committee on Aging, she has been a strong supporter of the Congressional Senior Intern Program, which sponsors older citizens to come to Washington and to sit in on briefings about programs and measures for the elderly. Her support of tax relief for married couples centers on concern for the elderly. "It is particularly sad when you hear about elderly couples who want to get married but choose not to because of the financial strain it would create," she wrote to her district in 1979. "And there are also the cases where couples on a tight budget contemplate divorce just to improve their tax situation." Closely related to the issue of the elderly is the economical woodburning stove issue, for which Byron supported energy tax credits as a benefit to "low- and middle-income energy-conscious families who want to reduce their dependence on costly non-renewable fuels and cannot afford the expense of purchasing alternative energy sources such as solar units." Another proposed bill for the elderly asked that the first $5,000 of retirement income be exempted from income taxes. Newsletters to her Sixth District emphasize the "relatively smooth transition" and the continuity constituents can expect of Byron's handling of "citizen problems with the federal government."

Beverly Byron, along with all other women serving in the 96th Congress, supports the Congresswomen's Caucus by her membership, though her contributions to their initiatives have been minimal. Her husband's view of women-related legislation was at best conservative, and Byron's comments at the outset of the 96th Congress reflected a hesitancy to commit herself on women's issues. "Legislation is not going to change discrimination," goes her argument. "That is like trying to legislate morality. The quality of representation is neither hindered nor helped by gender; the quality is with the individual." With Byron's election, however, the number of women representing Maryland rose to four (Spellman, Holt, and Mikulski are the others), bringing Maryland's representation by women in the House to 50%. Indeed, Maryland accounts for over 25% of women's participation in the entire 96th Congress.

Selected Speeches and Writings

Byron does not use written texts for her speeches.

Honors

Local honors for civic contributions.

Bibliography

Arnoff, Kathie-Jo. "The Women of the 96th Congress," *AAUW Magazine*, May/June 1979.

Ruby, Robert. "Mrs. Byron Will Do as Husband Did," [Baltimore] *Evening Sun*, December 15, 1978.

Schultz, Michael. "Mrs. Byron Probably to Get Husband's Slot," [Baltimore] *Evening Sun*, October 12, 1978.

Shirley Anita Chisholm
November 30, 1924-

B. Brooklyn, New York; D. Charles and Ruby Seale St. Hill; M. Conrad Chisholm, 1949; Served in U.S. House of Representatives as Democrat-New York, January 3, 1969- , 91st Congress- .

Petite and outspoken Shirley Chisholm, the first black woman to serve in Congress, arrived in Washington in 1969. One of her first political moves was to discomfit the established congressional committee system for assigning her to the Subcommittee on Rural Development and Forestry. The Brooklyn congresswoman moved quickly to resolve what she perceived to be a ridiculous oversight and an example of congressional inflexibility. "Apparently all they know in Washington about Brooklyn is that a tree grew there," argued Chisholm after she learned of her assignment. Promptly she was reassigned to Veterans Affairs. "There are a lot more veterans in my district than there are trees," she allowed after the unprecedented committee shift.

Her slogan, "Unbossed and Unbought," sums up her straight-speaking, beholden-to-no-one style. Combined with her firm, reasonable manner of championing social causes, "unbought and unbossed" was the concept on which she rode to Washington as representative of the 12th District. On her way to the top Chisholm spent more time with the people of her district working toward the community's social goals, especially in childhood education and child welfare, than she did in organized party-backed politics. Early on, she explains in her autobiography, she had decided, based on her experience with the Bedford-Stuyvesant Political League (BSPL), that politics "is a beautiful fraud that has been imposed on the people for years, whose practitioners exchange gilded promises for the most valuable thing their victims own, their votes." Organizing the people of her neighborhood for social change captured Chisholm's imagination, for she realized that improvements could be made only from within the community. After graduating from Brooklyn College (sociology, 1946, *cum laude*) and Columbia University (M.A., education, 1952), she poured her energies into local child care and community centers (Mt. Calvary Child Care Center and Hamilton-Madison Child Care Center) and established a distinguished reputation as an authority on child care in New York City, eventually serving as director of Hamilton-Madison and as a policy-making consultant to the New York City division of Day Care.

There has been little time for personal life in her crowded public schedule, though she is in her New York City office once a week. Chisholm describes her civil servant/social worker husband, who has supported her behind the scenes since 1949, as "a secure man in his own right." She grew up in Barbados, a background that accounts for the slight accent in her crisp, sometimes evangelical, rhetorical style. Her parents, emigrant Barbadians, worked in blue-collar occupations—her mother a seamstress, her father a factory worker and baker.

In 1964 Chisholm was drafted by people from the community to represent them in the New York Assembly. Greatly experienced, and familiar by then with the pressure points and needs of the community from her work with the BSPL, the League of Women Voters, and various grassroots community groups, she moved confidently into New York State politics, pressing vigorously for legislation that would benefit disadvantaged students, establish child care programs, and aid unemployed domestic workers—in short, to create programs for those who looked to her as their primary advocate in the Assembly. Though failing to win the support of the local political machine, she enjoyed enormous popular support, sailing into the Assembly with a 17,000-vote plurality on her first try. In 1968 Chisholm emerged as the women's choice for Congress from the Bedford-Stuyvesant area. Her opponent, James Farmer, staged a well-financed media campaign. Hers was an old-fashioned street corner campaign, which demonstrated her power advantage among welfare mothers and the Spanish-speaking of her district. Speaking Spanish was not incidental to winning the trust of her neighbors, and ultimately the seat for the 12th District. Her opponents, according to political observers, miscalculated badly when they failed to realize that over 50% more women than men were registered to vote in the 12th District.

Once in Washington, Chisholm practiced the maverick, true-to-her-conscience politics she had perfected in the ghetto. She considered herself at the outset to be more of an advocate than a legislator for the ethnic and racial minorities she represented. In 1972 she explained, "There isn't much I can do inside Congress in a legislative way. I work to be a major force for change outside the House even if I cannot be one within it. There is a great deal I can do for people of my district by using my office and the resources it opens up to me in helping individuals and groups." Her legislative strategy has been to co-sponsor bills vital to her constituency—education for minorities, welfare bills, and the like. Of necessity she has concentrated her energies on remedying the problems of the chronic poor: high unemployment, inadequate housing, the lack of medical and drug treatment facilities, understaffed schools with minimal resources to upgrade the skills of students from disadvantaged backgrounds. Her staff directs considerable energy toward grantsmanship for district projects.

Shirley Chisholm had galvanized the support of those traditionally overlooked by organized politics—youth, women, the elderly, Hispanics, Native Americans, drug addicts, gay activists—and based on this disparate following she waged a serious presidential campaign in 1972. "Although many considered my campaign symbolic of the emerging political awareness of women, blacks, and minorities, I did not run as a symbolic candidate but rather as one of many contenders in the quest for the Democratic nomination for president. I campaigned actively for nine months in both primary and non-primary states," she recalled after the 1972 campaign. Indeed, the courts upheld the legitimacy of her campaign when she sued the networks for equal air time, entitling her to the same public exposure as Democratic candidates McGovern and Humphrey. Chisholm stressed throughout the strenuous campaign that she was not a "gimmick" candidate, knowing the impossibility of her winning but never acknowledging the inevitability of failure even though she arrived at the 1972 Miami Democratic Convention with only 24.5 committed delegates. By convention's end, with 152 delegate votes, she claimed to have broken tradition, though she splintered the liberal vote at the convention and refused to endorse George McGovern during the 1972 presidential campaign. She struck out against blacks who derided her candidacy by indicting the Black Caucus members at the Democratic Convention: "I'm the only one among you who has the balls to run for president."

An iconoclast with priorities, Chisholm has refused to line up neatly behind liberal-identified issues when she sees no direct relation to the issues of her district. Of the environmental issue she once said, "I agree with an 85-year-old woman who said to me, 'Earth Day. Polluted water, polluted air. But I'm not going to get caught up in that. What we need is a campaign in America about polluted hearts.'" As a member of the Congressional Women's Caucus she has unflinchingly supported legislation touching upon equal rights, even when such support sets off fireworks from militant black groups who claim that she has staked out the women's issue at the expense of black welfare.

Because Chisholm, for all her candor and notoriety, seeks little personal recognition or aggrandizement, she often alienates those who seek to honor her, failing to appear at large gatherings of the "important people" in favor of smaller, powerless groups. The honors she has accepted generally come from small, social-change New York City groups. Though she has been criticized as politically unwise for choosing such audiences, she has held her own in the perilous political waters of New York's 12th District since 1968 by remembering well the people who elected her in the first place. "I've suffered worse discrimination as a woman than as a black," has been a familiar Chisholm refrain through the years. Her work and her votes, especially in the House Education and Labor Committee, on which she has served since the 92nd Congress, have consistently reflected her unflagging commitment to the fiery issue of equal rights—for women, blacks, and other oppressed Americans.

Selected Writings and Speeches

"Race, Revolution and Women," *Black Scholar*, Vol. 3, No. 4, 1971; *Congressional Record*, Representative Shirley Chisholm, floor remark, 91st Cong., 1st Sess., May 21, 1969; *Unbought and Unbossed* (1970); Reprint of Chisholm's testimony before U.S. Congress, House, *Subcommittee of the Education and Labor Committee: Hearings on the Equal Employment Opportunities Enforcement Act*, 92d Cong., 1st Sess., March 18, 1971; "Welfare Reform or Enforce Poverty," (Speech before National Welfare Rights Organization given July 31, 1971; "Dr. Welby Is Not the Answer" (American Association for the Advancement of Science, December 29, 1971); "Drug Addiction, a Social Problem," *Law Journal*, March 13, 1971; "Presidential Campaign Position Paper No. 1," *Foreign Aid*, House of Representatives, 1972; "Old Ivy Needs to Go," (Speech before North Carolina Education Association, April 7, 1972); "Needed Equal Educational Opportunity for All," *School and Society*, April 1972; *The Good Fight* (1973); "Black Politicians and the American Electorate," *Black Scholar*, October 1975; "Vote for the Individual, Not the Political Party," *Vital Speeches*, August 15, 1978; "Shirley Speaks Her Mind," *Ebony*, October 1978; Excerpt from Testimony on Proposed Department of Education, August 1, 1978, *Congressional Digest*, November 1978; Commencement address at Metropolitan State College (Denver, CO), May 11, 1980.

A more complete listing of Chisholm's public speeches may be found in B. Manning, *Index to American Women Speakers* (1980), pp. 81-82.

Honors

Numerous honorary degrees, among them Talladega College (1969); Wilmington College (1970); La Salle College, Pratt Institute (1972); Kenyon College (1973); Metropolitan State College,

Denver (1980). Citation for outstanding service in early childhood education and welfare by Sisterhood of Concord Baptist Church, Brooklyn (1965); Certificate of Honor Award for outstanding achievement in service to youth, Junior High School 271, Brooklyn (1965); and many others.

Bibliography

In Chamberlin, Hope. *A Minority of Members* (1973).

"An Interview on Title IX with Shirley Chisholm, ..." *Harvard Education Review*, No. 4, November 1979.

"The First Black Woman in Congress Speaks Out on Our Political System," *Chicago Tribune*, October 11, 1970.

Gant, Liz. "Black Women Organized for Action," *Essence*, October 1976.

Hunter, Charlayne. "Shirley Chisholm: Willing to Speak Out," *New York Times Biographical Edition*, May 27, 1970.

Jaquith, Cindy. "Where Is the Women's Political Caucus Going?," *International Socialist Review*, Vol. 33, No. 5, 1972.

Kuriansky, Joan, and Catherine Smith. "Shirley Chisholm," Ralph Nader Congress Project. Citizens Look at Congress (Series), Grossman, 1972.

Saxon, Bridget. "Shirley Chisholm for President," *Encore*, Spring 1972.

Schneir, Miriam. "The Woman Who Ran for President in 1972," *Ms.*, September 1972.

Steinem, Gloria. "The Ticket That Might Have Been ... President Chisholm," *Ms.*, January 1973.

In Stimpson, Catharine A., ed., in conjunction with the Congressional Information Service. "Discrimination against Women: Congressional Hearings on Equal Rights in Education and Employment," Bowker/CIS (1973).

Werner, Tom. "Chisholm: Pursuing the Dream." (Film 48mm, distr., New Line Cinema, New York City).

White, Joyce. "Women in Politics," *Essence*, October 1976.

Cardiss Robertson Collins
September 24, 1931-

B. St. Louis, Missouri; M. George W. Collins (widow); Served in U.S. House of Representatives as Democrat-Illinois, June 7, 1973- , 93rd Congress- .

Though numerous women have entered the Congress because of the untimely death of a spouse, Cardiss Collins is the first black woman to do so, actually one of the few black women ever to have served in the Congress. A public servant before becoming a representative, she had worked at the Illinois

Department of Revenue as a secretary and as an auditor while forging political connections in her 24th Ward as a Democratic committeewoman (she still maintains active ties with Chicago chapters of moderate black organizations such as the NAACP and the Urban League). Cardiss Collins is not the most vocal member of Congress, but she skillfully manages to maintain constituent support in her Seventh District on Chicago's West Side, where in 1980 she trounced her female opponent, attorney Mary Turner, by drawing 78% of the vote. There was no Republican candidate running in the district, which is distinctly Baptist and Democratic in makeup—two affiliations from which Collins gathers her legion of supporters.

Perhaps Representative Collins has been able to do well in her Seventh District because she is not so removed from the demographic and educational characteristics of the people she represents there. Her education is not notable, her political connections before she entered the House not particularly powerful, and her mien, not as impressive perhaps as some of her black congressional women colleagues of the past and present. However, she has slowly and without much attention risen to the position of chair of the Manpower and Housing Subcommittee of the Government Operations Committee.

Collins is uncompromising when it comes to seeing that the needs of the poor, the elderly, and women be met adequately by government programs. Social legislation has become her major concern, since she is well-acquainted with the plight of Chicago's poverty population who depend on Aid to Families with Dependent Children, day care, and job training programs. She has spoken out frequently in favor of federally funded abortions for poor women who demand them, and is a champion of other women-related health issues. She observes the Community Services Administration (formerly the Office of Economic Opportunity) with a critical eye, concerned that its programs be more responsive to the unemployment problems of minorities, especially those who lack the necessary background and training for productive employment. Perhaps because she sees the domestic effort on behalf of the nation's poor so lacking, Collins has not been a visible supporter of more globally directed relief needs—the congresswomen's mission to Cambodia, for example—although she is on the House International Relations Committee.

She has been very active in the Congressional Black Caucus, leading it during the 96th Congress. In the Congresswomen's Caucus, she gathered enough support to get an amendment added to the Comprehensive Education and Training Act Amendments which provided compensatory job training for eligible women. As Collins is enormously popular in her own district, her wins are spectacular ones, typically racking up 85% of the vote.

Bibliography

"Congressional Black Caucus: On the Issue toward a Development of a Positive U.S. Africa Policy," *Essence*, June 1976.

In Cummings, Bernice, and Victoria Schuck. *Women Organizing* (1979).

"Washington Notebook," *Ebony*, April 1979.

"Women in Government," *Ebony*, August 1977.

Nancy Dick
July 22, 1930-

B. Detroit, Michigan; D. Robert and Jessie Kilzer; M. Stephen Barnett, 1979; Served as Lieutenant Governor of Colorado, 1979- .

Nancy Dick will admit in the first few minutes of an interview that nothing in her background up to the age of 40 pointed to her becoming the highest ranking woman ever elected in the State of Colorado. Widowed as a young woman with three small children, scrambling to be both mother and provider, Nancy Dick had little time for political activities and even less interest. "I was totally naive about politics, and pretty anti-organizational," she relates. A few years after her husband's death, she moved from Colorado Springs to the skiing community of Aspen for a change of scene and to establish a new and more rural lifestyle for her family and herself, a risky move considering that the only paying job she had held since her marriage was as a typist. She did have a bachelor's degree in hotel management from Michigan State University, however; so she went to work at a number of part-time jobs—hostess, manager, salesperson, and the like—for Aspen tourist establishments near her home.

Her political career began, according to the lieutenant governor, when she accepted the position of Democratic party treasurer of Pitkin County in 1973, the major duty being "to write one or two checks a year." She is convinced that the person who asked her to take on this job was working down an alphabetized telephone list of names looking for a willing volunteer. "It was an accident," she willingly reveals. From this position she moved enthusiastically into other small-group political activities, such as the Democratic Party State Rules Committee, her first statewide activity, because "they were fascinating and there was little or no intimidation." She had never even been inside the State Capitol when she was asked by the Democratic party chair of her district (five counties on Colorado's Western Slope) to run for the traditionally Republican-held state representative's seat. Figuring she had little to lose politically, and assured that her family was behind her, Dick launched a vigorous five-county campaign in which she emphasized issues she had faced as a single parent, as a Coloradoan living on the Western Slope, and as a worker in the tourist industry. She credits her victory to another "fluke." The popular incumbent chose not to run for the seat that year.

The committees on which she served while in and out of the legislature dealt with rural, energy, and health issues: her resume reveals that she was chairperson of the Governor's Commission on Rural Health/Manpower Solutions (1977); a member of the Colorado Medical Society Rural Health Committee (1975-1978); a participant on the United States Oil Shale Environmental Advisory Panel (1974-1978); and finance chairperson for the Federation of Rocky Mountain States (1976). Though an avid ERA advocate and a vocal supporter of pregnancy insurance legislation while she served in the Colorado House, Dick is wary of becoming identified with women's issues at the expense of other pressing social issues. "I will no more advocate for women's groups than for minorities, children, and the aging," she has said. Her House committee memberships have spanned the gamut of legislative issues—Transportation, Agriculture; the Judiciary; Health, Welfare and Institutions. For her the legislature was a "fantastic learning experience," so challenging that she began to attend law school at night in an attempt to become a better legislator.

During her second term, interested Democrats (not the "heavy-duty Democratic regulars," she notes) scouted her out as a possibility for running in the lieutenant governor's race in 1978. At this point in her career, Nancy Dick was committed to finishing her law school program, though she understood well as a Democratic woman and a Western Slope resident that she had an attractive package of qualities to offer the Governor Richard Lamm ticket. She originally decided not to run so that she could complete law school, but a few months later, with encouragement from friends and concerned Democrats, she put law school on the back burner and announced her decision to enter the lieutenant's race. If she won, she would be the highest ranking elected woman in Colorado State government; if she lost, she would be a fulltime law student. An indication of Nancy Dick's distance from political ambition is her reminiscence that she did not really care which came through for her; both were palatable challenges. She made her candidacy for the lieutenant governor's slot a family affair once again, her children appearing with her throughout the grueling state campaign. When people commented on her resiliency she noted that her legislative constituency, spread over the mountainous terrain of five rural counties, had prepared her for the traveling. In her first bid for office she had logged more than 36,000 miles, a foot race compared to the lieutenant governor's contest.

Dick projected confidence throughout the campaign, possibly because she had never been defeated in a race. Women appreciated her because she related her own personal history with candor and humor. Her single-parent status, her commitment to ecology, and her interest in rural issues also proved popular among the electorate. The woman who never entertained a political ambition before 1970 was lieutenant governor by the end of the decade. Others who had underestimated her ability to conduct a campaign were more surprised than she by her victory. One advantage she had over her opponents: her genuine enthusiasm for trekking around the state meeting people. Lieutenant Governor Dick's victory in Colorado signaled a number of positive gains for all women—specifically, the message that "politics is not a closed group." She sees herself as a role model for those women who believe that only extraordinary women can compete successfully in the political marathon. Role models, she believes, demonstrate that women can speak responsibly, intelligently, and effectively to the important issues, problems, and decisions of our times.

Lieutenant Governor Dick's job does not require her to preside over the Senate, and she has a clear understanding with Governor Lamm that she will not be used as a legislative liaison between the executive branch and the legislature. Stomping the state to bring the executive branch to the people of outlying areas is a duty she performs effectively. The lieutenant governor's "capitol for a day program" goes out into the state, bringing together leaders of various communities to question and to dialogue with state officials, including the lieutenant governor, on issues ranging from displaced homemakers, to Colorado's housing problems, to cattle ranchers' water rights. Because of what staffers term "Nancy's frank and interested style," the program has been successful and has brought considerable visibility to the office of the lieutenant governor. Her statutory responsibilities include chairing the Colorado Commission on Indian Affairs and the State School District Budget Review Board.

Lieutenant Governor Dick commutes to Aspen to be with her physician husband on the weekends and her grown-up, dispersed family when they infrequently converge at Aspen. Hers is a lifestyle that mirrors many successful women who belong to the group sociologically christened "dual career couples." During her frequent public appearances, whether she is talking about the concerns of career women, single-parent families, widows, political women, or re-entry women, Dick brings credible messages to special-interest groups because of her wide range of ordinary life experiences, transcending the narrowly defined realm of formal politics. Knowing a little about many things has worked to her advantage.

Dick is fond of citing humanist scholars when talking about Colorado's struggle to balance technological and ecological resources; similarly, she invokes feminist writers and philosophers to underscore the increasing significance of women in the work force and women in politics. The career of Nancy Dick, former full-time housewife and mother, now lieutenant governor, suggests that voters have come to recognize the contributions of women in the political realm.

Selected Speeches and Writings

Speech presented to Colorado Vocational Association Summer Workshop (Ft. Collins, CO, August 2, 1979); Commencement Address to Ft. Lewis College Graduating Class of 1979 (April 21, 1979); "Growth: The Good News and the Bad News" (Keystone, CO, September 6, 1979); Speech delivered to the Colorado Trial Court Administrators Association (Greeley, CO, September 20, 1979); "Commentary: Shackled by the 7% 'Solution,'" *Rocky Mountain News*, February 20, 1980, p. 41.

Bibliography

Dean, Katie. "Nancy Dick: Colorado's New Lt. Governor," *Denver Post Empire Magazine*, December 31, 1978, pp. 16-17.

Morrow, Fred. "While Lamm's Away," *Rocky Mountain News*, January 28, 1979, p. 5.

Reifenberg, Anne. "Nancy Dick Eyes United Colorado," *Colorado Springs Sun* "Update," December 3, 1979, p. 2-A.

Helen Gahagan Douglas
November 25, 1900-June 28, 1980

B. Boonton, Morris County, New Jersey; D. Walter and Lillian Rose Mussen Gahagan; M. Melvyn Douglas, 1931; Served in U.S. House of Representatives as Democrat-California, January 1945 to January 1951, 79th through 81st Congress.

The daughter of Walter Gahagan, a civil engineer who had allegedly "filled in most of Long Island," and one of five children, Helen Gahagan was raised strictly and conservatively in a Republican, Episcopalian household. She attended public school in Brooklyn, followed by the Berkeley School for Girls, also in Brooklyn, and Miss Capon's School for Girls in Northampton, Massachusetts.

After two years of study at Barnard College, Columbia University, Helen Gahagan, despite the opposition of her father, set aside her academic pursuits for a part in a play of her own creation, *Shadows on the Moon*. Her role in this production was so impressive that she came to the immediate attention of several prominent theatre directors in New York, and her stage career began to gain momentum. She appeared in numerous successful Broadway productions between 1922 and 1928, including a part as Laura Simmons in John van Druten's *Young Woodley*, which ran for some 260 performances on Broadway.

After six years on stage, Helen Gahagan put down her acting career as spontaneously as she had acquired it—this time for a career in opera. Although untrained in voice, she went abroad in the company of a Russian woman who had been singing mistress at the Imperial Conservatory in St. Petersburg, and while staying in Italy totally immersed herself in the study of opera. She learned to sing Italian operas in the original language, while resident companies with which she performed in Czechoslovakia, Austria, and Germany sang in their native languages.

Upon returning to the stage in New York in 1930, Helen Gahagan met Melvyn Douglas, a member of the supporting cast, whom she married eight months later in April 1931. In 1932, enroute with her husband to her new home in California, she stumbled headlong into the rural migration of the Depression indigents, an experience that made a resounding impression upon her. "I was shocked, and I really came of age at that time. I watched the New Deal cope with these problems and I became convinced it was the most enlightened administration that we'd had. At the same time, I realized that the Republicans had allowed this situation to come to pass."

In 1937 Helen Douglas undertook a concert tour of Europe that included an appearance at the Salzburg Music Festival. So appalled was she by her observations of the growing menace of Nazism, that upon her return to the United States she threw herself into relief work, beginning with the Farm Security Administration on migratory workers' problems. In 1939 President Roosevelt appointed her to the National Advisory Committee of the Works Progress Administration, and she also served that year on the State Advisory

Committee of the National Youth Administration. She served as vice-chairman of the Democratic State Central Committee, responsible for the women's division from 1940-1944; as a Democratic national committeewoman for California during this same period; and as a member of the board of governors of the California Housing and Planning Association in 1942 and 1943, where, always working toward improved conditions for migratory workers, she was vocal on the subject of low-income housing. She was also appointed a member of the Voluntary Participation Committee, Office of Civilian Defense, by President Roosevelt.

In addition to her many activities during the war years, Douglas took sole responsibility for her household and the rearing of her three children (always "trying desperately to avoid elegance") while her husband was away in the service. In 1944 she ran successfully as a Democrat for Congress from California's 14th District, a predominantly Democratic, low-income polyglot comprising migrant workers, ethnic groups, and factory workers. During her campaign she received the support of various labor groups, including the ILGWU and the CIO. Shunning a campaign based on personal aspects (she was known for her remarkable beauty and wit, though she eschewed comparison to the Republicans' Clare Boothe Luce), Douglas was forthright in her presentation of the issues — equal rights for members of all races and creeds, food subsidies for the poor, respect for the rights of organized labor, full opportunity for honestly conducted private enterprise, protection of small farmers and small businesses, taxation based on ability to pay, the return of excess and unjust profits to the government, and renegotiation of war contracts.

As a delegate to the Democratic National Convention in July 1944, Douglas was chosen to address the assembled delegates. President Truman appointed her as alternate U.S. delegate to the United Nations Assembly. She served three terms in the Congress, during the 79th, 80th, and 81st sessions, and during her six years in office she consistently upheld the convictions expressed in her initial campaign. As a member of the House Foreign Affairs Committee she approved of aid for foreign countries, and, along with Clare Boothe Luce, was a proponent of the Atomic Energy Commission, recommending complete civilian control over the development and use of atomic energy. Douglas opposed cuts in funding of the Children's Bureau as well as reductions in National Labor Relations Board funding. She supported legislation that would break the Pacific Gas and Electric monopoly on electric power distribution in her district, favored the anti-poll tax bill, and battled for increased federal payments under the Social Security Act. She submitted an amendment, albeit unsuccessfully, authorizing a restoration of the rent controls provided under the Price Control Act of 1942, and was an early proponent of government support for cancer research. She supported a veterans' housing bill and an anti-lynching bill.

Amidst the hypersensitive political atmosphere of the McCarthy era, Douglas dared to criticize the behavior of the House Un-American Activities Committee, and to vehemently oppose the witchhunting tactics characteristic of the loyalty oath bill for federal government employees. When she ran in 1950 for California's vacated Senate seat, her Republican opponent from a neighboring congressional district, one Richard M. Nixon, in a virtually slanderous campaign by contemporary standards, branded her a "pink lady," "soft on communism." Writing of her in 1954 in a volume of biographical essays called *Ladies of Courage*, Eleanor Roosevelt summed up Douglas' political defeat: "Helen Douglas never indicated that she was even aware that politics was supposed to be a man's world. Had she been content to organize her women as idealistic window dressing, without trespassing into that area which the men call 'practical politics' and regard as belonging exclusively to themselves, she might be—to outward appearances—a leader in the Democratic party in California today."

Although this defeat ended her active political career, Douglas continued to lecture, to write, and to star in Broadway productions. In 1964 she was appointed by President Johnson as a special ambassador to head the United States delegation to the inauguration ceremonies of President Tubman of Liberia. During that same year she was a delegate for the Jane Addams Peace Association to the Soviet-American Women's Conference in Moscow, and served as co-chair of the Women's International League for Peace and Freedom. During the 1970s Douglas wore the mantle of doomsayer. "I'm frightened about what's happening to us as people. Something is eroding us at the very core," she reflected in a post-Watergate interview. In 1972 Douglas worked faithfully for George McGovern's presidential campaign, and continued her support of liberal candidates until her death in the summer of 1980, following a long bout with cancer.

Selected Writings and Speeches

"Impressions of the United Nations," *Annals American Academy*, July 1947; "The World I Want for Children," *Parents Magazine*, March 1949; "Why I Voted for Arms in Europe," *New Republic*, August 19, 1949; *The Eleanor Roosevelt We Remember* (1963).

Some oral history transcripts from 1972-1975 are held by Indiana University's Oral History Research Project in a closed collection. This collection is listed under Melvyn Douglas, and is chiefly about Melvyn Douglas' career.

A more complete listing of Douglas' public speeches may be found in B. Manning, *Index to American Women Speakers* (1980), p. 103.

Honors

Woman of the Year, New York Hadassah (1945); Outstanding Woman of the Year, National Council of Negro Women (1945).

Bibliography

"California Foot Race," *Newsweek*, June 5, 1950.

In Chamberlin, Hope. *A Minority of Members* (1973).

In Engelbarts, R. *Women in Congress* (1974).

Flannery, H. W. "Red Smear in California," *Commonweal*, December 8, 1950.

"Helen Gahagan Douglas," *New Republic*, September 20, 1948.

Ickes, H. L. "Helen Douglas and Tobey," *New Republic*, October 16, 1950.

Israel, Lee. "Helen Gahagan Douglas," *Ms.*, October 1973.

In Lemparski, Richard. *"Whatever Became of ...?"* (1967).

In Roosevelt, Eleanor, and L. A. Hickok. *Ladies of Courage* (1954).

Toledano, R. de. "Roaring Races," *Newsweek*, October 30, 1950.

Frances Tarlton (Sissy) Farenthold
October 2, 1926-

B. Corpus Christi, Texas; D. Benjamin Dudley and Catherine Bluntzert Tarlton; M. George E. Farenthold, 1950; Received 420 votes for United States Vice President, 1972; President of Wells College, 1976- .

Frances Tarlton Farenthold, whom everyone has called "Sissy" since her Texas childhood, has never held a major political office. She emerges as a major political figure of the last 10 years and as a woman to watch in the eighties because of her achievements as a legislator (the only woman in the Texas House from 1968 to 1972); as a candidate for major office (she ran primary campaigns for the Democratic gubernatorial nomination in Texas in both 1972 and 1974); as the first woman to seriously contend for the vice-presidency of the United States (1972); and as a college president (Wells College, Aurora, New York).

Born and bred a Texan, Sissy Farenthold was no stranger to eastern politics and the eastern elite. She graduated from Vassar in 1946, and from the University of Texas School of Law, where she was one of three women in a class of 800. She managed the traditional roles of wife, mother, and volunteer as well as a career, which took off in the mid-sixties when she came back to public life as a legal aid lawyer. From there she began sprinting to national prominence as a spokeswoman for feminist and civil liberties issues.

Farenthold's vita lists her impressive past and present organizational and institutional affiliations, from the Texas Advisory Committee to the U.S. Civil Rights Commission (1968-1975), to the Chair of the National Women's Political Caucus (1973-1975). But the most fascinating aspect of Farenthold's political profile is her uncanny ability to land on her feet, no matter how outspoken her opinions, how perilous her political gambles, how difficult her career and committee assignments.

She came to Wells College as its first woman president in 1976, when it appeared that her political career in Texas was waning. She had lost badly in the 1974 Democratic primary for governor, but her public portfolio at that time chronicled her impressive 400-delegate bid to be McGovern's vice-presidential running mate in 1972 (she lost to Senator Thomas Eagleton). At that time, she had been at the forefront of the feminist Democratic movement, and had held academic appointment teaching law at the University of Houston.

Wells College, in upstate New York, a tiny, private woman's college, seemed a long way from the national political limelight, and certainly a long way from Houston, where husband George, a wealthy steel and oil man, resides. In coming to Wells College, Farenthold inherited more than a prestigious position. Wells was half a million dollars in debt, and the new president was expected to grapple with financial problems as well as with the many issues that plagued women-centered education in a period when small private women's colleges were going out of style and out of business. Since assuming the leadership of Wells, she has become a frequent commentator on women's higher education. A firm believer that women must gain entree to nontraditional fields, President Farenthold has initiated programs in business and engineering that allow students to graduate with a liberal arts degree from Wells and a technical degree from cooperating institutions.

Perhaps her most stunning success at Wells has been the Public Leadership Education Network (PLEN), which she pioneered through the funding of the Carnegie Corporation. Like almost all of Farenthold's affiliations, PLEN is the first attempt of its kind—a network joining the resources of five small women's colleges (Carlow, Goucher, Spelman, Stephens, and Wells) for the primary purpose of fostering young women's political careers. In a recent interview Farenthold explained that the idea had come to her while analyzing her own career, which she described as "a stumbling process." "We'd like women to consider public life much, much earlier than they did before, so they don't just stumble into it in later years," she said in 1979.

Having become sensitive to the women's issue when as a young Texas lawyer she found she was allowed to practice law but not to serve on a jury, Farenthold has long considered the dearth of good women in high places. In a 1975 article for *Redbook* magazine, she wrote about the possibilities of turning the country around if women could break through the male power elite of national politics, and she named 45 women she felt could provide a leadership of "fresh thinking and new directions." Among the women nominated in her best-of-all-feminist-political-worlds fantasy were Patsy Mink, Barbara Tuchman, Bella Abzug, Barbara Jordan, Margaret Mead, Liz Carpenter, Gloria Steinem, and Barbara Mikulski. At that point, the only women who had ever served in Cabinet positions were Frances Perkins and Oveta Culp Hobby. Farenthold also speculated about the country's need for a department of peace with a Cabinet-level secretary and a Cabinet office for women-related affairs. "In today's world, we need all the help we can get," she wrote.

Some of the women mentioned in her *Redbook* article have since risen to major political positions; her suggestion for the women's office came true, to a certain extent, during the Carter administration with the nomination of Sarah Weddington. But Farenthold has not been one to placidly applaud change, especially when she catches any indication of sexism. In 1979 she protested Carter's firing of Bella Abzug from her job as co-chairperson of the National Advisory Council on Women, saying that Carter's action "demonstrates the revolting nature of the raw, unrestrained power" of the high office. She communicated her opinion in a letter personally delivered by her to the White House.

Of paramount concern to the feminist politician turned college administrator is the ratification of the Equal Rights Amendment, an issue she predicts can only be resolved with increased political participation and political pressure by women. In a 1978 interview she stated, "You change laws by changing lawmakers," an axiom that provides the mortar for her Public Leadership Education Network proposal. Elsewhere she has analyzed the ERA situation: "It is interesting to hear some of the arguments in opposition to the Equal Rights Amendment. Some of them are the same ones that were made at the time when women, after a tremendous thrust of energy and effort, were enfranchised.... There is no question that under ERA there will be debates at times, indecision at times, litigation at times. Has anyone proposed that we rescind the First Amendment on free speech because there is too much litigation over it? Has anyone suggested the same for the Fourteenth Amendment (and I don't suppose there has ever been a constitutional amendment with so much litigation)?"

When she is not at Wells putting out financial fires (she has almost done away with the Wells College debt by stringent budgeting and judicious pruning of programs and personnel), Farenthold travels the country organizing and participating in sessions such as the Conference for Women on SALT II (1978) or the Conference on National Philanthropy (1979), where she indicted foundations for their minimal support for women's ventures and programs. She is presently on the Vassar Board of Trustees, as well as the Board of Schlesinger Library on the History of Women at Radcliffe. Because of a dual-career marriage, she and her family commute back and forth between Aurora and Houston. But when she is on campus in the president's office at Wells, the students know of her presence by the Texas flag that flies outside her office window. Though she is a dedicated college president, Farenthold is first and foremost a political lady from Texas. She has made it clear in the press and in her speaking engagements that she "is not in political exile"; she is in training.

Selected Writings and Speeches

"44 Women Who Could Save America," *Redbook*, April 1975; "Are You Brave Enough to Be in Politics?," *Redbook*, May 1976; "Legal Rights" (Speech given at Vermont College, February 26, 1977, for International Women's Year); "Applied Politics for College Women: An Educator Looks at New Concepts," *The Christian Science Monitor*, August 21, 1978; "Does Jimmy Carter Respect Women?," *Newsday*, January 22, 1979; "A Case for Others" (Speech given at Conference of National Council on Philanthropy, Denver, CO, November 8, 1979).

Honors

Honorary degrees from Hood College and Boston University (1973); Yale Women's Forum Award for contributions to the women's movement (1978).

Bibliography

Anast, Dave. "Interview with Sissy Farenthold," *The Bakersfield Californian*, April 22, 1978.

Dunn, Si. "Why Sissy Farenthold Is Not in Political Exile," *Texas Woman*, March 1979.

"Farenthold Cooking with SALT," *Ithaca Times*, December 13, 1978.

Frappolo, Elizabeth. "The Ticket That Might Have Been ... Vice-President Farenthold," *Ms.*, January 1973.

Grossman, Ellie. "PLEN: Learning What Public Life Is All About," *Rocky Mountain News*, January 14, 1980.

Maeroff, Gene I. "Political Power for Women: Five Colleges Join to Pave the Way," *New York Times*, July 11, 1978.

Minns, Karen M. C. "Babypink: Sissy—A Retrospect," *The Courier* (Wells Student Newspaper), May 1977.

Dianne Feinstein
June 22, 1933-

B. San Francisco, California; D. Leon and Elizabeth Rosenberg Goldman; M. Richard Blum, 1979; Served as Mayor of San Francisco, November 28, 1978- .

Dianne Feinstein came to be mayor of San Francisco in the wake of a sensational assassination, in which Mayor George Moscone, the first avowed homosexual to achieve elective office in San Francisco, and Harvey Milk, a San Francisco supervisor, were murdered in City Hall by a former San Francisco commissioner. The murders divided San Francisco's community, pitting straight citizens against gay citizens. As Moscone's immediate successor, it was Feinstein's task to calm the tension and paranoia that had enveloped the city. "The situation was so stark, so unreal, so terrible that everybody [suffered] a great sense of shock," she recalled later. "What really had to be done was, one, reassure the people; two, put the books back together; and three, do what's best, because sometimes violence begets violence." In New York City and San Francisco, gay activists demonstrated, sometimes violently, to protest the murders of Moscone and Milk.

Mayor Feinstein was able to soothe the diverse elements of San Francisco society with her astute political appointments. She appointed a moderate declared homosexual to fill Harvey Milk's seat, and a woman to take over her own position on the Board of Supervisors, thereby placating both the homosexual community and women's groups. The mayor met with members of various sexual preference groups asking them for cooperation and moderation during the transition period. When former commissioner Dan White was found guilty of voluntary manslaughter for the deaths of Moscone and Milk, thousands marched on City Hall to protest the lenience of the verdict. Feinstein, recovering from the death of her husband, neurosurgeon Bertram Feinstein, was confronted with violent riots that resulted in numerous injuries and significant destruction to the city.

Feinstein's victory in the mayoral election of December 11, 1979 against Supervisor Quentin Kopp was due, in large part, to the endorsements given her by homosexual activist David Scott, a loser in the preliminary qualifying vote. Governor Jerry Brown backed Kopp, while President Carter took Feinstein's part in the 1979 election. She was well known to San Franciscans because of her membership on the influential San Francisco Board of Supervisors from 1969, serving as its president during 1970 to 1972, and 1974 to 1976. In 1971 she had unsuccessfully fought Joseph Alioto in the mayoral race.

Undoubtedly, Feinstein's major challenge since becoming mayor of San Francisco has been to establish a viable budget in the wake of Proposition 13, which had resulted in an immediate loss of nearly $150 million in revenue for the city. The mayor's problem has centered on the impossibility of meeting San Francisco's expenses without calling for huge reductions in city services (Feinstein proposed a $29 million cut in March 1980) and substantial hikes in mass transit fares. Though there seems little possibility that the state can muster the shortfall from San Francisco's revenues, since the entire California budget surplus was wiped out by the 1978 Proposition 13 situation, she has encountered resistance from the San Francisco Board of Supervisors in putting her budget-cutting plans into effect. Feinstein must cope with further possibilities of cuts in the summer of 1980, when Proposition 9, another drastic tax-cutting referendum, is brought before California voters.

Due to the dire financial situation in San Francisco, Feinstein, a Democrat in a non-partisan office, must confront the dismantling of many liberal programs that she personally favors. She had long been identified with California ecological groups—Friends of the Earth and the Sierra Club—as well as a long list of liberal causes, including the Bay Area Urban League and the Chinese Cultural Foundation. Political analysts have commented on Feinstein's increasingly conservative fiscal decisions based on her pragmatic knowledge of urban problems.

Feinstein, a graduate of Stanford (B.A., 1955, history and political science), became interested in criminal justice as a public affairs intern. She periodically flowed in and out of governmental positions—California Industrial Welfare Commission, California Women's Board of Terms and Paroles; San Francisco City and County Advisory Commission for Adult Detention, and the Mayor's Commission on Crime—but because of family exigencies (the birth of a daughter and the failure of a first marriage), she devoted full time to the learning process even when unpaid. Like Mayor Byrne of Chicago, she inherited an impossible financial situation, a no-win double bind challenging her to choose between the city's haves and the have-nots with the knowledge that budget cuts hit most acutely the low-income population.

Honors

Women of Achievement Award, Business and Professional Women's Clubs of San Francisco (1970); Distinguished Woman Award, *San Francisco Examiner* (1970).

Bibliography

Frequent references in the *San Francisco Examiner and Chronicle* and in *San Francisco Magazine*.

"All Hers at Last," *Time*, December 24, 1979.

"Healing Starts in a Troubled City," *U.S. News and World Report*, December 18, 1978.

"In More Big Cities It's Her Honor the Mayor," *U.S. News and World Report*, July 16, 1979.

"San Francisco: Feinstein Hangs On," *Newsweek*, December 24, 1979.

"San Francisco Mayor Dianne Feinstein Invokes Mutual Aid Pact and Puts Policemen from San Francisco and Neighboring Suburban Communities on Alert," *New York Times*, May 23, 1979, p. 1.

Millicent Hammond Fenwick
February 25, 1910-

B. New York City; D. Ogden Haggerty and Mary Stevens Hammond; Served in U.S. House of Representatives as Republican-New Jersey, January 1974- , 95th Congress- .

Millicent Fenwick, the septuagenarian Republican representative from New Jersey's Fifth District, reflects the upper-class background characteristic of this wealthy district's past leaders. While her natural elegance and cultured background of inherited wealth fit the patrician profile, her political style differs from that of Republican predecessors Charles Eaton, Peter Frelinghuysen, and others because of her liberal concern (going much beyond *noblesse oblige*) for the people whom she feels have been oppressed by the "terrifying" power of federal government. She sees herself as a protector of the beleaguered in her district—the aged, the minorities, and the poor—and attempts to personally grease the wheels of government to force the system to serve the needs of these constituents. In a sense, she has carried with her to Congress the consumer advocacy persona she cultivated in her former position as director of New Jersey's Division of Consumer Affairs from 1972 to 1974, a political appointment of Governor Cahill that drew her out of the New Jersey legislature to the executive branch.

Born in New York City, the daughter of Mary Stevens, the blue-blooded heiress and descendant of revolutionary heroes, and Ogden Haggerty Hammond, Millicent Hammond's childhood was tragically marred by the death of her mother on the ill-fated *Lusitania*. Her father remarried Marguerite McClure Howland in 1917, and it seems that Millicent and her stepmother did not get along well. Like Clare Boothe Luce, Millicent's academic background was unorthodox. She attended the Foxcroft school until 1925, when her father, who had been appointed ambassador to Spain by President Coolidge, took his daughters with him to Madrid. From her cosmopolitan childhood she acquired fluency in French and Spanish, a background later alluded to when she asked to be made a member of the Foreign Relations Committee in Congress. After returning to the United States, she took courses from Columbia University, and later studied philosophy under Bertrand Russell at the New School for Social Research. She was married early and unhappily to Hugh Fenwick, and by 1938 was alone with two small children, supporting her family on an elegant, small farm in Somerset, New Jersey. Reportedly, her husband had abandoned the family after squandering a great deal of his wife's capital, and Fenwick took a job with Condé Nast at *Vogue* to earn money for the household and to pay off her husband's substantial debts. If it had not been for the financial crisis imposed by these hard times, Millicent Fenwick might never have realized the potential she possessed for working well with people in government, for organizing, and for expressing herself confidently and clearly.

She served as an associate editor for Condé Nast Publications from 1938 to 1952. The earlier *Vogue* background is still apparent in her carriage and chic appearance even as she enters her seventies. Fenwick endorsed volunteerism in the pages of *Vogue*, where society women were portrayed as having more substantive and altruistic life goals than merely to dress and entertain well. Volunteerism and civic commitment were, after all, part of her heritage (her mother's death on the *Lusitania* occurred in the line of volunteer duty—she was sailing to Europe to organize a hospital for victims of World War I). Fenwick served on numerous committees for civic good during and after the Condé Nast years. She resigned from Condé Nast in 1958, due, in part, to a revival of her family fortune from income derived through her assets as owner of the Hoboken Land and Improvement Company, a fortune Fenwick has disclosed as in excess of $5 million. She became a member of the Bernardsville Borough Council, was vice-chair of the New Jersey Committee for the United States Commission on Civil Rights, and served on numerous other committees that worked toward protecting citizens' legal and economic rights. She also chaired the Governor's Committee on Equal Employment Opportunity. Fenwick's state committee memberships and her successful fundraising ventures for Republican candidates, notably for Senator Clifford Case and President Eisenhower, established New Jersey and eastern establishment political contacts that led eventually to her vice-chairmanship of the New Jersey Republican State Committee.

When her political ambitions became more defined in 1967 with her election to the New Jersey Legislature, sagacious politicos in the state began to tag Fenwick as a woman of talent who might serve the state in a greater capacity. She was easily reelected to the New Jersey Legislature in 1969 after demonstrating skill in dealing with problems associated with the aged, minorities, and unemployment, but left the Legislature for the directorship of the state's consumer affairs office, a newly created job she approached with considerable creativity in a time when vocal consumer indignation was beginning to escalate. Perhaps her greatest achievement in this position was to actively involve the lay public in the professional boards of the state, so that control of the professions became less self-serving than had previously been the case.

When Peter Frelinghuysen of the Fifth District decided not to seek reelection in 1974, Fenwick was mentioned in newspapers and political circles as a likely congressional candidate. The 64-year-old Fenwick beat a 38-year-old male opponent, Tom Kean, in the primary by a mere 84 votes and went on to defeat another young man, Democrat Fred Bohen, for the seat. In Peggy Lamson's biographical profile of Fenwick (*In the Vanguard*, p. 20), Bohen assesses his unusual opponent's political capabilities and personal style, describing her as "a tireless and expert campaigner, an excellent and witty speaker, very quick with one-line rejoinders.... She had an ability to turn complicated questions into simple, easily understood formulations that catch the popular fancy." An oft-quoted example of her quick wit concerns a debate she engaged in on behalf of the Equal Rights Amendment. A male colleague responded to her speech endorsing the amendment with a counterstatement of earnest disapproval: "I just don't like the amendment. I've always thought of women as kissable, cuddly and smelling good." Fenwick replied brightly and without malice, "That's the way I feel about men, too. I only hope for your sake that you haven't been disappointed as often as I have" (*Parade*, May 4, 1975).

Elected to the House of Representatives in 1974 and reelected in 1976, she has served as a member of the House Committee on Banking, Finance and

Urban Affairs; the Small Business Committee; and the Committee on Standards of Official Conduct. In addition, she served as a member of the Helsinki Commission on Security and Cooperation in Europe, a commission she created to monitor compliance with human rights provisions in the Helsinki Accords. Fenwick takes a conservative view to introducing legislation, though she herself has been remarkably successful in authoring and sponsoring new bills. Her conviction that the tentacles of bureaucracy have damaged the government's responsiveness to people's needs, and that less rather than more government may be part of the solution, is reflected in her statement that there is no point in introducing legislation unless an overwhelming good is to be realized from its adoption. Fenwick's successfully introduced legislation understandably leans toward protecting the consumer—a law to protect consumers in business bankruptcy cases, and a recommendation that Health, Education and Welfare allow more home visitations by patients without jeopardizing their Medicaid benefits, for example. She introduced the first bill in the House to permit Indochinese refugees to become permanent residents in the United States. Another bill geared toward providing solutions for those who have been hit by costly and tragic misfortune is her asbestos workers bill, which would provide adequate disability compensation for asbestos workers and their families without having to engage in lengthy and expensive litigation. Fenwick has called for the abolition of the "tax on marriage." Noting that people who live together without benefit of marriage pay less taxes, she has concluded that "the marriage tax penalty encourages this trend."

Fenwick has been a strong feminist by virtue of her life style and her commitment to independence, consistently supporting the ERA though not to the satisfaction of some feminists. On one occasion she debated Phyllis Schlafly in a televised debate on ERA. She asserts that the advancement of women in politics is contingent upon women performing well when they are in a position to shape legislation and public policy, and has said that the competency of political women will be measured "by a steady stream of accomplishments that affect the welfare of the nation." Nevertheless, she disapproves of a specifically female agenda: "What after all would we think if men all got together and kept doing things that were supposed to be in the interest of men?" A stern moralist when it comes to politics, Fenwick has noted that women don't often seem to be linked with political corruption. "I've never known a woman in politics who has been offered a bribe," she once commented.

Toward achieving this congressional standard of excellence, Millicent Fenwick devotes her life to the House (12 to 14 hours per day at the office). The congresswoman's personal style and preferences—from smoking a pipe, to forging an excellent professional relationship with a former Democratic colleague, Bella Abzug—suggest the difficulty of categorizing her. Though a Republican (she champions fiscal responsibility and a lessening of governmental interference in people's daily lives), Fenwick supports a great many so-called liberal causes. Surely her election to the House insures advocacy on behalf of many population groups outside the mainstream.

Writings and Selected Speeches

Commencement Address, Upsala College, *New York Times*, May 27, 1976.

Bibliography

Burks, Edward C. "Rep. Fenwick: Basics Her Forte," *New York Times*, May 13, 1979, N.J. p. 4.

Burnham, S. "Congresswoman Who Cares," *McCalls*, June 1977.

Carpenter, T. S. "Rating Our Congressmen: As a Delegation They're Getting Better," *New Jersey Monthly*, October 1978.

Glaser, V. "Millicent Fenwick at Home in the House," *Saturday Evening Post*, September 1975.

Hart, Jeffrey. "Millicent Fenwick and Those Vietnam 'Cliches,'" *Human Events*, August 16, 1975.

In Lamson, P. *In the Vanguard* (1979).

Reinhold, Robert. "Bill Offered by Senator Mathias and Repr. Fenwick That Would Allow Married Couples to File Separate Returns," *New York Times*, July 10, 1979.

"Republican Representative Millicent Fenwick of NY," *New York Times*, May 13, 1979.

Stafford, J. "Millicent Fenwick Makes an Adroit Politician," *Vogue*, June 1975.

Ungar, S. J. "Grandmother Is a Sophomore," *Atlantic*, July 1977.

Walker, Connecticut. "Rep. Millicent Fenwick: A Star of the New Congress," *Newark Sunday Star Ledger*, May 4, 1975.

Geraldine A. Ferraro
August 26, 1935-

B. Newburgh, New York; D. Dominick and Antonetta Corrieri Ferraro; M. John Zaccaro, 1960; Served in U.S. House of Representatives as Democrat-New York, January 3, 1979- , 96th Congress- .

A woman running for the United States Congress in New York State has a difficult course to sprint, especially if she is Catholic and running from a conservative district where the issue of abortion inevitably rears its head. Ferraro took a cautious stand during her campaign, stating her personal rejection of the concept of abortion; but she held that a woman should have the right to select abortion as an alternative and that, in fact, the federal government should fund abortions for poor women. She has stated that her opinion on abortion was strongly colored by her legal experience in the Queens County attorney's office, where she had worked extensively on child abuse. "Unwanted children become abused children," went her argument.

Ferraro maintains that her campaign was made particularly difficult by an opponent who lashed out against her husband, calling him a "slumlord" because of his involvement in real estate. Then, too, she suffered because of federal campaign financing laws that she considers discriminatory. "A candidate cannot borrow or receive more than one thousand dollars from her or his spouse, but can contribute unlimited amounts to his or her campaign. Given that in most marriages, most of the assets are in the husband's name, most married men running for office have access to a great deal more money than married women who are candidates" (*Ms.*, January 1979, p. 93).

A Democrat from the heavily populated Ninth Congressional District (Queens), Ferraro has been vigorous in defending her district's interests, concerns for decent pensions, medical care for the elderly, and the like, typical of districts populated by working class people and retirees. She clashed with Congresswoman Olympia Snowe in early February 1980 on the allocation formula the Maine legislator proposed to put a 12.5% cap on federal financial assistance designated for any one state under the targeted fiscal recessionary assistance program. Since the 12.5% proviso would cut the fiscal assistance rationing for only two states—New York and California—Ferraro argued that Snowe's amendment was biased against states with dense populations. "This type of parochialism and legislating is irresponsible," she protested. "I would not support a cap on the amount of grain price supports that Iowa, or Nebraska, or Kansas receive. Agricultural aid goes where it is needed, and so, too, should anti-recessionary assistance be targeted to those areas in the greatest need" (*Congressional Quarterly Weekly Reports*, 1980, p. 358).

During 1979 Ferraro opposed Carter issues in 26 cases, while she supported him in 66 votes. Present at almost 90% of the House sessions, she tends to agree with her Democratic colleagues on most votes, dissenting during 1979 on only 14% of House party unity votes (those roll calls that are taken when a majority of Democrats oppose a majority of Republicans on a given issue). A member of the Post Office and Civil Service Committee and its Postal Operations and Services Subcommittee, as well as Public Works and Transportation and its Aviation Subcommittee, Ferraro has taken the position that civil service pensions be protected at all costs. She is particularly interested in her assignment to the Select Aging Committee, especially with regard to retirement income and employment. The Congresswomen's Caucus has targeted the economic problems of aging women among the most shocking in the country, noting that one-half the female population over age 65 are living on less than $1,800 per year. Ferraro, though a member of the Congresswomen's Caucus and a strong supporter of ERA, has kept a low profile on women-related issues during her first term, and is seldom cited in Caucus news releases. She strongly advocates augmenting Social Security payments to the aged living in areas where the cost of living is highest, again a regional issue specifically dear to her Ninth District. Her office staff offers assistance to the elderly in straightening out Social Security and Medicare bureaucratic hitches.

Especially vocal in the struggle to obtain federal loans to assist New York City's water situation, in 1979 Ferraro was the only New York City voice on the Public Works and Transportation Committee, which voted some $25 million to complete the third water tunnel in the city. Though President Carter opposed House actions on a multibillion-dollar water projects authorization bill in January 1980, the congresswoman praised measures to refurbish existing water systems in major cities. "It is appropriate that Congress begin a shift of priorities from the new construction projects that have always dominated public works bills to rehabilitation and maintenance of existing facilities," she argued, taking her characteristic stand in favor of measures to benefit the federally abandoned inner-city (*Congressional Quarterly Weekly Reports*, 1980, p. 186).

Congresswomen have traditionally been concerned with consumer matters, and Ferraro, too, has publicly taken up the consumer cause, especially with regard to New York City food prices in 1979 and 1980. Her particular concern for older citizens who face the city's ever-increasing food price leaps revealed itself in hearings on food price trends held in New York City, which aired the views of food industry representatives and consumer advocates.

Geraldine Ferraro taught in the New York public schools from 1956 to 1961 while studying by night at Fordham Law School (L.L.B., 1960). From the early sixties to the mid-seventies she remained in private practice and devoted considerable energy to her children, striking out into public affairs as an assistant district attorney for Queens County in 1974. As a bureau chief supervising cases involving special victims, she authored a statute that defined child abuse as a felony offense in New York State. On battered spouse legislation and other domestic violence issues Ferraro was a visible and effective advocate for progressive reform. In 1978 she was admitted to argue before the U.S. Supreme Court, and became advisory counsel to the Civil Court of New York in that same year.

Clearly, Ferraro, who maintains a mobile office so that she can be accessible to her scattered Queens constituency, is a legislator much concerned with the problems of neighborhoods and of the ordinary people who inhabit them. She states: "I am convinced we can serve the real needs of our neighborhoods without huge budget deficits and government waste."

Bibliography

Numerous references in *New York Times*.

"Food Industry Representatives and Advocates Attend Hearings," *New York Times*, March 13, 1979, Sec. 2, p. 1.

Haberman, N., and A. Northrop. "Freshwomen in Congress," *Ms.*, January 1979.

"HR Public Works and Transportation Committee Votes," *New York Times*, July 30, 1979, Sec. 2, p. 3.

Radcliffe, Donna. "Rushing on the Hill," *The Washington Post*, December 6, 1978, p. C4.

Ella Grasso
May 10, 1919-

B. Windsor Locks, Connecticut; D. James and Maria Oliva Tambussi; M. Thomas Grasso, 1942; Served in U.S. House of Representatives as Republican-Connecticut, January 21, 1971 to January 3, 1975, 92nd through 93rd Congress; Served as Governor of Connecticut, January 8, 1975- .

Ella Grasso's career has spanned the range of public service. Her government experience includes state representative in the Connecticut General Assembly for two terms, the first woman floor leader in the state legislature, the first woman chairperson of the Democratic State Platform Committee, secretary of state for 12 years, and member of Congress for two terms. She is the first American woman ever to be elected governor without having followed her husband into office. A central fact of Grasso's political career is her unerring feel for political waters ever since she won the newly created additional state seat in the Connecticut House of Representatives in 1952. Her ethnic Italian upbringing combined with an impressive academic background (scholarships to the Chaffee School, 1936; Mount Holyoke College, B.S., 1940; M.S., 1942) have served her well as a public servant. In speeches and articles she deftly interweaves the concerns of big business with those of, say, the struggling young families in Connecticut's ethnic population—a skill she learned in the General Assembly and perfected during her secretary of state years (1958-1970). During that period she served as vice-chair of the Executive Committee of Human Rights and Opportunities and chairperson of the Planning Committee for the Governor's Commission on the Status of Women.

During her Connecticut legislature days, powerful Democratic figures called upon Grasso to serve on prestigious committees and commissions; John Kennedy appointed her to the Board of Foreign Scholarships, and Lyndon Johnson reappointed her. She received considerable attention from national political people in her roles as a member of the National Platform Committee in 1960 and co-chairperson of the Resolutions Committee of the Democratic National Convention in 1964 and 1968.

From the beginning Grasso displayed a finesse in political matters unequaled by other contemporary female politicians. When she arrived at the Connecticut statehouse in 1952, she had already attracted the favorable notice of Connecticut Democratic luminaries John Bailey, John Dempsey, and Abraham Ribicoff, who supported her progressive notions for streamlining state government through the elimination of Connecticut's county governments. In 1955, after an easy reelection to the Connecticut House, she was named floor leader. She enjoyed the wheeling and dealing that went with politics on the floor of the legislature and enthusiastically undertook the work of overhauling the Democratic platform in Connecticut.

Those who have written about Ella Grasso have talked about her gregarious, jovial manner with colleagues and constituents, her unthreatening, unfashionable, though pleasant appearance, her sensible manner of presenting valid arguments. Her mentor, the powerful Democrat John Bailey, in commenting on her self-confidence, points out that Ella was never known "to hide her light under a bushel." Her degrees in sociology and economics have provided her with credible credentials with politicians and business people, while her fluency in Italian and her loyalty to her ethnic roots have endeared her to the Connecticut population that first supported her. Though her *curriculum vitae* speaks of innumerable committees she has chaired, of countless organizations for which she has served as director or trustee, as well as her political offices and appointments, Ella Grasso is most admired and respected in her home state for the traditional qualities she possesses: a loyal daughter, she remained close to her parents in their old age and appears to lead an exemplary family life with her husband, Dr. Thomas Grasso, a retired high school principal, and her two grown children. In 1968 she announced that she would not run for the Sixth Congressional District seat due to overriding family concerns—aged parents, teenaged children, and a husband recuperating from two heart attacks. It is obvious that this personal decision scarcely nicked her political future. In the policy area Governor Grasso has translated her concerns for family well-being into support for comprehensive health care and other assistance programs for the aged, and has supported President Carter's National Health Plan and Hospital Cost Containment programs.

As governor, Grasso has experienced enormous success. Her campaign against Representative Robert A. Steele hit the issues of consumer concerns, inflation, and high sales tax. After the election, she brought in the Public Utilities Control Authority, a consumer-oriented group, to replace the Public Utilities Commission in Connecticut. She met the $71 million state debt she had inherited with strategies to tighten government spending, and set the tone for austerity by turning back her own salary raises to the state, even refusing to travel by limousine and private airplane. Connecticut's citizens responded well to Governor Grasso's frugality and commitment to "make do with little." Her stunning victory over Ronald A. Sarasin in 1978 brought her a second term as governor of Connecticut. She has been a leadership figure among governors, serving as chairperson of the Coalition of Northeastern Governors, 1979-1980; chairperson of the Democratic Governors Association, 1979-1980; and chairperson of the Credentials Committee of the 1980 Democratic National Convention.

Ella Grasso's dynamism and political intelligence have insured her a career apparently free of discrimination on the basis of sex. Though she supports expanded opportunities for women, she rarely hits upon the issue with reference to herself. She does associate herself with the feminist movement, however. In a typical 1975 speech on women in politics she allowed that there remains a need for women's contributions to public service, even though "it has been my good fortune not to experience any discernible discrimination, even from the earliest days of my public career." Grasso continued: "The 93rd Congress had 12 women members, the 94th Congress has 16, plus scores of women holding key elected positions in state and local governments.... In the future, an effective Congress will include many more women members—and the day will come when the nation's First Lady will be the nation's first woman President."

Grasso calls herself "a tough old bird." After undergoing surgery for cancer in the spring of 1980, the governor turned trauma into political hay with her pragmatic report to the press and her no-nonsense approach to further treatment, requiring extensive radiation therapy.

Writings and Selected Speeches

Message by Ella Grasso, Independence Day Celebration, Colebrook, CT (July 4, 1979); Remarks by Governor Ella Grasso, Danbury (CT) Rotary Club (October 3, 1979); Remarks by Governor Ella Grasso, Regional Forum of American Association of Retired Persons, Hartford, CT (September 12, 1979).

A more complete listing of Grasso's public speeches may be found in B. Manning, *Index to American Women Speakers* (1980), pp. 130-31.

Honors

Time magazine, one of 12 "Women of the Year" (1975); *Ladies Home Journal* "Woman of the Year" (1976); Numerous local awards from Connecticut communities and organizations, including the Silver Apple Award of the Connecticut Education Association; Thomas Jefferson Award, sponsored by several Texas media associations for distinguished service in defense of the press; Knight of the Order of Merit of the Italian Republic; Honorary doctorates from Mount Holyoke, Smith College, and from Sacred Heart University, Bridgeport, CT.

Bibliography

Buckley, W. F. "No Trespassing," *National Review*, October 13, 1978.

Burnham, A. "Governor Grasso's Troubles," *Progressive*, January 1978.

In Chamberlin, Hope. *A Minority of Members* (1973).

Collins, G. "A Democratic Love Story," *Connecticut*, April 1978.

In Engelbarts, Rudolf. *Women in the United States Congress* (1974).

"Grasso On Her Own," *Economist*, December 13, 1975.

In Lamson, Peggy. *Few Are Chosen: American Women in Political Life Today* (1968).

"Republican's Chance," *Connecticut Economist*, August 5, 1978.

Schlafly, Phyllis. "Grasso Proposes 40-Hour Work Week," *Human Events*, January 31, 1976.

"Surprises from Nation's Two Women Governors," *U.S. News and World Report*, October 10, 1977.

Treaster, Joseph B. "Ella Grasso of Connecticut: Running and Winning," *Ms.*, October 1974.

Weeghman, R. B. "Throwing Out the Baby," *Flying*, April 1976.

Edith Starrett Green
January 17, 1910-

B. Trent, South Dakota; D. James Vaughn and Julia Starrett; M. Arthur Green, 1933; Served in U.S. House of Representatives as Democrat-Oregon, January 5, 1955 to January 3, 1975, 84th through 93rd Congress.

Taken as a parcel, Edith Green's political decisions present many contradictions: a supporter of the Supreme Court's decision to abolish segregation, she opposed busing; an author of the Equal Pay Act (1963), she has never been an ERA supporter; the chairperson of liberal senator Bobby Kennedy's Oregon campaign in 1968, she backed right-wing senator Henry "Scoop" Jackson in 1972; a staunch supporter of educational programs, she deplored the proliferation of educational programs administered by the federal government. Possibly because she possessed staying power in the Congress, serving 20 years, she felt no compunction to line up as a liberal Democrat behind all issues, preferring rather to call the issues as she saw them.

Unlike women who entered Congress in the 1970s, Green counted the seniority system as the most powerful tool women could wield in order to gain power in Congress. Without it, she said, women would have no say on committees. Green used her committee assignment to Education and Labor and her position as chair of the special Subcommittee on Post-Secondary Education to push through some of the most significant educational legislation ever to come out of Congress, including the Higher Education acts of 1965 and 1967 and the Higher Education Facilities Act. Work study and grant programs for needy students were her brain children (she herself dropped out of college because of a lack of funds). Through her amendments to end discrimination in health and education Job Corps training, many women entered these fields. Called "Mrs. Education" in the media, Green was the true mother of Affirmative Action on college campuses receiving federal monies. Her higher education bill prohibited colleges and universities from discrimination during the admission process, as well as discriminatory hiring practices within the institution. Green's statement "Let us not deceive ourselves; our educational institutions have proven to be no bastions of democracy" is widely quoted. However, she received considerable bad press during the sixties in the wake of campus unrest because of her proposal that federally funded institutions of higher education submit their behavior codes to the government for approval.

Green came from a family of schoolteachers, and worked as a teacher herself for 15 years before launching a political career. Not that she wouldn't have preferred to train for another profession—her interest in law was squelched by her parents, who suggested that nursing and teaching were professions where women might be allowed to make meaningful contributions. If she went into law, they warned her, she could expect to be toiling unrecognized behind the scenes in a clerical position. Her path to a degree in education (B.S., University of Oregon, 1939) was interrupted by marriage, children, and teaching. Later she did some graduate work at Stanford.

Green opposed the many anti-poverty programs under the aegis of federal educational agencies. Fair wages, to her way of thinking, would do more in the way of reducing poverty because she believed people need to control their own lives and free themselves from government control. She voted against extending "the war on poverty" legislation because "I think that it has wasted millions of dollars in this country and the impact has been minimal." Instead, she became an advocate of vocational training programs: "I've always argued that it is just as desirable, just as possible, to have philosopher plumbers as philosopher kings," she told audiences.

She was rigorous in her examination of programs favoring groups termed "disadvantaged" by society-at-large. Addressing a Brigham Young University audience in 1977 she stated, "I have never believed that race, sex, religion, or national origin are valid criteria for either 'favorable' or 'unfavorable' treatment. This is one reason why I have been opposed to programs which give an advantage in job consideration and promotion to members of those groups who have suffered historic discrimination."

A pet peeve of Green's was being asked how she got into politics, which she translated as "how did you, a *woman*, get into politics?" She began in politics at the grassroots level as state legislative chair for the PTA in 1946, while living in Portland. School support was her issue then, as it remained even after her retirement in 1975. She ran the most difficult race of her career when she fought Tom McCall (later, Oregon's governor) for a seat from the Third District to the 84th Congress. Though Green enjoyed great popularity in Oregon during her 10 consecutive terms, she decided not to run for the Senate because of her commitment to the Education and Labor Committee; she stood to lose her seniority, thus her clout, if she left the Congress.

Green championed a library services bill during her first term in Congress to pump federal support into rural libraries, thus providing many millions of Americans access to a public library, a measure that passed into law in 1956. She was consistently a friend to libraries, schools, and agencies for the aged and the needy. Her dedication to educational issues extended into the international sector; she served as a delegate to numerous Unesco and NATO conferences, representing the United States on education.

After her divorce, Green retired to Charbonneau, Oregon, where she remains active in Oregon affairs, especially issues concerning education. Among her board memberships are Linfield College and the University of Oregon Health Sciences Center. During her congressional years she seemed to be constantly on the run; now, in the 1980s, she walks five miles a day. An armchair observer, she is still vocally critical of members of Congress who give politics a bad name.

Selected Speeches and Writings

"Education and the Public Good: The Federal Role in Education," in Walter P. Reuther, *The Challenge to Education in a Changing World* (1963); "The Future Is Now," *Colleges and Universities*, Fall 1975; "The Road Is Paved with Good Intentions: Title IX and What It Is Not," *Vital Speeches*, March 1, 1977.

The papers of Edith Green from 1956 to 1973 are held by the Oregon Historical Society in Portland, which also holds a recorded interview with Green.

A more complete listing of Green's public speeches may be found in B. Manning, *Index to American Women Speakers* (1980), p. 132.

Honors

Many honorary degrees, including University of Alaska (1956); Boston College and Yale University (1965); Reed College, Oberlin, Miami University, and Georgetown (1966); Northeastern University (1972); Portland's First Citizen Award (1979).

Bibliography

"Backer of Federal Aid Asks, What Went Wrong?," *Educational Digest*, April 1974.

In Chamberlin, Hope. *A Minority of Members* (1973).

"Disadvantaged Middle Class," *Journal of the National Association of College Admissions Counselors*, November 1973.

"Education's Federal Grab Bag," *Phi Delta Kappan*, October 1972.

"Interview with Representative Edith Green," *Urban Review*, Vol. 4, No. 1 (1969).

Miller, Norm C. "Representative Edith Green: A Bare Knuckle Fighter," *Wall Street Journal*, December 3, 1969.

"Political Profiles of the Eisenhower Years," *Facts on File*, 1977.

"Political Profiles of the Johnson Years," *Facts on File*, 1976.

"Political Profiles of the Kennedy Years," *Facts on File*, 1976.

Rosenberg, Marie C. Barovic. "Women in Politics: A Comparative Study of Edith Green and Julia Butler Hansen," *Dissertation Abstracts*, Vol. 35, No. 1 (1974), p. 542-A.

Sullivan, Ann. "Edith Green, Stateswoman Extraordinaire Still Serves," *The Oregonian*, February 15, 1979.

Wides, Louise. "Edith Green, Democratic Representative from Oregon," in Ralph Nader Citizens Look at Congress Project (Series), Grossman, 1972.

Martha Wright Griffiths
January 29, 1912-

B. Pierce City, Missouri; D. Charles Elbridge and Nell Sullinger Wright; M. Hicks Griffiths, 1933; Served in U.S. House of Representatives as Democrat-Michigan, January 5, 1955 to January 3, 1975, 84th through 93rd Congress.

Martha Griffiths' 20-year congressional career will be remembered most for her efforts to pass the Equal Rights Amendment (ERA). She set this difficult goal for herself saying, "This amendment, if passed, would be like a beacon which should awaken nine sleeping Rip Van Winkles to the fact that the twentieth century is passing into history. It is a different world and they [the Supreme Court] should speak for justice, not prejudice.... I seek justice, not in some distant tomorrow, not in some study commission, but now while I live." Elsewhere Griffiths had said, "My grandmother wanted to live long enough to vote for a woman president. I'll be satisfied if I live to see a woman go before the Supreme Court and hear the justices acknowledge, 'Gentlemen, she's human. She deserves the protection of our laws.' "

Griffiths, a lawyer (she earned her degree from the University of Michigan in 1940), and a former judge (the first woman judge of Recorder's Court, Detroit, Michigan), has been interested in legal reform, especially for laws affecting women, more than in any other single issue during her career. In the early 1970s her name was mentioned as a possibility for the first woman justice of the Supreme Court. In fact, her nine women colleagues in Congress pressed President Nixon to nominate her. Though a Supreme Court appointment has not materialized, and Griffiths' age may be a future impediment, she herself has not dismissed the future possibility of a Justice Griffiths.

Martha Griffiths used every legislative ploy available to her, on and off the floor, to insure support of ERA in the House and the Senate. Though she told congressional colleagues that their political careers hinged on supporting the amendment, and warned that legions of members from women's organizations would plague the campaigns of those opposing ERA, she named the Supreme Court, not the Congress, as the major culprit responsible for sex discrimination. This politic manner of persuasion assuaged the sensitive feelings of many representatives who were opposed to ERA; 350 representatives supported the amendment in the House, although Griffiths was forced to challenge Judiciary Committee chairman Emanuel Celler by obtaining a discharge petition to bring the amendment up for a vote. Not one to hesitate in using leverage, she opposed bills sponsored and signed by those against ERA. Gerald Ford, who was House minority leader when Griffiths was in the midst of the state ratification campaign for ERA, acknowledged plainly that the future constitutional amendment would be a "monument to Martha." In 1972 she was able to get 354 ERA votes in the House and 84 in the Senate. Since March 22, 1972, the amendment has been wading through the state ratification process. Though a staunch supporter of women's rights, Griffiths exhibited caution in embracing some controversial issues, such as abortion.

Though the fight for the amendment was Griffiths' most brilliant hour in Congress, many events in the sixties influenced the amendment question; for example, her feud with the Equal Employment Opportunities Commission (EEOC), an agency she claimed did not effectively enforce Title VII of the Civil Rights Act, designed in principle to ban sex discrimination in hiring practices. "They [the EEOC] are a bunch of jerks. Every one of them should be fired," she bluntly wrote to President Johnson in 1967. The widely publicized conflagration resulted in frequent statistical reports on women workers issued by the Labor Department. More, it galvanized women behind the equal employment issue; NOW (National Organization for Women) was born in June 1966 largely because of Griffiths' monitoring of EEOC developments.

The Social Security benefits of divorced women, widowers, and widows, now more frequently called "surviving spouses," have improved due to Griffiths' concern. She argued against laws excluding benefits for divorced women married over 20 years, as well as those laws that gave female survivors who had never been in the work force more Social Security benefits than married women who had worked outside the home all their lives. Why couldn't couples pool their Social Security credits for higher benefits, and why shouldn't the surviving children of mothers who had not worked for more than one year before death be entitled to benefits? Why were widows allowed to collect reduced benefits at age 60, while widowers were forced to wait until age 62? These were among the questions of inequity addressed in Griffiths' 1972 Social Security bill (HR 1).

National health insurance, an issue appealing to the auto worker constituency of Griffiths' 17th District, became one of the most controversial pieces of legislation in 1970. Later, the bill metamorphosed into the Kennedy-Corman-Griffiths proposal, lauded by labor and despised by insurance programs like Blue Cross and Blue Shield as well as the nation's physicians. The proposal called for an end to private patient fees and insurance costs and expanded health care delivery systems and cost-effective measures to encourage better use of facilities and medical personnel.

Since her first difficult campaign in 1952, which she lost to the GOP candidate, Griffiths has been a successful and easily reelected candidate. Her campaigns were managed by her lawyer husband, Hicks Griffiths, until 1974. Because she performed well on her early committee assignments—Banking and Currency, Government Operations, the Joint Economic Committee of the House and Senate—she eventually was able to climb aboard the most prestigious House committee, Ways and Means, which Wilbur Mills had chaired since the late 1950s. It appears that Griffiths regarded Mills as something of a mentor, a compliment which he returned with his public acknowledgment of respect for her considerable legislative skills. Reportedly she once admitted, "Chairman Mills is the only living person who knows about tax." Her voting record on the Ways and Means Committee reflects the confidence she had in Mills' technical knowledge of budgetary matters.

One of Griffiths' most ambitious undertakings as chair of the Joint Economic Committee Study of Welfare in 1972 involved her conducting national hearings to determine the actual needs of those less fortunate members of society for whose benefit the actual programs are designed. During the hearings, held on site in New York, Atlanta, and Detroit, she probed witnesses about "the tangled mess of welfare," looking for solutions to the unfair administration of welfare and to abuses against the welfare system. She counts her work on welfare and health problems as the most substantial contribution she made to the Ways and Means Committee.

Though Martha Griffiths was not reelected in 1974, she maintains active ties with the Congress, and remains the guiding light for state ratification of ERA. In 1978, following the founding of the Congresswomen's Caucus, a bipartisan group of women in the United States House and the Senate, the Women's Research and Education Institute (WREI) was formed to assist in policy formation for the Caucus, and to encourage political participation by women at the highest levels. The Honorable Martha Griffiths presides as president of the board of WREI.

Ever since their marriage, Griffiths' husband has been an important force behind her career. Because Harvard Law School did not accept women students, after their graduation from the University of Missouri in 1934 they both attended the University of Michigan. After law school they started a private practice with their law school friend, G. Mennen Williams, former governor of Michigan and political ally of Martha Griffiths through the years.

When political powers in the state tapped Martha to run for Congress (she had served as a state legislator for four years), her husband encouraged her to take on the challenge. During the Washington years, Hicks lived in Detroit while Martha enjoyed the limelight in Washington, though she often said that her husband's happiness was her first priority and that she would not hesitate to renounce politics if he ceased to approve of their lifestyle.

Like Juanita Kreps and other women who have retired from public life, Griffiths has become a "professional" board member; memberships on the boards of Chrysler Corporation, K-Mart, and Greyhound Corporation suggest the high-powered company she keeps. Politics continue to be the main course for Martha Griffiths, however, with such assignments as chairing the 1976 Rules Committee for the Democratic National Committee.

Selected Writings and Speeches

"The Law Must Reflect the New Image of Women," *The Hastings Law Journal*, November 23, 1971.

Papers of Martha Griffiths are held by the Bentley Historical Library at the University of Michigan (at the time of this writing the papers comprise 206 feet of congressional office file material)..

A more complete listing of Griffiths' public speeches may be found in B. Manning, *Index to American Women Speakers* (1980), pp. 133-34.

Bibliography

Many articles about Griffiths in the *Detroit Free Press* and the *Detroit News*.

Abramson, Marcia. "Martha Griffiths," Ralph Nader Citizens Look at Congress Project (Series), Grossman, 1972.

"Analysis of Health Insurance Proposals Introduced in the 92nd Congress," House Ways and Means Committee, August 1971.

Anderson, Jack. *Washington Post*, September 7, 1966 (column).

Carpenter, L. "Six Women Who Could Be President," *Redbook*, November 1975.

In Chamberlin, Hope. *A Minority of Members* (1973).

Congressional Quarterly Almanac, 1970, pp. 1051-1067.

Congressional Quarterly Weekly Report, August 14, 1970, p. 2041.

"Equal Rights," *U.S. News and World Report*, August 24, 1970.

Foley, E. "Quitting While She Is Ahead," *Biography News*, April 1974.

Hunter, Marjorie. "Martha Wright Griffiths," *New York Times Biographical Edition*, August 11, 1970, p. 1955.

King, P. C. "Martha Griffiths ... and Some Personal Memories of Her by a College Chum at U. of M.," *Biography News*, November 1974.

"Ladies Home Journal 'Women of the Year'," *Ladies Home Journal*, April 1974.

In Lamson, P. *Few Are Chosen* (1968).

In MacPhearson, Myra. *Power Lovers* (1975).

"Martha Griffiths: Graceful Feminist," *Time*, August 24, 1970.

United States Women's Bureau. *Women of the 88th Congress* (1963).

Wandres, J. "Unretiring Congresswomen," *Retirement Living*, August 1974 (interview).

Julia Butler Hansen
June 14, 1907-

B. Portland, Oregon; D. Donald C. Butler; M. Henry Hansen, 1939; Served in U.S. House of Representatives as Democrat-Washington, January 3, 1961 to January 3, 1975, 86th through 93rd Congress.

Julia Butler Hansen's background, at first glance, appears to be a contradiction of what one usually expects of a prominent and influential political figure. She grew up and spent much of her life in the tiny town of Cathlamet in southeast Washington, where her father had settled in 1891. Her degree from the University of Washington (1930) was in home economics. She distinguished herself in children's literature by writing a juvenile book, *Singing Paddles* (1935), about life in Cathlamet and Vancouver. She was married late (age 32) to a lumberman, a marriage which lasted for over 35 years, though her husband's interest in politics was minimal. Her only son was born to her at age 38. Yet, after leading a quiet, uncomplicated life for many years, as chairwoman of the Interior Subcommittee for Interior Appropriations Hansen has managed budgets of over $2 billion. It is reported that her reputation during her long tenure in Congress was formidable enough to cause many colleagues to tremble at the notion of crossing her, no doubt an asset during her years in Washington state politics as chair of the Committee on Roads and Bridges, and her term beginning in 1955 as the first woman speaker pro tem in the Washington House. She has had many opportunities to exert her strong personality. In 1949 she fought off a statehouse colleague for the chair of the influential Committee on Roads and Bridges. When her opponent argued that his masculinity and his residence in Washington's King County were reasons for his election, Hansen informed him that his calculations were off, as she held all the votes.

Julia Butler Hansen got into politics at the grassroots level as Wahkiakum County Democratic chair in 1936 with the help of a seat on the state Democratic Executive Committee. Her name was little known outside of Cathlamet, Washington, where she wrote, worked for a title company, and served on the Cathlamet City Council as its first elected woman member. In 1938, with the recognition of her children's book, she gained notoriety outside of Cathlamet. These accomplishments combined fortuitously with the

Democratic connections she had begun to forge on the state level and Hansen easily won a Washington House seat in 1938, where she served effectively until 1960. Though she left state politics ostensibly for private life back in Cathlamet, she was drafted for the seat representing the Third Congressional District in the U.S. House, replacing Russell Mack, the late Republican representative.

Hansen came to Washington, DC, when Kennedy began his presidency in 1960, and was appointed to the Interior and Insular Affairs Committee, as well as to the Education and Labor Committee. By 1963 she was serving on the 55-member Appropriations Committee, the most influential House committee. When she became chair of the House Appropriations Subcommittee of the Interior, which controls the purse strings for the Department of the Interior, including the National Parks Service, the Bureau of Indian Affairs, and the Bureau of Mines, as well as for all national arts and humanities projects, Hansen established herself as one of the most powerful members of Congress, the first woman to chair a key appropriations subcommittee. The acreage from Alaska to Maine and from the Great Lakes to the Trust Territories that the subcommittee fiscally administered is vast, and Hansen's balancing act was to fairly address the interests of the ecology and preservation people at one end of the spectrum, and the developers and manufacturing interests on the other. During budget hearings Hansen frequently invoked her own regional background in the forest country when challenged by ecologists. Her voting record suggests that she leaned toward business interests when they conflicted with ecological concerns for her state. Her work with the Indian reservations, most of which she visited personally over the years in her commitment to the improvement of Indian living conditions and education, gave her great satisfaction.

Throughout her political career, Hansen was often the lone woman in a powerful position among scores of men. Though she claimed it never bothered her ("I went into politics as a citizen, not as a woman"), she was offended by the male power system as it operated in Congress, and worked toward revamping it. "We had a lot of greedy old men hogging all the power," stated Hansen with characteristic directness. Her House career was successful in part because of her command of the House rules and her skilled political maneuverings behind the scenes to obtain favorable legislation for her state—bills involving the fishing and lumber industries, for example. Her relatively easy victories at election time demonstrated strong constituent support. In return, her campaign pledges to constituents affirmed her determination to continue to do what she had done all along—endorse large federal expenditures for public works.

Though she shifted to a more conservative position in the early 1970s, Hansen remained pro-union, voted to cut off funding for the Vietnam War after June 1972, and supported the Equal Rights Amendment. According to the Ralph Nader "Citizens Look at Congress" profile, Representative Julia Hansen believes that her greatest legislative contributions have been in creating greater public awareness of the education and health problems faced by Indians; in advancing major appropriations for arts and humanities programs; and in fostering major appropriations for more ecological land management and reforestation.

Writings

Singing Paddles (1935).

Julia Butler Hansen's papers (1948-1970) are open to the public in the University of Washington Libraries, Archives and Manuscripts Division. These include legislative and personal correspondence, and scrapbooks.

Honors

Julia Ellsworth Ford Foundation Award for Juvenile Literature for *Singing Paddles* (1935); Washington Mother of the Year (1960).

Bibliography

In Chamberlin, Hope. *A Minority of Members* (1973).

Darmstadter, Ruth. "Julia Butler Hansen," Ralph Nader Citizens Look at Congress Project (Series), Grossman, 1972.

In Engelbarts, Rudolf. *Women in the United States Congress* (1974).

"Hansen's Reply," *Washington Post*, August 17, 1972.

Heywood, Mike. "Julia Butler Hansen: Alive, Well, Persnickety," *Bellingham, Washington Herald*, April 11, 1979, p. 9A.

Meyer, Eugene L. "Bicentennial Commission Deeply Involved in Politics," *Washington Post*, August 14, 1972.

Rosenberg, Marie C. Barovic. "Women in Politics: A Comparative Study of Congresswomen Edith Green and Julia Butler Hansen," *Dissertation Abstracts*, Vol. 35, No. 1 (1974), p. 542 A.

Patricia Roberts Harris
May 31, 1924-

B. Mattoon, Illinois; D. Hildren Roberts; M. William Beasley Harris; Served as U.S. Ambassador to Luxembourg, 1965-1967; Secretary, U.S. Department of Housing and Urban Development, 1977-1979; Secretary, U.S. Department of Health, Education and Welfare, July 27, 1979- .

Patricia Roberts Harris became the nation's first black woman Cabinet member in January 1977, when President Carter appointed her secretary of the unwieldy Department of Housing and Urban Development (HUD). She took over HUD with a sheaf of academic, diplomatic, political, and business credentials—law professor; ambassador to Luxembourg (1965-1967); an attorney with a prominent Washington law firm (1970-1977); membership on the boards of Chase Manhattan Bank, IBM, and other large corporations; and four years as the District of Columbia's national committeewoman (1973-1977). Harris was the first black woman ever to occupy many of these positions.

During her two years as secretary of HUD, Carter found her to be among his staunchest supporters, a translator of his policies and programs to many Democratic political groups. During her confirmation hearings for the position of secretary of Health, Education and Welfare (now the Department of Health and Human Resources), Harris affirmed her loyalty to President Carter's administration: "The programs of the president of the United States are the programs of this administration, and I certainly would support them and do support them," she testified in front of the Senate Finance Committee. President Carter was similarly unequivocal in his praise for Harris at her swearing-in ceremony as secretary of Health, Education and Welfare on August 3, 1979. "The Department [HUD] was poorly organized and its effectiveness was severely in doubt," said the president. "Pat Harris came in as secretary of HUD and with her superb management capabilities, she transformed this weak department into one of the most strong, able, effective, and sensitive in government." Patricia Roberts Harris took Carter's endorsement of her strong administrative skills at face value. By November 1979, only a few months after her appointment, she had launched a vigorous anti-smoking drive, the same issue that got her predecessor, Joseph Califano, into difficulty with the tobacco industry. She minced no words in telling the tobacco manufacturers to stop using "sexy guys and gals" in the ads to promote their product. Realizing that firm departmental administration called for one person to express an HEW position on legislation and policy, in December 1979 Harris intrepidly issued orders to her subordinates (thousands of employees at the Department of Health and Human Resources) to clear all outside communications about HEW policy with her.

Most critics and supporters agree that Harris knew little about housing when she came into her first Cabinet post, the HUD position, a department that handles an $11 billion annual budget. She won over supporters by inviting mayors and interested citizen groups to talk with her about urban problems. UDAG (Urban Development Action Grants), designed to stimulate private investment in urban development projects, emerged as a priority legislative task for HUD. UDAG has been called President Carter's most outstanding domestic program, much of the praise due to Harris' "sterling performance as a manager with a heart." Revamping the loan policies of "Fannie Mae" (Federal National Mortgage Association) was another coup. In 1978, under Harris, 155,000 federally assisted housing starts were recorded. Perhaps her notable interpersonal skills were developed during her diplomatic days as ambassador to Luxembourg (1965-1967), a position she received as a political reward from President Johnson, whose nomination she seconded at the 1964 Democratic Convention. Yet, she is known to be outspoken and abrupt about issues involving social justice.

Her sense of egalitarianism within HUD was noted during her first week on the job, when surprised department workers watched her with astonishment as she lined up for lunch with other employees in the HUD cafeteria. And, though her reputation for a sharp tongue has been remarked upon in the press, so has her sense of humor. After HEW hearings in which Senator Birch Bayh was addressing the marijuana issue, Harris was asked to clarify the fact that Bayh used oregano, not marijuana, to "roll a joint." Mirthfully she responded, "I wonder what he puts on his pizza."

When she took on the job as HEW secretary, Harris realized Carter's intention of making the Department of Education an entirely separate department from health and welfare, a controversial move that critics termed "a further expansion of bureaucracy." At her swearing-in Harris loyally asserted, "I want to assure everyone in this room and all others who view or hear this event that I will work tirelessly and resolutely to establish a separate Department of Education—and to bring reform and dignity to the American welfare system—and to enact national health insurance." HEW's budget, which in 1979 stood at $73 billion, not counting Medicare, welfare, and other large entitlement programs, has a reputation for being ungovernable. The previous secretary, Joseph Califano, had gotten the boot from President Carter on July 19, 1979, because he disagreed with the president on means and methods of controlling HEW's spending. However, since Califano was fired during the same purge that took Treasury Secretary Blumenthal and Energy Secretary Schlesinger, many political observers suggested "that politics, rather than managerial competence" accounted for changes in Cabinet personnel (*Wall Street Journal* editorial, July 23, 1979).

Perhaps because Harris arrived at HEW via a route of elite educational institutions (*summa cum laude* from Howard University; the University of Chicago; and first in her class at George Washington University Law School), as well as lucrative and prestigious positions in corporate and public life, critics have called Harris an unrepresentative black, especially in the sensitive areas of housing and welfare. Senator William Proxmire asked Harris during her confirmation hearings if she could possibly understand the views of society's disadvantaged citizens. She replied, "I am one of them. I am a black woman, the daughter of a dining car waiter. You do not seem to understand who I am." As for being a political woman, it would seem that Harris aimed for a power position more because of her color than her sex. In a 1979 *Chicago Tribune* interview she related several unpleasant racial incidents she had experienced while growing up in southside Chicago: "Those incidents were not so hurtful as they were strengthening," explained Harris. "You might say I have always wanted to be Number One, but I wanted power solely to help the poor and the disadvantaged."

Selected Speeches and Writings

"Law and Moral Issues," *Journal of Religious Thought*, Harvard University Press, 1964; "Developmental Problems in the Concept of Citizenship," *Howard Law Journal* 15 (1964); "The Negro College and Its Community," *Daedalus*, Summer 1971; "Socially Responsible Corporations and the Political Process," in *Managing the Socially Responsible Corporation*, Melvin Anchen, ed. (1974); "Successful Housing Policies Depend on Meshing Private Investment and Public Expenditure," *Journal of Housing*, January 1979; "The Role of the American Intellectual Community in Redefining Our National Purpose" (delivered at Harvard University, May 2, 1979), *Vital Speeches*, July 15, 1979.

A more complete listing of Harris' public speeches may be found in B. Manning, *Index to American Women Speakers* (1980), p. 142.

Honors

Distinguished Alumni Award, Howard University (1966); Ladies Home Journal Woman of the Year in Business and the Professions (1974); Order of the Crown, Luxembourg (1967); Yale Women's Forum, Medal of Achievement (1976); Phi Beta Kappa, Order of the Coif; Elected to the American Academy of Arts and Letters; PUSH Award for Excellence (1978). Many other honors, including honorary degrees from over 40 universities and colleges.

Bibliography

"American Women: Givers, Doers, Changers," *Vogue*, May 1968.

Avery, P. "Top Women Bureaucrats Talk about Jobs, Bias, and Their Changing Roles," *U.S. News and World Report*, September 5, 1977.

"Behind the White House Purge," *U.S. News and World Report*, July 30, 1979.

"Black Woman Joins Three Boards," *Business Week*, May 29, 1971.

"Blacks on the Carter Team," *Ebony*, March 1977.

"Feminists Applaud HEW Secretary Patricia Harris for Hiring More Women and Minorities," *Wall Street Journal*, December 21, 1979, p. 1, col. 5.

Gregg, Gail. "Harris Did 'Good Enough' Job Ex-Critics Said," *Congressional Quarterly*, July 28, 1979.

"How Patricia Harris, a Tough Team Player, Is Likely to Fare as New Secretary of HEW," *Chronicle of Higher Education*, July 30, 1979, pp. 9-10.

"HUD's Harris: Balance for Carter, Letdown for Builders," *Professional Builder and Apartment Business*, February 1977.

"Ladies Home Journal Women of the Year, 1974," *Ladies Home Journal*, April 1974.

"Madam Secretary," *Crisis*, January 1977.

Nickel, H. "Carter's Cactus Flower at HUD," *Fortune*, November 6, 1978.

Nye, P. "Conversation with Patricia Roberts Harris," *Nation's Cities*, August 1977.

Nye, P. "Patricia Roberts Harris," *Nation's Cities*, March 1977.

"Patricia Roberts Harris Is President Carter's Choice for Secretary of the Department of Housing and Urban Development," *Journal of Housing*, December 31, 1976.

Poinsett, A. "Patricia Harris: HUD's Velvet Gloved Iron Hand," *Ebony*, July 1979.

Sanders, C. "Ambassador Is a Lady," *Ebony*, January 1966.

"Senate Approves Harris for HEW," *Chronicle of Higher Education*, August 6, 1979, p. 12.

"Targets for HEW: Hospital Costs and Welfare Reform," *U.S. News and World Report*, November 26, 1979.

U.S. Congress. Senate. Committee on Finance. *The Nomination of Patricia Harris to Be Secretary of Health, Education, and Welfare.* Hearings, 96th Congress, 1st Session, July 25-26, 1979.

Washington, E. "Patricia Harris: Blunt New Voice in the Boardroom," *Life*, September 24, 1971.

"What You Can Expect from Carter's Cabinet," *U.S. News and World Report*, January 10, 1977.

Williams, D.A., et al. "Question of Loyalty," *Newsweek*, July 30, 1979.

Margaret O'Shaughnessy Heckler
June 21, 1931-

B. Flushing, New York; D. John and Alice O'Shaughnessy; M. John M. Heckler, 1953; Served in U.S. House of Representatives as Republican-Massachusetts, January 10, 1967- , 90th Congress- .

Margaret Heckler is another congresswoman who made it into the United States House because she remained undaunted in the face of criticism and lack of support from her party's leaders. When she decided to run for Congress in 1966 from Massachusetts' 10th District, she was pitted against Joseph W. Martin, a prominent though aged Republican who had served in Congress for 42 years. During the primary, Heckler dared not mention Martin's age as an issue for fear of alienating the voters, and she could not outline differences in their political views since they had few. Even Governor Volpe would not endorse Heckler publicly, though she had served on the Governor's Council for four years. Periodically the governor stated in the newspapers and on television that he had "asked Margaret not to run."

After winning the nomination, Heckler went on to campaign against Democrat Patrick J. Harrington, an experienced politician backed by the Massachusetts Democratic party and endorsed by the Kennedys. She defeated her opponent, unbeholden to her party for anything but negative criticism of her candidacy, and later credited women's support for her victory. Her public statements during this period and her vigorous campaign demonstrated a natural political personality lacking any traces of timidity. During this first campaign for Congress and throughout her congressional career in Washington, self-confidence and daring have characterized her political style, though she leans conservatively on a number of issues, mainly economic and defense-related. "Massachusetts needs a Heckler in the House" has been her winning campaign slogan over the years.

Her political ambitions began to ferment in college (Albertus Magnus, B.A., 1953), where as a political science major she participated zealously in the state student legislature. She campaigned for speaker of the student house and won, with her future husband, John Heckler, acting as campaign manager. Over the years he has actively supported his spouse's political ambitions, a factor that has undoubtedly contributed to her success. In a 1968 profile, journalist Peggy Lamson wrote of Heckler's personal political capital:

> Her home life was well organized. Her husband, an established stockbroker, was strongly in favor of her career. Her three beautiful children, aged nine, seven, and six, were well cared for by the Norwegian girls the Hecklers imported each year to live with the family and act as mother's helpers. She had been a practicing lawyer for ten years, having established her own firm with some of her law school classmates when she discovered the paucity of openings for women lawyers in Boston's "best" and staid law firms. At Boston College Law School she had been editor of the law review and an active competitor in the Moot Court. (*Few Are Chosen*, p. 117)

Once in Washington, Heckler unabashedly asked to be on the Judiciary Committee and was firmly refused, appointed instead to Government Operations and Veterans Affairs. By 1972 she was often at odds with Nixon's war policies, questioning "Vietnamization" strategies and calling for withdrawal of American forces from Vietnam. In recent years, however, her energies have been directed toward numerous women-related issues.

"Women are the one minority group it is still considered fashionable to discriminate against," the representative stated in 1970. Margaret Heckler's record in Congress has been one of support for women-related issues even when such interests cut against the cloth of Republican administration policy. During the 1968 Republican convention she criticized Nixon's position on limiting child-care funding for working mothers, defending her position by pointing to the women of her district's industrial towns who needed strong child-care programs in order to continue working. As a member of the Banking and Currency Committee she has worked for measures that would change unequal credit laws. In 1973 she argued:

> Women now constitute 44 percent of the labor force and in these changing times deserve as much right to access to credit as do men. It is documented that creditors are often unwilling to extend credit to a married woman in her own name—despite the fact that in some instances she may be the major breadwinner in the family.

After Congress passed the ERA in 1972, Heckler worked for the ratification of the amendment in the Massachusetts legislature, and publicly declared that the drafting of women was "a totally theoretical situation that could occur whether or not Equal Rights passes." She pressed hard for the creation of an all-volunteer army, which for a time muted the "women and the draft" concern over ERA. The representative also served on the National Commission on the Observance of International Women's Year.

Heckler, together with Elizabeth Holtzman, founded the Congresswomen's Caucus, a bipartisan group of women in the House and Senate working on legislative issues "to improve the rights, representation, and status of women in America." She and Holtzman have chaired the group since its inception in April 1977 and have worked with the caucus in achieving extension of ratification for ERA, passage of Congresswoman Schroeder's Federal Employee Part-time Career Employment Act and additional labor legislation to facilitate women's entry into the labor force, revisions in the Social Security system's treatment of women, and improvements in the monitoring of programs and procedures specifically directed to women's health. Other legislative efforts of the caucus have been directed toward displaced homemakers, sexism in public education, women in small business, domestic violence, legal rights of women, child-care recommendations, and America's older women.

In December 1979, Heckler, along with the Congresswomen's Caucus, endorsed the Revson Foundation's program to provide internship money for women to work directly with policymakers in Washington. "Since women comprise over 50% of the U.S. population and only 4% of the U.S. Congress," noted Heckler, "I believe the students can make significant contributions on the federal level by identifying and diminishing sexual discrimination."

Heckler and seven other congresswomen flew to Southeast Asia during the Vietnamese-Cambodian crisis in early November 1979 to urge the Cambodian government to allow food and medical supplies to be distributed to the masses of Cambodians dying from starvation and disease. "Our conscience dictates that we go and try," Heckler announced before the trip. "The conscience of the world demands that the problem be solved." To the world's amazement, the efforts of the congresswomen resulted in the government's expansion of air-relief efforts.

Heckler lives in middle-class Wellesley, Massachusetts, a comfortable suburb far removed from the problems of the state's mill towns, but appears to be closely in touch with the concerns of her diverse constituency. In her 1970 campaign she underscored human needs as her primary legislative goal, "housing, medical care, transportation, reversal of environmental pollution and urban decay, and employment with conversion of defense-dependent industry to peace-oriented production." Since she arrived in Washington in 1967, politics Heckler-style has been a liberal affair and often crosses party lines.

A strict moralist when discussing the motives of politicians, she has advocated four-year terms for members of Congress as a way of counteracting the tendency of elected officials to vote on legislation solely for vote-getting back home.

Perhaps the strict morality Representative Heckler has advocated through the years, some say "preached," accounts for her wide appeal among the female electorate. Her speeches frequently invoke the idealism of public service: "Once you start to separate public service from the enormous influence of the 'fat cats' of society, you rob the vested interests of their most valuable weapons." Her career, a dynamic illustration of tenacity and temerity, demonstrates that women can effectively challenge the political "fat cats" and emerge as winners.

Selected Speeches and Writings

See a listing of Heckler's public speeches in B. Manning, *Index to American Women Speakers* (1980), p. 145.

Honors

Honorary degrees from Northwestern University, Emmanuel College, Stonehill College, Regis College, Albertus Magnus (1972); Outstanding Young Woman (1965).

Bibliography

In Chamberlin, Hope. *A Minority of Members* (1973).

"The Congresswomen's Caucus: Our Friend on Capitol Hill," *Women's Agenda*, March/April 1979.

"Homemakers Would Be Able to Set Up Their Deductible Retirement Accounts," *Wall Street Journal*, February 21, 1979.

In Lamson, Peggy. *Few Are Chosen* (1968).

"No Time for Sentiment," *Time*, September 23, 1966.

"The Women of the 96th Congress," *AAUW Magazine, 1st Edition*, May/June 1979.

Carla Anderson Hills
January 3, 1934-

B. Los Angeles, California; D. Carl and Edith Hume Anderson (Wagner); M. Roderick Maltman Hills, 1958; Served as Secretary of Housing and Urban Development, March 10, 1975 to January 3, 1977.

When President Ford named Carla Anderson Hills to head the Department of Housing and Urban Development (HUD) in 1975, she became the third woman Cabinet member in American history, preceded only by Franklin Roosevelt's secretary of labor, Frances Perkins, and Dwight Eisenhower's HEW secretary, Oveta Culp Hobby.

Hills, a Republican, was the Ford administration's sole Cabinet-level woman; and though many liberal senators and representatives balked at her appointment saying that she lacked experience for the HUD post, she encountered little vocal opposition during the confirmation proceedings because of her excellent credentials. Some pointed to Ford's need for a top-level woman to demonstrate a pro-woman stance before the 1976 presidential campaign. Senator William Proxmire, chairman of the Senate Committee on Banking, Housing, and Urban Affairs, was perhaps the most blunt and outspoken against the Hills nomination. During her confirmation hearings he charged her with "not having a winning record in housing or in other urban problems. You have no record," he went on, "winning or losing." According to Proxmire, "the bottom line in all this ... is that you are a woman and many have said that this is the ace card in this situation."

Previous to her Cabinet appointment, Hills served as assistant attorney general in the Civil Division of the Department of Justice, where 450 people reported to her, most of them attorneys, a job which gained her a reputation as a tough and able administrator. She was the highest ranking woman in the Justice Department at the time of her nomination to HUD. Hills served on the Standing Committee on Discipline of the United States District Court, as well as on the corrections task force for the California Council on Criminal Justice before coming to Washington.

Carla Anderson Hills' personal background is one of money, ambition, and success. Her father, a self-made millionaire in the building supplies business, encouraged his daughter to excel in sports. She showed horses and played tennis competitively during high school and college, winning the university women's double championship at Stanford several times. Before graduating from Stanford *magna cum laude* in 1955, she spent a year at Oxford University, St. Hilda's College.

Even in grade school Hills talked of a life of public service as a lawyer. After Stanford came Yale Law School, where she graduated twentieth in her class of 167 in 1958. Reportedly, her father discouraged her from attending law school, hoping that she would become involved in the family business. Undeterred, she paid her own way through the first year at Yale doing odd jobs. After completing law school, she married attorney Roderick Hills, and spent two years as an assistant attorney in the Civil Division of the Department of Justice in Los Angeles, also teaching at the UCLA Law School. The Hillses have worked together a great deal during their marriage, practicing in their Los Angeles law firm from 1962 until 1974, when Carla Hills came to the Justice Department.

Opportunities for the couple have surfaced readily it would seem. When Elliot Richardson was secretary of defense he tried to recruit Mr. Hills as an assistant secretary. Though Roderick Hills was not prepared to make a commitment to Washington at the time, Richardson remembered Carla Hills' excellent credentials after he moved over to the attorney general's spot, and offered her a job as assistant attorney general. She accepted, just as Richardson resigned in the midst of the Nixon Watergate scandal during the "Saturday Night Massacre," and Carla Hills successfully negotiated the assistant attorney general's job with Richardson's successor, William Saxbe. The transition from private practice to the federal milieu was a major change requiring Hills to demonstrate significant managerial and administrative skill in handling cases brought against the government on constitutional questions affecting federal programs. Her stellar performance was noted by President Ford during her first year at the Department of Justice. Among the qualities frequently reported in the press, she has been praised for "undeniable femininity" blended with a "tough as nails" administrative style. At this time, Roderick Hills became chair of the Securities and Exchange Commission.

Carla Anderson Hills favored the restoration of urban centers to their former roles of city centerpieces, but opposed adding the expense of such projects to the bloated national deficit. Thus, many city mayors and urban planning commissions saw her as a threat to their federal funding sources. In her public speeches, however, she attempted to allay those fears by projecting a positive HUD posture toward the solution of urban problems. In a 1975 speech at the Washington Press Club she summarized the urban development question: "Our studies conclude statistically what we should have concluded intelligently more than a decade ago: that it is far less costly to recycle a city than to build a suburb" (*National Observer*, October 18, 1975).

After Ford's defeat in the 1976 presidential election, the Hillses were besieged with offers from law firms and foundations to take on prime assignments. With ample prestige and money, Carla and Roderick Hills announced their plans to take their time during the Democratic reign of Carter, possibly in hopes that a new Republican administration would once again tap their formidable talents, allowing them to continue their careers in public service. For Carla Anderson Hills, a return to private life signalled admission into the elite corps of women serving in corporate board positions. Among her directorships she counts IBM, American Airlines, and Standard Oil. In addition, she serves in trusteeship or advisory capacities to major intellectual institutions—the Woodrow Wilson School at Princeton, and the Yale Law School, just two examples of her prestigious assignments.

Selected Speeches and Writings

Federal Civil Practice, California Continuing Education of the Bar (1961); *Antitrust Adviser* (1971); "The Crisis of the Cities," U.S. Conference of Mayors, 1975; Speech at Washington Press Club, *National Observer*, October 18, 1975; Speech at U.S. Conference of Mayors, June 30, 1976.

Honors

Honorary degrees include Pepperdine University (1975).

Bibliography

"Call Her Madam," *Washington Post*, February 26, 1975.

Cannon, Lou. "Supporters Rally behind Mrs. Hills," *Washington Post*, February 15, 1975.

"Carla Anderson Hills Is President Ford's Nominee for HUD Secretary," *Journal of Housing*, March 1975.

"Excellent Choices," *Washington Star-News*, February 17, 1975.

Kobenschlag, M. "Carla Hills Jeered at Home Owners Protest Hearing in Chicago," *House and Home*, December 1975.

"Lady Prepares To Move In," *Economist*, March 1, 1975.

"The Nomination of Mrs. Hills," *Washington Post*, February 16, 1975.

Pritchard, A. "Whither HUD with Carla Anderson Hills?," *Nations Cities*, March 1975.

Ross, I. "Carla Hills Gives the Woman's Touch a Brand New Meaning," *Fortune*, December 1975.

"Secretary of HUD Quells Any Doubt about Her Support of Ford; Stepped Up Her Speechmaking with Appearance in Many States," *Wall Street Journal*, September 24, 1976.

"Some Used Fords on the Market," *Time*, November 22, 1976.

"Tough, Charming Cabinet Woman," *Time*, February 24, 1975.

United States Congress. Senate. Committee on Banking, Housing, and Urban Affairs. *Nomination of Carla Hills To Be Secretary of Housing and Urban Development*. Hearings, 94th Congress, 1st Session, February 24 and 27, 1975.

Oveta Culp Hobby
January 19, 1905-

B. Killeen, Texas; D. Isaac William and Emma Hoover Culp; M. William Pettus Hobby, 1931; Served as First Secretary of Health, Education and Welfare, April 11, 1953 to 1955.

Reportedly, when Oveta Culp Hobby, the second woman in United States history to achieve Cabinet rank, resigned as the first secretary of Health, Education and Welfare in 1955, Secretary of the Treasury George M. Humphrey commented, "What? — the best man in the Cabinet?" Before she began the job at HEW at President Eisenhower's request, Hobby had been in the public eye for many years as the co-editor and publisher of her husband's newspaper, the Houston *Post*, and as the first director of the Women's Army Corps during World War II. She had established herself as a woman of administrative skill, a hard worker reported to keep a 12-hour work day six days a week. Unlike many women who have achieved high public office, Hobby denied frequently in public statements and speeches that being a woman in the highest echelons of public life presented problems; she could not understand why more women had not surfaced to the highest ranks of government. At HEW she asked to be addressed as "Mrs. Secretary."

From girlhood Oveta Culp leaned toward law as a career. She attended but did not graduate from Mary Hardin-Baylor College and the University of Texas Law School, and studied law in her father's office. She went to the Texas House of Representatives as a parliamentarian at the age of 20, staying at this post until 1931. At the same time she became active in Texas Democratic politics, and clerked for the Texas State Banking Department, then in the process of codifying Texas banking laws.

When Oveta Culp married at age 26 her husband had already served as governor of Texas, and was the publisher of the Houston *Post*, Texas' biggest newspaper. She immediately became involved in the *Post*, working as a research editor, a book editor, and finally, in 1938, as executive vice-president. During this period she moved in the most active and powerful Texas civic, social, and business circles, serving as director of a bank and a radio station, as a member of many cultural and educational boards, and as president of the Texas League of Women Voters.

The mother of two children, the wife of a powerful man, and capable in her own right, Oveta Culp Hobby was the very model of the successful married woman, just the right person, it was thought, to lead the women's division of the War Department's Bureau of Public Relations. In this job she acted as the liaison between the War Department and the families of soldiers. A high-placed public relations figure, she was to keep morale high and the war effort going strong by informing the public of the well-being of their servicemen. General George Marshall, chief of staff, found her to be so effective in this position that he asked her to take over the organization and administration of the Women's Auxiliary Army Corps (later the WACs), newly created by Congress. As a colonel in this first U.S. women's army it fell to her to recruit women officers and enlistees, a task on which she worked closely with Eleanor Roosevelt. With no American prototype for such an organization of women, Hobby was able to say upon her retirement from the Army in 1945 that she had brought the fledgling effort from zero to a smooth-running operation numbering 100,000 women.

Back at the Houston *Post* Hobby again assumed her publishing and editorial duties along with myriad civic and professional assignments, until Eisenhower, whom both Oveta Hobby and her husband had supported in their newspaper, asked her to head the Federal Security Agency in Washington, not a Cabinet position in 1952. Eisenhower had several reasons for appointing Oveta Hobby: he knew of her accomplishments when as Lieutenant Colonel Oveta Hobby she had headed up the WACs; he needed someone from Texas in a high-ranking position; he wanted to put a known woman into a position of power in his administration; and the Hobbys had done much for his candidacy in Texas, though they actively maintained Democratic connections on the local level. When the Federal Security Agency, which then housed the Office of Education, the Bureau of Old Age and Survivors Insurance, the Food and Drug Administration, and the Public Health Office, metamorphosed into the much more complex Department of Health, Education and Welfare, Hobby had the job of pulling more than 25 bureaus together in order for HEW to function as a cohesive unit. While her husband stayed in Houston, Oveta Culp Hobby worked on the expansion of Social Security benefits, the Salk vaccine program, and a blueprint for a national health system.

The Salk vaccine program became one of the most controversial issues of Hobby's career at HEW due to the fact that at least 14 reported fatalities occurred shortly after the nationwide vaccination program was initiated. These deaths captured national headlines and called into question the safety of the vaccine and the competence of HEW in overseeing the program. Even though Hobby rode out the crisis and the Salk vaccine eventually was put back on the market, she decided to resign after the furor died down; her husband was ill in Houston, and the *Post* needed her attentive hand. After her husband's death in 1964, her son carried on the political tradition, and became lieutenant governor of Texas in the late 1970s. Oveta Hobby stayed on at the *Post* and served on numerous boards and councils, including those of Rice University, the Eleanor Roosevelt Memorial Foundation, and the Houston Symphony.

Selected Speeches and Writings

"What Community Recreation Programs Can Do for Service Women," *Recreation*, April 1952; "Citizen Responsibilities," *Vital Speeches*, December 15, 1954; "Are You Getting Your Share of Social Security?," *American Magazine*, April 1955; many speech excerpts from 1953-1955 in *School Life*, a government periodical; "Houston: The Race Is On," *Saturday Review* 22 (May 1965).

The Library of Congress Manuscripts Division holds papers and assorted memorabilia that trace Hobby's years with the U.S. War Department during the 1943-1945 period when she served as director of the WACs with the rank of U.S. Army colonel.

The Dwight D. Eisenhower Library holds correspondence, speeches, writings, and other printed material documenting Hobby's years as HEW Secretary (1953-1955), and much material related to her support of Eisenhower during the 1952 campaign.

Other manuscripts pertaining to Hobby can be located in Andrea Hinding's *Women's History Sources* (1979).

Additional public speeches made by Hobby may be found in B. Manning, *Index to American Women Speakers* (1980), p. 150.

Honors

Honorary degrees from Baylor University (1943); Sam Houston State Teachers College (1943); University of Chattanooga (1943); Bard College (1950); Texas Press Association Award; University of Missouri Distinguished Service in Journalism; Philippine Military Medal; Army Distinguished Service Medal; Publisher of the Year (1960); Honor Award, National Jewish Hospital (1962).

Bibliography

Many articles on Hobby in Houston *Post*. Her syndicated column was called "Mr. Chairman."

"Among Presidential Appointees," *Independent Woman*, January 1953.

"End of Hobby?," *Newsweek*, May 30, 1955.

Fortune, August 1950 [Portrait].

"More Than Orchid-Bearers," *Time*, November 24, 1952.

"New Look at Welfare Plans," *U.S. News and World Report*, December 26, 1952 [Interview].

New York Times, September 1, 1953 [Speech at Fifty-Fifth American Hospital Association Meeting, San Francisco].

New York Times Magazine, February 22, 1953 [Portrait].

"Voluntary Action on Polio Vaccine," *The Reporter*, May 19, 1955.

Woodbury, C. "America's Glamorous Godmother," *American Magazine*, May 1953.

Marjorie S. Holt
September 17, 1920-

B. Birmingham, Alabama; D. Edward R. and Juanita Felts Sewell; M. Duncan M. Holt, 1940; Served in U.S. House of Representatives as Republican-Maryland, January 3, 1973- , 93rd Congress- .

Marjorie S. Holt is somewhat of an anomaly among the United States congresswomen due to her outspoken and uncompromising conservatism. She rejects, for example, racial quotas in schools as well as busing to achieve racial equality, and she has been particularly vocal in her criticism of the Department of Health, Education and Welfare (HEW) for what she believes to be "harassment" of local school districts. Holt believes that quality education for all will only come about when there is less government control of school programs and increased autonomy in school districts.

She kept heavy political company during the Nixon era, and during her 1972 campaign relied on administration support, especially upon campaign appearances on her behalf by Spiro Agnew. When she was elected, Holt commented to reporters that she and Agnew had a "special relationship," one that would put her "in a good position to get advice and counsel, and cooperation."

Holt's record on women's issues has a peculiar history. In her 1972 campaign she underscored the importance of preserving family life and "feminine roles," despite her own exceptional accomplishments in male-dominated situations (she was one of only five women to graduate from the University of Florida College of Law in 1949 and was a member of the *Law Review* staff there). While she had called upon the Congresswomen's Caucus to "place greater emphasis on constructive studies and realistic proposals on issues affecting women," Holt complained bitterly in 1976 of an anti-feminine bias among her peers which she said prevented her from winning the leadership role of the GOP House Research Committee. Instead, the committee chose moderate-to-liberal representative Bill Frenzel of Minnesota. Of her role as a political woman Holt has noted that she was the first woman from Maryland elected to Congress in a general election: "I feel somehow responsible for the fact that there are now 323 women serving in elected positions in my state." Regarding abortion as a symptom of family deterioration, she has irritated feminists by her many votes against the use of federal funds to pay for abortions requested by low-income women.

Congresswoman Holt has honed in on national security and budgetary issues from the very beginning of her tenure in Washington. Ultraconservative in her speeches and voting record, she deplores the regulation of natural gas prices, calls for the balancing of the federal budget, and supports the tightening up of what she considers to be spendthrift welfare and food stamp programs. As a "law and order" woman, Holt favors stiff penalties for those committing crimes with guns, while she defends the citizen's right to bear arms. She termed the 94th Congress the "worst" in history for accelerating double-digit inflation and violating the ideals of Jeffersonian government. "While the Congress pours our wealth into a thousand domestic programs administered by a monstrous bureaucracy fiddling with statistics, charts, and reports weighing tons, it cuts the strength of our national defense to perilous weakness," she scolded in 1976. The congresswoman proposes zero-base budgeting as a solution for many of the country's fiscal ills.

Marjorie Holt's Fourth Congressional District, comprised of Anne Arundel and southern Prince Georges counties, overwhelmingly elected her in pro-Nixon year 1972 and returned her to Congress with hefty margins in 1974, 1976, and 1978. Previous to her election to Congress she practiced law, served as clerk of the Circuit Court of Anne Arundel County (1966-1972), and was a prominent and active member of Maryland's Republican Party, attending the Republican National Convention as a delegate in 1968. Her committee memberships in Congress include the Committee on Armed Services (subcommittees on Military Personnel and Intelligence and Military Application of Nuclear Energy) and the House Budget Committee. In 1975-1976 she served as chair of the Republican Study Committee, a group of conservative members of Congress who protest the growth of central government and place strong emphasis on national defense.

When asked to comment on the role of women in politics Holt points to the need for men and women to work as a team, but believes that the snowballing effect of women running for legislative office may very possibly result in the election of a woman president. She credits her own success as a congresswoman to hard work, an excellent staff, and a supportive family, noting that the hours required of her would not be possible if a woman had young children, or lacked the stamina for a rigorous schedule. Although the national media have focused on Holt's legislative efforts to slow down federal spending, the congresswoman counts the National Homestead Act, a program which encourages citizens to buy deteriorated homes for a nominal sum in return for their restoration work on these dwellings, as one of her most successful programs.

Selected Writings and Speeches

"Spendthrift Trusts," *University of Florida Law Review*, Fall 1949; *The Case against the Reckless House* (1976); "Women in Politics," *Challenge*, June 1979; "Statement of the Honorable Marjorie S. Holt before the Republican Platform Committee," January 14, 1980.

See Holt's listing of speeches in B. Manning, *Index to American Women Speakers* (1980), p. 152.

Honors

Distinguished Alumna, University of Florida Law School (1976).

Bibliography

"Budget Sham," *Wall Street Journal*, September 10, 1979 (editorial).

In Chamberlin, Hope. *A Minority of Members* (1973).

"Democrats Beat Back Holt Spending Limit," *Human Events*, August 26, 1978.

Edsall, Thomas B. "Holt Loses Bid for Position in House GOP Leadership," *The Sun*, December 9, 1976.

Freed, Bruce. "Mrs. Holt Building GOP Support," *Baltimore Morning Sun*, June 9, 1971.

"An Interview with Marjorie Holt," *New Guard*, September 1974.

Patterson, Sue McCauley. "From Maryland with Praise and Reservations," *Ms.*, April 1975.

Elizabeth Holtzman
August 11, 1941-

B. *Brooklyn, New York; D. Sidney and Filia Ravitz Holtzman; Single; Served in U.S. House of Representatives as Democrat-New York, January 3, 1973- , 93rd Congress- .*

When "Liz" Holtzman defeated her opponent in the 1972 election, she became the youngest woman to date ever elected to the Congress. Interestingly, she unseated one of the oldest members of Congress, the crusty Emanuel Celler, powerful Democratic chair of the House Judiciary Committee and the representative of the 16th District for half a century. His fatal error: he took "Liz the Lion Killer" too lightly, terming her a "nonentity," and conducted a casual campaign while Holtzman was out with her workers beating the pavement to get out the primary vote. In the predominantly Jewish, Democratic 16th District, winning the Democratic primary was tantamount to winning the election; and since Holtzman was long on supporters but short on cash, her strategy was to take her campaign to the streets, picking up votes at grocery stores, movie theatres, neighborhood gatherings—in short, where the people were. A former assistant to Mayor John Lindsay and a Democratic committeewoman from 1970 to 1972, she was a relative newcomer but not a neophyte to neighborhood New York politics, just beneath the notice of Democratic powers in her district.

Holtzman's winning primary campaign centered on people-related issues. What were the bureaucrats doing to make public agencies respond to ordinary people? she asked during her campaign. She charged the bureaucracy with being "all screwed up," and accused Celler of insensitivity to the needs of the 16th District—Social Security benefits, health care for the elderly, the Equal Rights Amendment, educational problems—pointing out to all who would listen that Celler, wrapped up in his own world of power in Washington, was out of touch with the people and their problems. Sounding Celler's own campaign slogan of 50 years before ("Time for a Change"), she attacked his hawkish stand on Vietnam, his votes for costly weapons and extravagant space technology, and his support of the seniority system, which virtually excluded all newcomers from effectively representing their districts unless they found favor with committee chairs. To his protestations that he had done much for the district, she countered that his special interests in New York actually prevented him from acting in the best interests of the district. These human issues, the core of the first Holtzman campaign, have become her platform in Congress, where she has used every opportunity to say "no" to discrimination, to seniority, to war, and to excessive military expenditures, and "yes" to socially conscious, progressive legislation favoring the interests of ordinary low- and middle-income citizens.

In her first term in the House Holtzman and Barbara Jordan were given seats on the House Judiciary Committee, ironically Celler's old committee. The assignment proved to be one of historic importance, for it was the 38-member Judiciary that confronted the impeachment process and approved the "Articles of Impeachment" in the case of former president Richard Nixon. "We came into a situation in which we saw the kind of abuse of power that was so inconsistent with a democratic system. There was something very fundamental here. The majority of the committee clearly came down and reasserted their commitment to the values of the Founding Fathers," she recalled in a *Ms.* magazine interview (November 1974).

Perhaps no amount of experience could have adequately prepared a person to deal with the shocking events of Watergate with its profound constitutional resonance, but Representative Holtzman's tough academic training (Radcliffe College, B.A. *magna cum laude*, 1962; and Harvard Law School, J.D., 1965), her intellectual family background, her attention to detail and preparation, and her years with the Lindsay office served her well in this situation. In the televised hearings and the reportage of the Watergate hearings, Holtzman appeared calm though indignant, knowledgeable about the legal issues, and sensitive to the implications of impeachment for the entire country and its citizens. "I feel very deeply that the President's impeachment and removal from office is the only remedy for the acts we have seen," was her recommendation to the Judiciary, televised before millions. Some critics accused her of being overly zealous in her moral indictment of Nixon.

Before Watergate, Holtzman had begun her first term in Congress with a startling public action: she initiated a law suit against the Nixon administration charging that the United States' bombing of Cambodia was illegal and unconstitutional. The Federal District Court agreed with Holtzman's charges of presidential abuse of power, though the Federal Court of Appeals later reversed this decision. Holtzman, however, stands as the first person in American history to declare war unconstitutional, and her historic legal action showed that she was unafraid of challenging authority at the highest levels to preserve the constitutional rights of the Congress and of the ordinary citizenry.

She established a reputation early on for fearlessly confronting corruption. After Nixon's resignation, the congresswoman demanded the details of the pardon by President Ford, saying that the American public had a right to know what had transpired between the two men in terms of "a deal." She voted against Ford's nomination to succeed to the presidency. Using the experience of Watergate, she justified the introduction of legislation to allow the appointment of independent special prosecutors to investigate corruption in the highest echelons of government, including investigation of congressional malfeasance.

Not surprisingly, Holtzman came to the fore as one of the leaders in uncovering the "Koreagate" scandal, repeatedly demanding, during the 95th Congress, that the Justice Department push further in its investigation of congressional wrongdoing.

Especially aware of mismanagement of the taxpayers' funds, Holtzman uncovered millions of dollars of fraud in the New York City Summer Food Program in its Summer Youth Employment Program, a cheat on both the taxpayers and the recipients of benefits from these programs. At a national level, she takes a vigorous stance against defense spending: "If the mood of the country is for fiscal responsibility, then let's get at that area of government which is the biggest *waster* of funds—the Defense Department." Holtzman suggests, "If we make it use its billions in unobligated funds *before* coming to us for new funds, unlike their customary practice, we could eventually cut $20 billion from the defense budget."

At the core of her political philosophy lies the question of public accountability. Thus in dealing with the most demanding issues of the day—the oil shortage and windfall profits of the oil industry, for example—Holtzman states, "Unless the oil companies are prepared to show us accurate figures on both their profits and their reserves, it hardly makes sense for us to present them with more giveaways." She would protect the privacy and integrity of individuals, and expand the disclosure and accountability responsibilities of government and industry. Her advocacy of legislation to protect the privacy of rape victims in federal courts and to compensate victims of all crimes illustrates her approach to civil liberties issues.

The extension of the Equal Rights Amendment ratification deadline is largely due to Holtzman's legislative expertise. As the co-founder, with Margaret Heckler, of the Congresswomen's Caucus, the first bipartisan congressional coalition of women in American history, she has taken great interest in women-related legislation affecting every aspect of women's socioeconomic existence, especially job discrimination, and has been particularly vocal against the Hyde Amendment, which denies Medicaid assistance to poor women seeking abortions. "The issue is whether as a country we should deny some women—because of their poverty—the access to a medically safe abortion," she argued. "Cutting off federal funds for medically safe abortions is discriminatory and wrong."

In 1977 Holtzman was selected by the Speaker of the House to be one of the two House members on the President's Commission on the Observance of International Women's Year, during which a national agenda for responding to the problems facing American women was drafted. Legislation she has authored—from a bill to make the Social Security Act more responsive to the needs of working women, to one which would provide Medicare funding for breast cancer detection—provides the legal scaffolding for her view of feminist societal change.

As chair of the Subcommittee on Immigration, Refugees, and International Law under the Judiciary committee, Holtzman has introduced legislation to take action against Nazi war criminals residing in the United States, calling for the deportation of any individual "who ordered, incited, assisted, or otherwise participated in the persecution of any person because of race, religion, national origin or political opinion." She has consistently supported pro-Israel policies, as one would expect of a Jewish woman representing a Jewish district. She also serves on the House Budget Committee, which monitors government spending, and chairs that committee's Task Force on State and Local Government.

Like other congresswomen, Representative Holtzman is keenly aware of the problems of the elderly, and has been since 1979 a member of the Select Committee on Aging. She calls America's older women "the poorest segment of our population," and has authored legislation to improve the health care, housing, employment, pensions, and Social Security benefits of all older Americans, with special attention to the "often devastating problems of America's older women."

As for her personal life, Holtzman's consuming dedication to work and her weekly commuting schedule between Washington and Brooklyn allow little time for activities outside of the Congress, even for the tennis, swimming, and sailing she is known to enjoy. There appear to be strong ties among the Holtzman family, an ambitious and achieving lot of professionals. Her twin brother chose neurosurgery as his career, and both sister and brother had the benefit of career-oriented parents—the father an attorney, and the mother a scholar of Russian studies and a teacher at Hunter College. According to columnists, Liz Holtzman "reads every piece of paper her staff can find for her, and works til midnight." If this is a hardship for her, she has not revealed it.

Though Holtzman's distinguished legislative record has guaranteed her state and national press since her arrival in Congress, and her political maneuvering has been adept and often audacious, she has not won popularity prizes except with women's and consumerist groups. She has been described as "overly serious" by some, and "abrasive" by others. She faced the problem that sooner or later confronts all skilled and ambitious political women when in her third term she decided to seek the U.S. Senate seat from New York. Running a Senate campaign in New York State presented Holtzman with enormous financial problems, in contrast to the personal, relatively inexpensive congressional campaigns of the 16th District. Beholden to no one, she did not attract the special interest money in her primary campaign against former mayor John Lindsay and former New York City Consumer Affairs commissioner Bess Myerson. Holtzman promises to remain in the vanguard of political women in the 1980s, even if she should lose the Senate race.

Selected Speeches and Writings

"Corporal Punishment: The Scandal in Our Schools," March 1976; "Excerpt from Remarks on Proposal to Amend the Hatch Act," June 16, 1977, in *Congressional Digest*, December 1977.

Papers of Holtzman from her years as assistant to Lindsay are housed in the New York City Municipal Archives; other tapes and transcripts are located in the American Jewish Committee's William E. Wiener Oral History Library. The congressional papers of Elizabeth Holtzman will be deposited with the Schlesinger Library at Radcliffe College.

See B. Manning, *Index to American Women Speakers* (1980), p. 152.

Honors

Outstanding Achievement Award by the editors of *Mademoiselle* magazine (1972); Annette Pinsky Award, New York Civil Liberties Union (1975); Outstanding Woman of the Year Award, Kew Gardens Hadassah (1976); Tribute Medallion, Brooklyn Coalition for Soviet Jewry (1976); Albert Einstein College of Medicine, Spirit of Achievement Award (1977); cited as "hero" by Consumer Federation of America for her 100% pro-consumer voting record (1978).

Bibliography

In Chamberlin, Hope. *A Minority of Members* (1973).

In Lamson, Peggy. *In the Vanguard* (1979).

"Liz the Lion Killer," *Time*, July 3, 1972.

"More Time to Ratify ERA. Pro and Con," *U.S. News and World Report*, August 14, 1978 [Interview].

Phillips, B. "Recognizing the Gentleladies of the Judiciary Committee," *Ms.*, November 1974.

Purnick, J. "Senate 1980: See How They Run," *New York*, March 19, 1979.

"Representative Elizabeth Holtzman Becomes Chair of HR Committee on Immigration, Refugees, and International Law," *New York Times*, February 8, 1979.

Wall Street Journal, July 21, 1979 [editorial on Holtzman's amendment to immigration law].

"Watergate Anticlimax," *Nation*, December 27, 1975.

Weschler, Jill. "Dealing with Illegal Aliens," *Dun's Review*, July 1979.

Shirley Mount Hufstedler
1925-

B. Denver, Colorado; D. Earl Stanley Mount; M. Seth Hufstedler, 1950; First United States Secretary of Education, December 6, 1979- .

When President Carter chose Shirley Hufstedler, a Federal Appeals Court judge, to head the newborn Department of Education in November 1979, many observers found the appointment inappropriate because of her lack of experience in the educational field. However, the Carter administration contended that the new secretary, the thirteenth Cabinet member, was picked precisely because she owed no allegiance to the feuding education groups. Since Hufstedler stipulated in accepting the secretary of education slot that she would nevertheless expect to be in the running should a position on the United States Supreme Court open up, it is widely thought that for the secretary, new to politics and to management, the Department of Education is a stepping stone to the Supreme Court.

Despite educationists' charges that Hufstedler is incapable of speaking to the myriad legal, social, and pedagogical problems that plague American schools and colleges, she has demonstrated expertise in confronting the social injustices which separate som students from learning. While serving on the Ninth United States Court of Appeals in 1973, she filed a dissent against the ruling that it was not discriminatory for San Francisco teachers to refuse to teach English to Chinese-speaking students, an opinion upheld by the Supreme Court. At her swearing-in ceremony (December 6, 1979), Hufstedler called for "new coalitions, new hope, new charity, and new dedication to the concept of education."

A graduate of the University of New Mexico (business administration, 1945) and Stanford Law School (1949), she was a top-ranked student. In 1950 she married a fellow student from Stanford, Seth Hufstedler, and worked as a general civil lawyer until Governor "Pat" Brown appointed her a Los Angeles

County Superior Court judge in 1961. An able jurist, Hufstedler was named to the California Court of Appeals in 1966 by Brown, and two years later to the U.S. Ninth Circuit Court of Appeals by President Johnson.

Hufstedler's post at the Department of Education will call upon her creative and diplomatic energies to ease tensions among elementary, secondary, and higher education groups, all contenders for federal funds. In addition she faces the huge management assignment of administering a department of 17,000 employees and a budget of $14.2 billion annually. Her budgetary baptism occurred, according to the *Wall Street Journal*, soon after she arrived in Washington. In response to her request for $500,000 for a departmental program, the new secretary was informed that in budget making Washington style it was customary to round off to the nearest million.

Publicly she has said of herself, "I am not a political creature." Since the Department of Education, however, was a major political promise made by President Carter to the American people, Hufstedler's handling of essentially political educational problems will probably affect the administration's success or failure in the 1980 election. The big issues are: the desegregation of southern colleges; programs especially designed for handicapped students; federal involvement in primary and secondary education; and government loans for college students. All of these issues Secretary Hufstedler believes should be tackled with government's causing "minimum disruption and domination." She has spoken of creating educational environments where "students can learn, and teachers can teach." Watching on the sidelines are hundreds of education lobbyists ready to pounce should Hufstedler tread on the toes of any special interest group, from bilingual students to re-entry women. Her chief accomplishment since taking over the Department of Education has been to win several funding bouts in the 1981 budget process on behalf of educational programs for the disadvantaged.

Because the Department of Education is in its fledgling stages, Hufstedler's success will depend greatly on whether the transformation of HEW into separate departments of Health and Human Resources and Education comes off smoothly, so that the 17,000 employees of Education can work in concert rather than in chaos. It is the orchestration of this new department, staffed with people of conflicting loyalties, that may prove the most taxing of her tasks, calling not so much for the skills of an educator, as critics have charged, but for the fairness of a Solomon, requiring precisely the credentials Hufstedler possesses.

Selected Speeches and Writings

"Courtship and Other Legal Arts: The Appellate System," *Vital Speeches*, March 15, 1974; "In the Name of Justice: The Unending Rush to the Courts," *Vital Speeches*, July 1, 1977.

Bibliography

"Carter's Choice: A Judge for Education," *Time*, November 12, 1979.

Cookson, C. "Carter Makes Surprise Choice to Head New Department," *New York Times Educational Supplement*, November 16, 1979.

Fields, C. M. "Surprise Choice for Education Secretary Is Greeted with Praise and Uncertainty," *Chronicle of Higher Education*, November 5, 1979.

Lublin, Joann S. "HEW Minus 'E' Equals Headaches for Top Educators: Secretary Hufstedler Fights Red Tape and Turf Wars; Is It the DED or ED?," *Wall Street Journal*, January 22, 1980.

Lublin, Joann S. "The Testing of Shirley Hufstedler," *Wall Street Journal*, February 12, 1980.

"Nation's New Schoolmistress," *Newsweek*, November 12, 1979.

"Shirley Hufstedler Confirmed by the Senate as the Nation's First Secretary of Education," *Wall Street Journal*, December 3, 1979.

Sweet, Ellen. "Shirley Hufstedler and the Supremes," *Ms.*, May 1980.

Muriel Buck Humphrey
February 12, 1912-

B. Huron, South Dakota; D. Andrew E. and Jessie May Buck; M. Hubert Horatio Humphrey, 1936 (widow); Served in U.S. Senate as Democrat-Minnesota, January 26, 1978 to January 3, 1979, 95th Congress.

Definitely a "political wife" more than a political woman, Muriel Humphrey stepped into the breach in January 1978, after her husband, the popular Democrat Hubert Humphrey, died following a long bout with cancer. During her brief stay in the Senate, she stood out as the only woman among the 99 male senators, and followed her husband's legislative footprints by supporting liberal legislation, including the expansion of the Humphrey-Hawkins Full Employment Act (husband Hubert's brainchild) to include special considerations for women. The original bill had no provisions for the lowering of female unemployment to keep pace with other labor force participants; nor did Humphrey-Hawkins provide for skill training and on-the-job training without sex bias. Other special additions to the Humphrey-Hawkins bill demanded by Senator Muriel Humphrey and her colleagues of the Congresswomen's Caucus were child-care services for working mothers and part-time and flexible work scheduling. Since federal jobs programs have in the past favored males in low-income households, usually excluding wives, she supported the Congresswomen's Caucus efforts to assure that the higher unemployment rate for women would receive serious study and recommendations for remedy by the secretary of Labor.

Senator Muriel Humphrey moved with deliberate political caution after her husband's death, sidestepping the limelight as much as she was able to do given her unique situation in the Senate. President Carter found her to be a steady ally, and she came through for him on more than one crucial vote. In May 1978 she gave him the vote he needed in order to effect an important arms sale to the Mideast, and in the same year hers was the key vote in the Panama Canal neutrality pact. Possibly because Carter found the mild-mannered

Senator Muriel politically compatible, he approached her in the white heat of his firing of Bella Abzug about taking over the chair of his Women's Advisory Panel. But she would have none of it, and stayed afield of the incendiary women's questions that plagued the Carter administration in 1978 and 1979.

Muriel Humphrey met her senator husband, then an aspiring politician, in the 1930s and remained by his side in all his political endeavors, choosing to keep a low profile at all times. Reticent about interviews, and unwilling to claim any contributions to politics in her own right, Muriel Humphrey filled out her husband's term while a successor was being chosen by Minnesota Democratic regulars. With her resignation, however, the Republicans claimed Minnesota's vacant Senate seat with the election of Rudy Boschwitz.

Selected Speeches and Writings

The Minnesota Historical Society Audio Visual Library holds taped interview material of Muriel Humphrey pertaining to her life as a political wife.

Bibliography

Clifford, G. "What Would Hubert Have Done?," *People*, April 24, 1978.

Feldman, T. B. "Muriel Humphrey," *Ladies Home Journal*, October 1978.

"Guaranteeing Workers' Rights," *New Leader*, June 5, 1978.

"Muriel Humphrey, the 65-Year-Old Widow of Minnesota Democrat Hubert Humphrey, Will Fill Her Husband's Seat," *Wall Street Journal*, January 26, 1978.

"Nothing So Honored Hubert Humphrey in Death as the Valor of the Woman He Chose 41 Years Ago," *People*, January 30, 1978.

"Senator Muriel: Following in a Tradition," *U.S. News and World Report*, February 6, 1978.

"Senator Muriel Humphrey Will Give Carter Key Vote in Senate Foreign Relations...," *Wall Street Journal*, May 11, 1978.

Thimmesch, N. "Surprising Senator Named Muriel Humphrey: Interview," *McCall's*, June 1978.

Barbara Jordan
February 21, 1936-

B. Houston, Texas; D. Benjamin M. and Arlyne Jordan; Single; Served in U.S. House of Representatives as Democrat-Texas, January 3, 1973 to January 3, 1978, 93rd through 95th Congress.

To many political observers Barbara Jordan's career has been something of an enigma. When she came to Congress in 1973 with a string of "firsts" already behind her (first black elected to the Texas Senate since Reconstruction; first woman president pro tem of the Texas State Senate; first black woman elected to the United States Congress from the South), she distinguished herself by refusing to act in the normal, reticent manner of first-term members of Congress. She made an appointment with old-time Texas political mentor President Lyndon B. Johnson, who called Speaker of the House Carl Albert, who in turn saw to Barbara Jordan's assignment to the Judiciary Committee—a most unusual first appointment. "All civil rights legislation, questions regarding the administration of justice, constitutional amendments are handled by the Judiciary Committee. I wanted to be on it. I could never have foreseen that we would deal first with the confirmation of a Vice-President, the nomination of Gerald R. Ford to replace Spiro T. Agnew and then with the matter of the impeachment of the President" (*Ms.*, November 1974). Yet, when she left Congress a national figure six years later for private life and a prestigious academic appointment to the LBJ School of Public Affairs she stated in her autobiography, "I thought that my role now was to be one of the voices in the country defining where we were, where we were going. I felt I was more in an instructive role than a legislative role."

Though Barbara Jordan authored surprisingly little legislation while in Washington, people seemed to overlook this because of her memorable rhetorical style and ability to convey a special presence, a dominance, in whatever gathering she chanced to be—whether in the committee rooms of the Judiciary or in her own small pink house in Houston's 18th District which she has shared with her mother. Jordan, a physically imposing figure, built a legend in Texas as well as in Washington for delivering brilliant oratory in a resonant, authoritative voice characteristic of southern evangelists. Indeed, Jordan, the daughter of a Baptist minister and a champion debater in college, was so skilled in public speaking that for many Americans watching the Nixon impeachment proceedings on television hers was the only memorable voice during the entire Watergate legislative sessions. Solemnly, deliberately, she spoke on August 6, 1974, "My faith in the Constitution is whole, it is complete, it is total. I am not going to sit here and be an idle spectator to the diminution, the subversion, the destruction of the Constitution." For millions watching these televised debates, Jordan became the symbol of integrity in the midst of corruption—a voice who spoke for the masses, articulating the shock of a nation. Predictions soon surfaced in the press that Jordan would move on from Congress to higher elective or appointive office.

Barbara Jordan, in 1974, was acting out on a national stage the grandiose political presence Texans had become accustomed to when she was elected to the Texas State Senate in 1966—the lone female among 31 male senators. She had spent four years attempting to get into the Texas legislature, losing in 1962 and in 1964, and finally winning in 1966 after a dramatic increase in black voter registration. A consummately skilled, innate politician, she respected Lyndon Johnson as a typical Texas politician—"tough, expansive, and pragmatic," she called him—and decided to throw in her lot with this type of politician in the Texas Senate, wooing the Senate members with her brilliant rhetoric, placating them with a moderate brand of black politics. Playing politics with "the good old boys" was a game she mastered early on in Texas. Her message to students in 1967 was to use judgment and reason instead of bricks to register dissent, a point not lost on her Texas Senate colleagues, who respected her speaking style and her well-executed political maneuvers. She chalked up many legislative victories—the definition of a minimum wage law for Texas domestic and rural workers not covered by the federal wage laws, the establishment of the Texas Fair Employment Practices Commission, and the writing of other fair labor legislation—and devoted all of her time to the Texas Senate during the six years she served, chairing the Labor and Management Relations Committee. She engineered her own successful congressional campaign in 1972, with the newly created 18th Congressional District delivering to her a supportive black and ethnic Houston constituency. With the support of the Democratic powers-that-be in Texas, she won her first congressional race with a margin of 66,000 votes over her Republican opponent, Paul Merritt, and went to Washington in 1973.

At times Jordan was accused of "Uncle Tom-ism" by the black community, even by the Congressional Black Caucus on occasion, because she advocated a strict adherence to constitutional law, saying that blacks would gain equality in education and employment opportunity only on the merits of strict constitutional interpretation. She eloquently championed issues which addressed social change for the benefit of minorities, the aged, the ill, and the rejected segments of society. Feminism and black identity appeared to be secondary to her dedication to justice for all, though she consistently took up the cause of the economically deprived. With Martha Griffiths (D-Michigan), for example, she co-sponsored a Social Security bill that would include homemakers. As for legislation to benefit Houston, she supported bills to expand transit, to rebuild cities, to increase aid to schools, and to increase allocations for school lunch programs. Though she praised the 1954 Supreme Court busing decision, she believed that busing alone could not transform the educational system into one where equal educational opportunities existed for all. Unlike her black colleague, Representative Shirley Chisholm, Barbara Jordan publicly supported such interests as environmental protection and anti-pollution legislation. Above all, she opposed military expenditures, especially as related to the Vietnam War.

When Jordan announced her intention to leave Congress in 1978, there was wide speculation about the reasons for this surprising move, especially because she had demonstrated considerable political ambition on her way to the top. While accepting Jordan's autobiographical statement that she had tired of the Washington grind, and preferred the intellectual stimulation of teaching graduate seminars in political ethics and intergovernmental relations, it is nevertheless noteworthy that the black woman who practiced general civil law on the kitchen table of her parents' home after her graduation from Boston University Law School (1959) has moved into the rarified atmosphere of corporation boardrooms. She accepted a handsomely compensated directorship on the Board of the Mead Corporation in 1979, citing her concern for consumers as the major factor in her decision to serve. Many rumors have appeared in the press concerning Jordan's health; she had taken to walking with a cane during her second congressional term. Tersely denying reports of a bone cancer condition, she announced that she would significantly limit her speaking schedule.

Before her retirement from Congress Jordan told the press that she had no plans for a "grand finale," and though she never officially closed the door on a political future, she has remained taciturn about her political plans since retiring to academia. Her life in 1980 is centered around the LBJ School and a country home in Austin.

Selected Writings and Speeches

"Who Then Will Speak for the Common Good," *Vital Speeches*, August 15, 1976 [Democratic Convention Keynote Address, 1976]; *A Self-Portrait*, 1978 (with Shelby Hearon).

In April 1978 Barbara Jordan donated her personal and career papers to Texas Southern University, her alma mater (1956); these include letters, speeches, film and video segments, and memorabilia.

Honors

"Women of the Year," *Ladies Home Journal* (1975); "Women of the Decade," *Ladies Home Journal* (1979).

Bibliography

Numerous articles in *Houston Chronicle, Austin American-Statesman*, and *Houston Post*.

Bryant, Ira B. *Barbara Jordan: From the Ghetto to the Capitol* (1977).

"Comet in Congress: Barbara Jordan's Star," *Wall Street Journal*, February 6, 1975.

"Former Rep. Barbara Jordan Intent on Decision to Withdraw from Politics," *New York Times*, February 13, 1979.

Haskins, James. *Barbara Jordan* (1977).

Phillips, B. J. "Recognizing the Gentleladies of the Judiciary Committee...," *Ms.*, November 1974.

Thompson, Wayne N. "Barbara Jordan's Keynote Address: The Juxtaposition of Contradictory Values," *The Southern Speech Communication Journal*, Spring 1979.

Wiessler, J. "No Grand Finale for Rep. Jordan," *Houston Chronicle*, June 18, 1978.

Florence Prag Kahn
November 9, 1868-November 16, 1948

B. Salt Lake City, Utah; D. Conrad and Mary Goldsmith Prag; M. Julius Kahn, 1899; Served in U.S. House of Representatives as Republican-California, March 4, 1925 to January 3, 1937, 69th through 74th Congress.

Journalists and colleagues termed her "one of the most dynamic women of her generation." Known for her quick wit, Kahn was the subject of a Washington legend: "You always know how Florence Kahn is going to vote

(Republican) but only God has the slightest inkling of what she's going to say." Large crowds were attracted to the congressional galleries in the hope of hearing her exchange acerb remarks with the likes of Representative Fiorello La Guardia from New York, who accused her, among other things, of being a follower of "that reactionary Senator George H. Moses of New Hampshire." Not one to be nonplussed, Congresswoman Kahn raised her formidable voice and fired back, "Why shouldn't I choose Moses as my leader? Haven't my people been following him for ages?"

Among her numerous "firsts," Florence Kahn was the first woman appointed to succeed her spouse in the Congress, though the 26 years of unpaid service she had rendered to the San Francisco Fourth District as her husband's Washington assistant had given her unprecedented training in negotiating the political intricacies of the House. Certainly few could have served San Francisco's interests as well as Congresswoman Kahn, who fought and won for San Francisco numerous defense contracts, public works projects, and construction funding. San Francisco's Marine Hospital, federal building, mint, improvements for the harbor and Presidio, Hamilton Field, Sunnyvale U.S. Naval Station, Alameda Naval Air Base, the San Francisco–Oakland and Golden Gate bridges owe their funding, and ultimately their existence, to Congresswoman Kahn's skillful political maneuverings. Though unembarrassedly unstylish, overweight, and poorly groomed, wearing floppy hats to cover her unkempt hair and ill-fitting clothing, she had the wit to remark when asked about her strategy of gaining and keeping political clout in the Congress, "It's my sex appeal, of course!"

As was not the case with the flamboyant Bella Abzug, no one seemed to take offense at Kahn's congressional style, perhaps due to her long-standing presence in the House, but most likely because of her unabashed support of popular issues: increased funds for the FBI, the repeal of the resented prohibition laws, and military preparedness. "Preparedness," she bellowed frequently, "never caused a war and unpreparedness never prevented one." Unlike earlier female colleague, Jeannette Rankin, Kahn supported military strength, and, as the first woman member of the powerful Appropriations Committee and the Military Affairs Committee, was in a position to translate her pro-military feelings into law.

From her childhood to her death in 1948, Florence Kahn displayed limitless energy and enthusiasm, despite invalidism in her later years. She taught mathematics in San Francisco's public schools after her graduation from Berkeley (1887) and before her marriage to actor-turned-politician Julius Kahn. The mother of two sons, Kahn drew up legislation to establish the FBI, defending its existence against critics as an institution to allay the fears of America's mothers, "who demand protection for their children." Director Hoover returned Kahn's favors by proclaiming her "Mother of the FBI." Florence Kahn skated into Congress term after term until 1936, when she met her match in a man who reflected the Democratic progressive tide of the times, Frank Havenner. After retiring to her home in San Francisco, she continued to delight the town with her zesty and visible presence. Remaining active in Republican and women's organizations, Kahn encouraged political participation by women—as long as it was accomplished with flair and a sense of humor.

Bibliography

The *San Francisco Examiner and Chronicle* contains numerous references to Kahn.

Anspacher, Carolyn. "Florence Kahn Dies: Former S.F. Congresswoman Dead at 82," *San Francisco Chronicle*, November 17, 1948.

In Chamberlin, Hope. *A Minority of Members* (1973).

Gilfond, D. "Gentlewoman of the House," *American Mercury*, October 1929.

Keyes, F. P. "Lady from California," *Delineator*, February 1931.

Maddux, E. "New Congresswoman," *Woman Citizen*, March 7, 1925.

New York Times, November 17, 1948 [Obituary].

"Portrait of Florence Kahn," *Current History*, June 1929.

Rinehart, M. R. "Women of the Year," *Pictorial Review*, January 1935.

Time, November 29, 1948 [Obituary].

Nancy Landon Kassebaum
July 29, 1932-

B. Topeka, Kansas; D. Alfred M. and Theo L. Landon; Served in U.S. Senate as Republican-Kansas, January 3, 1979- , 96th Congress- .

With her election, Kassebaum became the only woman U.S. senator, a fact remarkable enough without considering that before her election to the Senate she had held only one other political office—a seat on the local school board many years before. As the daughter of a political father, Alfred Mossman Landon, an "also ran" against FDR in 1936 and a distinguished governor of Kansas for many years, Kassebaum had first-hand knowledge of big league politics, even without elective experience.

Before her separation from her husband in the 1970s, Nancy Kassebaum had little interest in a political career, however. Her interests ran to civic affairs, business management as a vice-president of a family-owned radio station corporation, and family life with her four children. Though she had good academic credentials—a B.A. in political science from the University of Kansas (1954), and an M.A. in diplomatic history from the University of Michigan (1956)—she never made overtures to establish a political career until three years before the election, when she went to Washington with her children in 1975 to work for Senator James Pearson. When Pearson resigned in 1977, Kassebaum ran for the seat with idealistic hopes of making government more efficient and responsive to the ordinary citizens of Kansas.

As a candidate she alienated many special interest groups by taking an individualistic approach to issues: she opposed the extension of the ratification deadline for the Equal Rights Amendment, for example, and lost the endorsement of the Kansas Women's Political Caucus to her opponent, William Roy. Her father publicly discouraged her candidacy on many occasions.

A pragmatist, Kassebaum held no strong hopes for winning the Senate seat, and she has stated several times since then that she is reluctant to serve more than two terms. In fact, she introduced a joint resolution calling for a constitutional amendment to limit congressional terms. "The professional politician, with his eye on the next election, quite naturally seeks to temporize or completely avoid potentially controversial issues.... The result is often the subjugation of the nation's common welfare." Although many believe that the Landon name helped her in the 1978 election, finally it was Kassebaum's dedication to the restoration of traditional Madisonian political concepts and her commitment to public service rather than to self-interest that accounted for her appeal to Kansas voters. Her periodic reports to her Kansan constituency emphasize the need for individual self-discipline in an inflated economy to prevent the president's gaining wage and price control authority.

Kassebaum has spoken out frequently on the immaturity of American foreign policy, indicting the political delays which prevent open debate on the Strategic Arms Limitation Treaty (SALT II) on the Senate floor. In a 1979 address she defined a "mature foreign policy" as "one hospitable to the combination of principles with pragmatism, one willing to live with contradictions, to play an active role without excessive costs, to pursue arms control without any illusions about detente." She has repeatedly asked the Senate to "pursue assurances that [the SALT negotiations] produce significant and substantial reductions in strategic arms."

Her committee memberships include the Banking, Housing, and Urban Affairs Committee and its International Finance and Rural Housing subcommittees; the Commerce, Science, and Transportation Committee and its Surface Transportation and Aviation subcommittees; the Budget Committee; and the special Committee on Aging. During her first term Kassebaum co-sponsored legislation that provided cotton, wheat, and feed grain producers with parity prices for the 1979-1980 crops (S. 418) and legislation to expand home health services under Medicare (S. 489).

As the first woman elected to the Senate without her husband preceding her, and as an individual who on the surface does not appear to be imbued with consuming political ambition, Nancy Kassebaum is a political maverick. "Sen. Nancy Kassebaum's rise from mid-western farm wife to member of America's 'exclusive men's club' looks easier than it really was," Barbara Williams notes in *Breakthrough: Women in Politics*. "Kassebaum is not really a Senate Cinderella but a millionaire who spent one hundred thousand dollars of her own money in the campaign, a tireless worker, and a shrewd strategist who had grown up listening to political pros from behind curtains and through furnace vents" (p. 128).

Selected Speeches and Writings

"The Dynamics of Foreign Policy: Consensus and Coherence," Baker Awards dinner speech (March 24, 1979); "Leadership," Center for the Study of the Presidency (April 28, 1979); "Perspective on SALT II," Women's Task Force on SALT II (June 22, 1979).

Honors

Recipient of the Women in Communications Matrix Award.

Bibliography

Bartel, Dave. "Kassebaum: The Person behind All Those Labels," *Wichita Eagle/Beacon*, December 17, 1978, pp. 1, 6A, 7A, 8A.

Becker, Randall. "Lady in Waiting," *The Olathe, Kansas Daily News*, February 2, 1979, p. 5; February 3, 1979, p. 5; February 6, 1979, p. 5; February 7, 1979, p. 5; February 9, 1979, p. 5.

Erickson, Mary. "Here I Am!," *Lawrence, Kansas Journal-World*, February 11, 1979, pp. 1, 8A.

Haberman, Nancy, and Ann Northrop. "The Freshwomen in Congress," *Ms.*, January 1979.

Hendrickson, Paul. "His Daughter, the Senator-Elect from Kansas," *The Washington Post*, November 30, 1978, pp. G1, G3.

Leonard, Susan. "Rookie on Capitol Hill Retains Candid Outlook," *The Arizona Republic*, June 28, 1979, p. 10.

Martin, Frank W. "Freed to Run by Her Broken Marriage, Mrs. Kassebaum Goes to Washington," *People*, January 8, 1979.

Paschal, Jan. "One in 100," *Working Woman*, October 1, 1979.

Robb, Lynda Johnson. "Nancy Kassebaum: Making Political History," *Ladies Home Journal*, April 1979.

Rohner, Mark. "The Darling of the Senate," *Coffeyville, Kansas Journal*, June 10, 1979, pp. 9-12.

"Senate's Only Woman Prepares for January 15 Session," *Capper's Weekly*, January 9, 1979, p. 1.

Stevens, Paul. "Nancy Kassebaum Approaches Senate Job Head-On," *Tulsa World*, January 7, 1979, p. 10A.

Sutphin, Sam. "She's Met the Wonderful Wizards of Oz, D.C.," *The Saturday Evening Post*, September 1979.

Sweeney, Louise. "Senator Nancy," *Christian Science Monitor*, January 9, 1979, pp. B2-5, 14.

Whittemore, Hank. "A Kansas Landon Goes to Washington," *Parade*, March 18, 1979.

Williams, Barbara. *Breakthrough: Women in Politics* (1979).

Martha Keys
August 10, 1930-

B. Hutchinson, Kansas; D. Rev. S. T. and Clara Krey Ludwig; M. Andrew Jacobs, Jr., 1976; Served in U.S. House of Representatives as Democrat-Kansas, January 3, 1975 to January 3, 1978, 94th through 95th Congress.

Kansas, during the mid to late 1970s, took a leadership role in electing women to national political positions. Both Congresswoman Martha Keys and Senator Nancy Kassebaum, newcomers to the political scene, surprised politicians and political observers by their ability to outdistance opponents and to win in a state whose only other congressional woman was Kathryn O'Loughlin McCarthy, who served one term (1933-1935).

The centerpiece of both the Keys and Kassebaum campaigns has been an appeal to ordinary citizens. During her 1974 campaign, Keys hit on the issues of the "ordinary people just living out there" who had received "insensitive treatment" from the government on matters of unemployment and programs for the disadvantaged and the elderly. She called for numerous public works projects, while decrying government defense spending (differing sharply from Kassebaum's hawkish position). She became the only woman nominated to the prestigious Ways and Means Committee and the first Kansan on the committee since 1946. Though neither avoiding nor stressing feminism in her campaign ("I wasn't a women's rights candidate. I was running for a job I could do well"), Keys sought and obtained the endorsement of the Women's Political Caucus for the position on Ways and Means. High on her agenda of important national concerns were election reform, energy policy, and improved national health care programs. Subcommittee assignments on Health and Unemployment Compensation dovetailed nicely with her legislative interests.

Though Keys had served as the Kansas coordinator for the 1972 McGovern presidential campaign and in other leadership positions in state voluntary organizations, when she ran for Congress in 1974 the newspapers habitually identified her with her first husband, Samuel Keys, who was dean of the College of Education at Kansas State University. This proved an embarrassment for Martha Keys, often dubbed the "pretty homemaker from Manhattan," when during her first term in 1975 she divorced her husband and announced plans to marry Indiana congressman Andrew Jacobs. Interestingly, what concerned the Second District constituency most about the divorce and remarriage was the possibility that her loyalties to Kansas would be jeopardized because of her husband's affiliation with Indiana.

Keys' campaign for reelection to Congress hinged on this very debate. She constantly reminded the voters of her Kansan roots. She had two children in Kansas colleges, she said, and her weekends belonged to Kansas, not to Indiana. She had maintained her name and her Kansas residency by prenuptial agreement. Representative Jacobs, also divorced, seems not to have experienced the same problems. In a *Wall Street Journal* interview conducted during the 1976 campaign, when Jacobs frequently visited Keys' district, he admitted, "No one ever suggested my loyalty to Indiana has been diminished by my marriage." Rather, he stressed that Indiana's need for Kansas wheat made the two states natural political allies. Keys won her second term by a narrow margin, becoming the second Democrat to be returned to Congress from the Second District since the Civil War, and more unusually, a partner in the first husband-wife team ever to serve concurrently in Congress. Keys and Jacobs also became the first congressional couple to hold membership in the "Spouses Club" (formerly the "Wives Club") of the Congress. Keys had another well-known relative in the Senate, brother-in-law Senator Gary Hart from Colorado, who provided political entree for her in 1972 when he managed the national McGovern campaign.

Martha Keys' career underscores the fact that women who have pursued the homemaking role *can* make it to the national political arena. Her educational background was traditionally centered in music (University of Kansas City, now the University of Missouri), though she found later that she "had no interest in teaching music." Born and reared in Kansas, she moved around the country following the academic career route of her first husband while her four children were growing up, a mobility pattern that turned into a campaign plus. "I will be working with representatives from other areas. I have to be able to understand the needs and drives these representatives have for being able to achieve things for their areas," she said during her first campaign. Parochial during her first term, Keys concentrated on introducing Kansas-identified legislation to benefit farm families and agricultural interests. She was the only Kansas member of the Congressional Rural Caucus.

The daughter of a clergyman, Keys recalls that she has always thought of her life in terms of public responsibility. When she was defeated by conservative Republican Jim Jeffries in her third bid for Congress (the margin was about 52% to 48%), she moved into HEW as an assistant secretary with the Agency on Aging. A specialist on Social Security as it relates to women, Keys frequently takes on public speaking assignments to inform women about developments in the system.

Selected Writings and Speeches

The Martha Keys papers are located at Kansas State University in Manhattan.

See B. Manning, *Index to American Women Speakers* (1980), p. 171.

Bibliography

"Crackdown on the Three Martini Lunch?," *U.S. News and World Report*, February 27, 1978 [Interview].

Doles, Jill. "Rep. Keys to Wed Rep. Jacobs in Private Rites," *Topeka Capital-Journal*, January 4, 1976.

Dworkin, S. "These Freshperson Congresspersons," *Ms.*, April 1975.

Ferguson, Lew. "Martha Keys Thinks Maturity Main Issue," *Topeka Capital-Journal*, October 17, 1974.

Fraker, S., and H. Hubbard. "Choice Races," *Newsweek*, November 1, 1976.

"Keys Named to House Committee," *Topeka Pictorial-Times*, January 23, 1975.

"Keys Recites Oath of Office," *Topeka Journal*, January 14, 1975.

Kronholz, June. "For Congresswoman, Issue in Kansas Race Is a 'Messy' Divorce," *Wall Street Journal*, October 7, 1976.

Myers, Roger. "Keys Announces Marriage Plans," *Topeka Journal*, November 20, 1975.

Myers, Roger. "Mrs. Keys Wins Second Term," *Topeka Capital*, November 3, 1976.

Myers, Roger. "Mrs. Keys Wins Nomination to Top Committee of House," *Topeka Capital-Journal*, December 12, 1974.

Nuss, Susie. "Fiance Introduced by Keys," *Topeka Capital-Journal*, December 14, 1975.

Peterson, Ken. "Keys Makes It Official; She's in Race," *Topeka Journal*, May 17, 1976.

Scott, Laura. "Homemaking, Politicking Blend for Martha Keys," *Kansas City Times*, January 13, 1975.

Smith, Gene. "Congressional Seat to Mrs. Keys," *Topeka Capital*, November 6, 1974.

Smith, Gene. "Keys, Peterson Winners in 2nd District," *Topeka Capital*, August 7, 1974.

Walters, Robert, and Lisa Myers. "Politics Makes Estranged Bedfellows ... Also the First Married Couple to Serve in Congress," *Topeka Capital-Journal* (*Parade Magazine*), September 26, 1976.

Coya Knutson
August 22, 1912-

B. Edmore, North Dakota; D. Christian and Christine Anderson Gjesdal; M. Andrew Knutson, 1940 (divorced 1962); Served in U.S. House of Representatives as Democrat-Minnesota, January 5, 1955 to January 3, 1959; 84th through 85th Congress.

For many people Coya Knutson (born Cornelia) triggers the memory of the infamous "Coya, Come Home" letter, a highly publicized missive instructing the congresswoman to return to family duties. The letter, written by her husband in 1958, effectively ended Knutson's political career. In the present social milieu where the situation of women politicians is widely discussed, Coya Knutson's traumatic experience testifies to the double standard applied to personal conduct in the political realm. According to political biographer Hope Chamberlin, before Knutson announced her intention of seeking a third term, her husband Andy, in a drunken rage, "wrote a letter picturing himself as a lonely, neglected castoff. 'Our home life has deteriorated to the extent that it is practically nonexistent,' he declared. Soon afterward he signed a press release accusing Coya of improprieties with handsome, young (30) Bill Kjeldahl, her administrative assistant, and threatened him with a $200,000 alienation of affections suit" (*A Minority of Members*, p. 264). Letters poured in lambasting Knutson for dereliction of duty to her husband and teen-aged son. Despite the fact that a special House elections subcommittee found Andrew Knutson to have been a "contributing cause to her defeat," and heard testimony largely negating his slanderous charges, many aspects of Coya Knutson's distinguished legislative record were overlooked, even forgotten by the public.

Coya Knutson began her career in the Red River Valley, where she and her husband owned and operated a local cafe and hotel; at the same time she put her training from Concordia College and Juilliard School of Music to work teaching school, while managing and directing the local Lutheran church choir. Since her parents had been farmers during her childhood in North Dakota, Coya Knutson found a natural issue in championing the cause of the family farm in her district, where she served as an agent of the Red Lake County Agricultural Adjustment Committee (1941-1944) and later as a member of the Democratic Farmer-Labor (DFL) party. Party regulars in that traditional district soon identified her as legislative material, and the outgoing, attractive candidate won a seat in the state legislature after a vigorous personal campaign. Though she made no waves, Knutson built a solid base of support, effectively working on the pressing issues of her district—agricultural matters and Indian affairs. In many ways her early days in the Minnesota Legislature, where she strongly supported state aid for health and education programs, mirrored her legislative interests in the United States Congress. She scored a significant political victory in her first U.S. congressional campaign in 1954, when she defeated four men in the primary and finally unseated the incumbent, Republican Harold Hagen.

In the Congress Knutson faithfully watchdogged the interests of her district by introducing legislation to support the school lunch program and aid to Indians. As the first woman on the Agricultural Committee she hammered away at the Eisenhower administration, protesting Secretary Ezra Taft Benson's pro-agrabusiness policies, which she claimed operated at the expense of the family farm. The contribution for which Knutson is most remembered is her successful establishment of the student loan program. Thousands have gone through school via funding from Title II of the National Education Defense Act, legislation she designed with the interests of poor farm youth in mind.

Because of the "Coya, Come Home" controversy, she lost the 1958 election to Republican Odin Langen, an unprecedented defeat in her Democratic district, but this did not signal a return to home and hearth for the energetic former congresswoman. She mustered her Democratic forces together for the 1960 campaign, in which she went down in defeat along with DFL-endorsed Governor Freeman. President Kennedy, for whom Knutson had diligently worked in the 1960 campaign, found a spot for her in the Civil Defense Agency.

A weird footnote accompanies the Coya Knutson saga. After years of dedicated civil service, she again set her sights on Congress in a special 1977 Seventh Congressional District primary. Her campaign was a losing one (she never did regain her former momentum), and who should turn up as one of her opponents in the primary race but former administrative aide, Bill Kjeldahl.

Bibliography

In Chamberlin, H. *A Minority of Members* (1973).

In Engelbarts, R. *Women in the United States Congress* (1974).

"Four-Way Democratic Primary Fight between Sullivan, Knutson, Kjeldahl, and Anderson," *New York Times*, February 8, 1977.

"Notes on People," *New York Times*, January 27, 1977.

In Stuhler, Barbara, and Gretchen Kneuter. *Women of Minnesota* (1977).

Juanita Kreps
January 11, 1921-

B. Lynch, Kentucky; D. Elmer M. and Cenia Blair Morris; M. Clifton H. Kreps, 1944; Secretary of Commerce, January 3, 1977 to October 31, 1979.

It is a long way from the mining community of Lynch, Kentucky, where Juanita Morris, daughter of a mine operator, grew up, to Washington, D.C., where Juanita Kreps, Carter Cabinet appointee, assumed control of the Department of Commerce, responsible for and to the nation's business interests. Kreps' *vita* is an example of a thoughtfully calculated political career. In tracing her extraordinary performance—from her student days at the noted work/study institution, Berea College, located in her native Kentucky, through the Phi Beta Kappa years at Duke when Kreps was training to become an economist during the early 1940s, into her academic career where she specialized in economic issues related to women and the aged during her various teaching assignments (Duke, Denison, Hofstra, Queens), and finally to the administrative level in the mid-1970s as vice-president of Duke University—it appears that Juanita Kreps made all the right career moves at the appropriate times.

She was probably one of a handful of women "qualified" to assume the position of secretary of Commerce in 1977, reportedly President Carter's second choice after he was turned down by Jane Cahill Pfeiffer of IBM. Kreps herself acknowledged upon accepting the job that use of the term "qualified women" usually indicates that a woman possesses credentials in the areas of business and government. From the first day with the Carter administration she emphasized the need for more creative searching strategies on the parts of those in power in order to recruit women and minorities for service at the highest level of government. She herself has publicly stated on numerous occasions that she carefully cultivated board directorships for herself (J. C. Penney, R. J. Reynolds Industries, Eastman Kodak, Western Electric, Teachers Insurance and Annuity) in order to gain the business experience acknowledged as credible by power wielders in government and industry.

In her work with influential boards and as a high-ranking administrator at Duke, Kreps has been singled out as the "first woman" and the "only woman" in countless situations. Perhaps because of her status of "uniqueness" in so many situations (first woman member of the New York Stock Exchange Board, for example) and because of her perspective as an economist, she has taken issue with many prevailing egalitarian notions of the feminist movement with regard to women and work. In Kreps' view, women cannot make significant inroads into the most valued segments of the economy (business, industry, and the professions) if they continue to offer themselves in excessive supply in the less valued, service-oriented sectors of the economy (clerical work, elementary school teaching, and nursing). In her position as secretary of Commerce she took a keen interest in seeing women with excellent educations move to a fast-track career pattern, and she encouraged Commerce's establishment of the President's Interagency Task Force on Women Business Owners (1977). At the same time she has half-humorously remarked that women, even at the highest levels, rarely are treated as equal participants. "I'd like to get to the point where I can be just as mediocre as a man," she once commented.

In a 1977 *Ms.* magazine article, Kreps supported flexitime, maternity and paternity leaves, permanent reduced workloads, and other creative labor arrangements to effect "improvements in time allocation and ultimately in the quality of life available in American families." Kreps' experiences in the academic labor market may account for her sensitivity to the reentry labor issues faced by women, no matter how high their academic attainment. She spent almost eight years after earning her Ph.D. in the struggle to get on tenure-track at a major university, finally accomplishing this at Duke, where her husband, Clifton Kreps, had been appointed Wachovia Professor of Banking in the 1950s. During this period she and her husband reared three children.

When Kreps' opportunity for the move to government came after her many years and roles at Duke—a professor, dean of the Women's College, assistant provost, and vice-president (1973-1977)—she made the decision, according to biographer Peggy Lamson, with some degree of negative critical advice from her husband. Lamson quotes Kreps: "So, he [Clifton] reminded me that I had not lived in an apartment in a city for a very long time, and I hadn't lived alone for more than thirty years. He [my husband] thought I would find that lonely. He also pointed out that I was already doing a wide range of very important things and I should not forget what my goals were in those areas" (*In the Vanguard*, p. 60). The unfortunate footnote to this conversation is that Kreps resigned her position as secretary in October 1979 for "personal reasons," after her husband sustained major injuries from self-inflicted bullet wounds.

As secretary of Commerce Kreps steered a host of subagencies, among them the National Technical Information Service (NTIS); the National Bureau of Standards (NBS); the Domestic International Business Administration (DIBA); and the Bureau of Economic Affairs (BEA), which handles census and gross national product statistics through its subagencies. She received high marks from the business community. As Commerce's first economist in the role of secretary, she forged linkages between business and economic interests by communicating frequently with the controllers of economic policy, though she was forced to fight for inclusion in high-level economic policy-setting sessions. She cites the growth and increase of effectiveness of the Economic

Development Administration (EDA) as one of her most significant contributions to Commerce. Through her efforts, EDA resources were made available to encourage business and industry in the cities. Commerce designed a governmental policy to designate minority businesses for at least 10% of federal purchasing and construction contracts, a policy opposed by non-minority contractors and the construction industry as a whole. To those who balked at the proposed solutions Kreps countered, "Americans are spoiled. We are so accustomed to growth and expansion that we think we can find a painless solution to every problem.... But solutions are never free; they are merely cheaper than non-solutions."

Kreps' political profile emerges as one of moderation and studied understatement, tempered by well-timed and calm assertiveness. It is unfortunate that her winning streak at Commerce was cut short by her premature departure, for she inspired praise from both the economics and business communities in the United States and abroad. As she has advocated so often in her public talks the importance of women's visibility in obtaining positions of power, one hopes that Kreps will remain visible in her private life, so that those at the highest echelons of government will look to her to fill some political position in the future.

Selected Writings and Speeches

Lifetime Allocation of Work and Income (1971); *Sex in the Marketplace: American Women at Work* (1971); "Who Is Responsible for the Quality of Life?," *Vital Speeches*, May 15, 1975; *Women and the American Economy: A Look at the 1980's* (1976); "Thoughts about Government and Business," *Vital Speeches*, August 1, 1977; *Los Angeles Times*, June 24, 1977 [Interview]; *Los Angeles Herald Examiner*, July 18, 1978 [Interview]; "An Exchange of Views on the U.S. Trade Policy," *Washington Post*, January 17 and 29, 1979; "Why No Recession in '79: Interview with Secretary of Commerce Juanita M. Kreps, *U.S. News and World Report*, April 30, 1979.

A more complete listing of Kreps' public speeches may be found in B. Manning, *Index to American Women Speakers* (1980), pp. 175-76.

Honors

Phi Beta Kappa (Berea College, B.A.; Duke University, M.A. and Ph.D.); honorary degrees from Denison University, Cornell College, St. Lawrence University, University of Kentucky, University of North Carolina, Queens College; Duke University Scholar and Fellowship (1942-1945); Ford Faculty Fellow (1964-1965); North Carolina Public Service Award (1976).

Bibliography

"Business Executives Laud Juanita Kreps's Trade Achievements; Outgoing Secretary Is Praised Particularly for Getting Business in China," *Wall Street Journal*, October 5, 1979.

"Catch-up for Calculating Women," *Time*, January 8, 1979.

"Commerce Secretary Juanita Kreps, Citing Personal Reasons, Will Leave Her Job at the End of October," *Wall Street Journal*, October 3, 1979.

"Commerce Secretary Kreps Said That If the Fed Does Decide to Tighten Credit, the Action Should Be Quite Modest," *Wall Street Journal*, April 13, 1979.

"Former U.S. Commerce Secretary Juanita Kreps, Elected Director of R. J. Reynolds Co.," *Wall Street Journal*, November 16, 1979.

In Furniss and Graham, eds. *Women in Higher Education* (1974).

"Is Rejoining Board of Eastman Kodak," *Wall Street Journal*, November 12, 1979.

"Juanita Kreps Elected Director of J. C. Penney," *Wall Street Journal*, November 29, 1979.

"Juanita Kreps: More Active Role for Commerce," *Nation's Business*, September 1977.

In Lamson, Peggy. *In the Vanguard* (1979).

In McBee, Mary L., and Kathryn A. Blake, eds. *The American Woman: Who Will She Be?* (1974).

"Secretary Kreps Defines Department's Goals," *Commerce American*, February 14, 1977.

Silk, L. "Candid Academic at Commerce," *New York Times Biographical Service*, May 1977.

Starr, H. G. "In Carter Cabinet, Some CPI Alumni," *Chemical Week*, January 19, 1977.

"U.S. Commerce Secretary Kreps Will Begin Talks Designed to Expand the Emerging Economic Relationship with China," *Wall Street Journal*, May 7, 1979.

"What Can You Expect from Carter's Cabinet?," *U.S. News and World Report*, January 10, 1977.

Mary Anne Krupsak
March 26, 1932-

B. Schenectady, New York; D. Ambrose M. and Mary Regina Wytrwal Krupsak; M. Edwin Margolis, 1969; Served as Lieutenant Governor of New York, January 1975 to January 1979.

Mary Anne Krupsak has never passed up an opportunity during her more than 30 years in politics to point out that she is not "one of the boys." Indeed, she ran her 1974 campaign for lieutenant governor of New York on the political slogan "She's Not Just One of the Boys," a campaign staffed by feminists and endorsed by New York Democratic leaders, from Bella Abzug to former governor Robert Wagner.

Once elected, Krupsak set out to prove to Governor Carey, party regulars, and the people of New York that the office of lieutenant governor could be a vital and dynamic force for political change in the state. With little advice or encouragement from Governor Carey, Krupsak turned her office into the ear of state government. She organized a series of enormously popular forums all over the state to which she and her staff would travel to listen and respond to the concerns of interested citizen groups. This program, which attempted to bring government to the people, contributed greatly to Krupsak's popularity. She was able to respond to the needs of the state, especially in the areas of tourism and local transportation, because of these pulse-taking sessions; and because of her visibility around the state, particularly in the upstate area, Krupsak was able to maintain the popularity she had cultivated in the 1974 lieutenant governor's primary.

By 1975, the highest-ranking elected woman official in New York's history was, according to some polls, more popular than Governor Carey himself. Despite Carey's disagreements with his lieutenant governor, he counted on her effectiveness at the grassroots political level, and the two maintained their expedient but hardly romantic political marriage through better and worse. At a political "roast" hosted by the New York press, Krupsak wittily commented on her relationship with Carey, saying that she wanted to destroy the myth that she and the governor did not share a close professional rapport. "The governor and I have a marvelous relationship," related Krupsak. "Why, he always stops and says, 'Hello, *how* are you?' Now that's progress. Three months ago, he would say, 'Hello, *who* are you?' "

As Krupsak developed an easy and humorous style with the press, she began to receive the press coverage necessary to underscore her pet issues and programs: her community forums around the state; her activities on behalf of women (with Bella Abzug she co-chaired the National Women's Conference in Houston); her preservation campaign to save Radio City Music Hall; her position as leader of the New York State delegation to the White House Conference on Balanced National Growth and Public Policy. Her view that New York City should take more responsibility for shouldering its own fiscal burden made her especially popular with upstaters. She supported an income tax hike for New York City commuters, and charged that a proposed gasoline hike would work against the interests of upstate New Yorkers, who did not have access to the level of mass transportation available to metropolitan New Yorkers.

Perhaps Krupsak's most controversial political stand centered around the issue of abortion. While serving as a New York State legislator in 1970 she voted to liberalize New York's abortion bill. Though a devout Catholic herself, she explained to the press, "... you cannot codify one group's religious or ethical beliefs into statutory law, and penalize the entire community, under penalty of imprisonment, for their differing beliefs." In her public talks she has repeatedly spoken out for women's issues, recommending to feminists the use of the elected political forum rather than the streets to bring women-related issues to public attention.

Krupsak's pharmacist parents instilled an early desire in their daughter to enter politics. Her father, descended from Catholic, Polish immigrant stock, participated in local politics. Mary Anne studied history and music in college and immediately went on to a master's program in public communications (1955) at Boston University, establishing good credentials for the volunteer campaign work she was to undertake for Democratic gubernatorial candidate Averell Harriman. When he won in 1956, she joined his office as an aide in the consumer relations area. In 1958 she joined New York congressman Samuel Stratton's Washington office for a year before seeking her law degree at the University of Chicago. Upon her return to New York in 1962 Krupsak practiced private and corporate law for a time before getting back into the mainstream of New York State government.

She worked at assistant counsel positions in the state senate and assembly before deciding to seek elective office in the densely Republican 104th District. In these early years Krupsak campaigned against the deeply entrenched Republican patronage in New York, and championed welfare projects over Republican-inspired public works programs. She challenged Governor Nelson Rockefeller at every turn, often referring to his "edifice complex," which she claimed was the reason for his building the Albany mall at the expense of human services programs. Krupsak's sprightly performance in the assembly eased her way into the state senate in 1972, where she continued to fight for legislative reforms, improved health and welfare benefits for women, and expanded and improved mass transit in New York. Because she had defeated Robert Lynch, a strong Republican candidate, for a state senate seat in 1972, Democratic leaders looked favorably on a Krupsak candidacy for a major office in 1974. But she decided that capturing the lieutenant governor's slot was her best political move.

In a 1978 *Ms.* article, aide Ginny Corsi assessed what has proved to be Krupsak's most valuable managerial asset in the tough New York political scene. Corsi explains that Krupsak is not one to save the day single-handedly, "but she'll get people into a small room who have never been willing to talk together, and she will force them to deal with common problems." Not a mean accomplishment in the diverse political terrain of New York State. Although Krupsak was replaced by Mario M. Cuomo, a former rival, in 1978 (she had chosen to challenge Governor Carey for his position in the primary and lost), she has remained visible on the national scene. She was a delegate to the Democratic National Convention in 1972 and 1976, and many suggest that hers will be a political career on the fast-track into the 1980s.

Selected Writings and Speeches

In New York Commission on Human Rights. *Women's Role in Contemporary Society, September 21-25, 1970* (testimony), Avon, 1972.

See B. Manning, *Index to American Women Speakers* (1980), p. 176.

Honors

Honorary LHD degree from Russell Sage College (1973).

Bibliography

Greenhouse, Linda. "The Rise and Rise ... and Rise of Mary Anne Krupsak," *Ms.*, April 1978.

Holt, D., and S. Agrest. "Parting Shot," *Newsweek*, June 26, 1978.

Logan, A. "Around City Hall," *New Yorker*, August 7, 1978.

Weisman, S. R. "Strong Minded Candidate," *New York Times Biography Service*, June 1978.

Madeleine May Kunin
September 28, 1933-

B. Zurich, Switzerland; D. Ferdinand and Renee Bloch May; M. Arthur S. Kunin; Served as Lieutenant Governor of Vermont, 1978- .

Madeleine Kunin came to politics by way of a writing career. Formally trained as a writer at the University of Massachusetts, Amherst (B.A., 1956), the Columbia School of Journalism (M.S., 1957), and the University of Vermont (M.A., English, 1967), Kunin has worked as a journalist, a television producer, and public relations woman. During the 1970s she taught at Trinity College in Burlington, and did freelance writing, specializing in nature and travel writing with a Vermont focus. During this period she actively courted Democratic support in Chittenden County, her first political experience being a seat on the Governor's Commission on the Status of Women (1964-1968).

Kunin seems to have scored political success with every try. She became the Burlington representative to the Vermont House of Representatives in 1973. During her tenure in the House (1973-1978), she won the Democratic whip post in 1975 and became chair of the Vermont House Appropriations Committee in 1977. Gaining notoriety by serving on numerous governor's commissions—the Governor's Commission on Children and Youth, 1973-1977; the Governor's Commission on the Administration of Justice, 1976-1977—she was elected lieutenant governor in 1978 with significant legislative experience behind her gleaned from legislative stints on the Joint Fiscal Committee (1977-1978), the Committee on Special Offenders (1975), and the Emergency Board (1977-1978).

Kunin's career parallels those of other successful political women who have achieved a certain local prominence by their writings, such as former representative Julia Hansen, Lieutenant Governor Nancy Stevenson, and former ambassador Clare Boothe Luce. Kunin's *Big Green Book: A Four Season Guide to Vermont* was quite successful in her home state, which relies heavily on the seasonal tourist traffic. She combines her political and writing careers with sizeable family obligations as the mother of four children.

Selected Writings and Speeches

Kunin, Madeleine, and Marilyn Stout. *Big Green Book: A Four Season Guide to Vermont* (1976).

Honors

Selected outstanding state legislator at the Eagleton Institute of Politics, Rutgers University (1975).

Bibliography

Numerous articles in local Burlington newspapers.

Clare Boothe Luce
April 10, 1903-

B. New York City; D. William F. and Ann Snyder Boothe; M. Henry Robinson Luce, 1935 (widow); Served in U.S. House of Representatives as Republican-Connecticut, January 6, 1943 to January 3, 1947, 78th through 79th Congress; Ambassador to Italy, March 2, 1953 to January 5, 1957.

Everyone who has written about Clare Boothe Luce has commented upon her being one of those extraordinarily gifted women who combines the natural assets of beauty and intelligence with the acquired privileges of social status and money. She has appeared on every sort of "outstanding" list, from "outstanding woman personality" to "best dressed." In 1953 the Gallup Poll reported that she ranked fourth in their survey of "most admired woman in the world."

As playwright, novelist, editor, politician, diplomat, and activist, Clare Luce earned respect and occupied celebrity status. She also achieved distinction in the smaller circles of high fashion and glamor. Yet her childhood had not pointed to the glittering success she would one day attain. As a child she was shuffled with her family from place to place, mainly in New York and New Jersey. Her mother, Ann Clare Snyder, had worked as a dancer before she married William F. Boothe, who called himself a "professional fiddlest." After her father deserted the family, Clare's mother worked as a saleswoman in the years of "genteel poverty." Just before World War I, Ann Boothe took her daughter to Paris for a year, where the cost of living was low and Clare would have opportunities to expand her cultural horizons. Of those years Luce later recalled, "I went to museums, learned French with children playing in the park and read incessantly. No matter how little money we had, mother never refused to buy me a book."

After returning to the States, Clare's mother married her physician, Albert Austin, and Clare began attending private schools. She graduated *summa cum laude* in 1919 from Miss Mason's Castle School in Tarrytown, New York. In 1921, on an extended trip to Europe with her family, she met Mrs. Oliver H. P. Belmont, a feminist looking for recruits to work on behalf of the National Women's Party. It was there that Clare Boothe began her lifelong commitment to women's causes by working for Alice Paul, the original equal rights advocate, in the same year that the amendment went up to the Hill. Stephen Shadegg, her biographer, talks of her distributing handbills from the air, while precariously perched in the open cockpit of a World War I plane. Her six-year marriage to multimillionaire George Brokaw, a clothing manufacturer 23 years her senior, ended in divorce in 1929. Brokaw died in 1935, and their only child, Ann Clare Brokaw, was killed in a tragic automobile accident in California in 1944.

After her divorce from Brokaw, Clare began her literary career by working for *Vogue* at $20 per week. By 1933 she had become managing editor of *Vanity Fair* magazine, a well-paid position she left one year later in order to freelance. She was well on her way to developing her talents as a playwright and columnist when in 1935 she married Henry Robinson Luce, publisher/founder of *Time, Life, Sports Illustrated,* and *Fortune* magazines. Concentrating on her own literary career during the late 1930s, Clare Luce authored several hit plays. *The Women* (1937), a sprightly and brittle comedy about divorce among the idle rich, was perhaps her most successful play and was later made into a film. *Kiss the Boys Goodbye* (1938) and *Margin for Error* (1940) also did well. A fast writer, as later she was to be quick in the art of verbal rebuttal in Congress, she claims to have spent less than one week writing *The Women*. Her introduction to *Europe in the Spring* (1940), a book of reminiscences of Europe before the war, calls for American patriotism and immediate action against Hitler. One finds here, as in many of her articles and speeches in later years, a note of modesty and a non-expert observer approach. "You must understand I am not a historian nor a philosopher, nor an economist nor a political columnist nor even a professional journalist," wrote Clare Boothe. "I am just a curious American and sometime scribbler (of plays) who happened to be in Europe all this spring, and who lived like everybody else there in the invisible shadow of the Blitzkrieg that has now almost destroyed it."

Although Clare Boothe Luce in later years became a staunch conservative, supporting right-wing American politics and leaders like Barry Goldwater and Ronald Reagan, she began her political career as a campaign worker for Roosevelt in his "Kitchen Cabinet" while she was at *Vanity Fair*. In 1935 she switched to the Republican party upon her marriage to Henry Luce. To feminists who charged that she had changed parties to please her husband, Luce replied, "I wasn't going to spend the rest of my life quarreling with him about politics, but, at about that time, I became very disillusioned with Mr. Roosevelt's foreign policy, so it was no great strain on my conscience." In 1940 she dazzled Republicans at a huge Willkie rally in Madison Square Garden with a speech that effectively launched her political career. Politics had never been alien to her; her stepfather had represented Connecticut's Fourth Congressional District and her husband was in the thick of current affairs. With this background and her natural poise and intelligence, it is not surprising that, after her war correspondent years in the Far East and the Pacific with *Life* magazine during 1941 and 1942, she became the Republican congresswoman from Connecticut.

Luce served the Fourth Congressional District in the 78th and 79th Congresses. Her maiden speech in the House attracted much controversy when she indicted Vice-President Wallace's freedom of the air proposal as "global thinking [that] no matter how you slice it is globaloney." Her verbal attacks sometimes created formidable problems. In her political campaign of 1944 she made the statement that Roosevelt "lied us into war," a remark that Luce lived with for many years, eventually resurfacing as an issue in her confirmation hearings as Eisenhower's ambassador to Brazil in 1959. During her years as congresswoman, Luce exercised her wit most frequently at the expense of the Democratic administration, calling Roosevelt and his inner circle a group of "ram squaddled, do-gooding New Deal bureaucrats." Even though she criticized Roosevelt's soft foreign policy on the floor of the Senate, her voting record generally supported the administration she had accused of "dictatorial bumbledom." Repeatedly in her public appearances and writings she stated her abhorrence of Fascist and Communist totalitarian dictatorships, and professed her uncertainty as to whether Russia and Germany espoused "real difference in the two ideologies." Her campaign slogan in 1942 against LeRoy Downs was, "Let's fight a hard war instead of a soft war."

Particularly incensed following the 1945 Yalta and Potsdam conferences by the approach taken by the Western negotiators, Luce expressed fears about America's "leaning over backward" to accommodate Soviet operations in Eastern Europe, Iran, and Korea. Her criticisms of foreign policy were made from a position of strength, as she had toured the battle fronts of Burma, India, and China, among others, as a war correspondent, and in 1945 as the only woman member of the House Military Affairs Committee. Moreover, she had interviewed key figures like General and Madame Chiang Kai-shek, Prime Minister Nehru, and many U.S. generals. Though Congresswoman Luce was all business as a journalist and politician, her femininity always received comment, as in this description of her firing a 155-mm howitzer: "Mrs. Luce pulled the lanyard like a veteran, but the concussion almost straightened out her blond curls."

Her wariness of atomic controls manifested itself when as a member of the Joint Committee on Atomic Energy she advocated a bill to insure civilian control of the atom under the Atomic Energy Commission. Later, she called for "the creation of appropriate international machinery within the framework of the United Nations Organization for international control and reduction of armaments and weapons, especially those involving atomic power."

Throughout her congressional career, Luce consistently championed social causes. Though she herself was a member of the Daughters of the American Revolution, she publicly deplored certain DAR policies, among them the ban on blacks in the membership and the restriction of DAR facilities to whites. Her legislation addressed social progress issues: she introduced bills to abolish discrimination against blacks in the armed forces and to prevent discrimination against Indian and Chinese groups. Another bill urged Congress to establish a special bureau in the Department of Labor that would insure workers equal pay for equal work, regardless of race, color, or creed. Unfortunately, most of her bills were killed in committee or buried before they even reached committee.

By the end of her second term of office Luce, formerly an Episcopalian, had converted to the Catholic Church, and announced that she would not seek the Republican nomination for Connecticut's U.S. Senate seat. Instead, she decided to step back from public life and turn her energies to writing articles, films, and essays. The period 1946 to 1948 was devoted to writing about Catholicism and matters of the faith. Her 1948 farewell to politics, delivered at the Republican National Convention, decried leadership styles and political maneuvers in the Democratic party. Without war and depression, jibed Luce, the Democrats lacked viable campaign issues.

But in 1952 Luce emerged from her semiretirement to make over 40 speeches on behalf of Eisenhower's presidential candidacy. At the same time she unsuccessfully sought the Republican nomination for the Connecticut Senate seat. As it turned out, Eisenhower rewarded Luce by nominating her for the Italian ambassadorial position. Perhaps because of her publicized conversion to Catholicism and her extensive work with the Italian war victims during World War II, her nomination, made public on February 7, 1953, brought praise in the United States and Italy with the exception of some ultraconservative and Communist Italian cliques. These groups complained respectively that being a woman she was unsuited for the post, and being a Catholic she would be in league with the Vatican. After testifying before the Senate Foreign Relations Committee, affirming her belief in the separation of church and state, she was confirmed by the Senate and presented her credentials in Rome in April 1953.

Luce became America's second woman ambassador and the first woman chief of mission to a major European power. Her position placed her in charge of all U.S. government operations in Italy and some 1,250 American and Italian embassy, consulate, information center, and Foreign Operations people. "Because I am a woman," she stated, "I must make unusual efforts to succeed. If I fail, no one will say, 'She doesn't have what it takes.' They will say, 'Women don't have what it takes.' Success by a woman makes it easier for other able women." Ambassador Luce's record during her tenure in Italy was by most reports competent. She was well received by the Italian people, and worked successfully through diplomatic channels to settle the Trieste dispute between Italy and Yugoslavia. As supervisor of the Military Assistance Advisory Group she substantially expanded U.S. military and economic assistance programs to augment Italy's defense agenda as established by NATO. Predictably, she did not enjoy popularity with the Italian Communists. She resigned from her ambassadorial post on January 5, 1957, after a bizarre illness reportedly caused by arsenic poisoning from chipping plaster in her villa bedroom. Later in life she was to consider her work in Italy as the most useful contribution of her career.

President Eisenhower recruited her again for diplomatic service in 1959, this time to be ambassador to Brazil. Although the Senate approved the nomination, Luce declined after an unpleasant campaign against her nomination led by Democrat Wayne Morse of Oregon. Although Luce managed to respond wittily to Morse's charge that she exhibited "part of an old pattern of mental instability," she resigned, saying: "The climate of good will was poisoned by thousands of words of extraordinarily ugly charges against my person, and of distrust of the mission I was going to undertake."

After her husband's death in 1967, Luce moved to Honolulu, Hawaii, where she continued her writing (as a columnist for *McCall's* and a contributor to current events periodicals), her commitment to civic and cultural activities, and her keen interest in the world of power and politics. Among her governmental consulting appointments, she served on the White House Preservation Committee (1970-1977); the President's Foreign Intelligence Advisory Board (1973-1977); and as consultant in American letters of the Library of Congress. She counts the U.S. Committee for Refugees, the United Nations Association of the U.S.A., and the International Women's Year Commission among her many board assignments. Into her late seventies, Luce has become a staunch advocate of increased U.S. military preparedness and a sharp critic of the SALT negotiations: "If [the SALT devotees] cannot be awakened," she writes, "the dream will turn into the nightmare of World War III." Her faith and her patriotism are recurrent themes in speeches and writings.

Through the years, Luce has consistently advocated women's rights, though her politics have evolved into increasing conservatism. Her stand against abortion is unequivocal. "I do not accept the extraordinary proposition that women cannot achieve equal rights before the law until all women are given the legal right to empty their wombs at will—and at the expense of the taxpayer," she stated in a 1978 interview. In public talks she has regretted the trivialization of marriage, the loss of fidelity and commitment in modern marriages. "Marriage is terribly important," she states. "It helps one to define oneself."

Of women's progress in politics she has observed, "There are no more women in Congress now [1979] than when I was a Congresswoman 35 years ago." And in forecasting women's political possibilities for the future: "Though we have a woman Prime Minister in Britain, I think it will be a long time before we have a woman President in this country." At the beginning of the 1980s the ERA is still a concern for Luce. In 1979 correspondence she wrote, "ERA was conceived as a bill to wipe out in one single stroke all the laws on the books which denied equality before the law to women. In the past half-century, women have won many rights they did not have when ERA was dropped into the hopper. But even so, I believe that the passage of ERA would bring the evolutionary process of legal equality to completion."

Plays and Books

Stuffed Shirts (1933); *Abide with Me* (1935); *The Women* (1937); *Kiss the Boys Goodbye* (1938); *Margin for Error* (1940); *Europe in the Spring* (1940); *Saints for Now* (1952).

Selected Articles and Speeches

"Call to Women: Have Confidence in America," *Ladies Home Journal*, March 1974; "What's Happening to America's Values," *U.S. News and World Report*, June 24, 1974; "Woman: A Technological Castaway," *Saturday Evening Post*, January 1974; "Coalition in Italy," *National Review*, November 7, 1975; "Time to Grow Up," *Reader's Digest*, April 1975; "Trend Away from Democracy: Interview," *Current*, September 1975; "Ultimatum to the UN," *National Review*, January 31, 1975; "Light at the End of the Tunnel of Love," *National Review*, November 12, 1976; "Message of the Fourth," *Reader's Digest*, July 1976; "When Women Will Be Superior to Men," *McCall's*, April 1976; "Equality Begins at Home," *Saturday Evening Post*, October 1977; "High Human Price of Detente," *National Review*, November 11, 1977; "Is the Republican Party Dead?," *National Review*, March 18, 1977; "Is the New Morality Destroying America?," speech for the Ethics and Public Policy Center of Georgetown University (1979); "History and the Nature of Man," Vernon A. Walters Lectures in History, U.S. Naval Academy (1979).

The official papers of Clare Boothe Luce are held by the Library of Congress but are not available to the public.

Note: Because of Luce's extensive journalistic output, users are advised to check bibliographies in all works about Luce and to check standard periodical indexing services.

A more complete listing of Luce's public speeches may be found in B. Manning, *Index to American Women Speakers* (1980), pp. 189-90.

Honors

Honorary degrees from Colby, Fordham, Mundelein, Temple, Creighton, Georgetown, Seton Hall, Mt. Holyoke, St. John's, and Boston University; Awarded Knight of the Grand Cross; Dame of Malta; Dag Hammarskjold Medal; Laetare Medal; Order of Lafayette; Cardinal Newman Award; Poor Richard Award; American Statesman Medal; The Trinity Award; Golden Plate Award; Fourth Estate Award; Horatio Alger Award; Amita Award; Award for International Achievement; Sylvanus Thayer Award.

Bibliography

Alexander, Shana. "Listening to Clare Boothe Luce," *Newsweek*, November 26, 1973.

Baldridge, Letitia. *Roman Candle* (1956).

Barzini, L. "Ambassador Luce as the Italians See Her," *Harper's*, July 1955.

In Chamberlin, Hope. *A Minority of Members* (1973).

In Diehl, Digby. *Supertalk* (1974).

In Engelbarts, Rudolf. *Women in the United States Congress* (1974).

In Frost, David. *The Americans* (1970).

Hatch, Alden. *Ambassador Extraordinary* (1956).

Lawrenson, H. "The Woman," *Esquire*, August 1974.

In Roosevelt, Felicia Warburg. *Doers and Dowagers* (1975).

Shadegg, Stephen. *Clare Boothe Luce* (1970).

In St. Johns, Adela (Rogers). *Some Are Born Great* (1974).

"This World," *San Francisco Examiner and Chronicle*, June 4, 1978 [Interview].

Helen Stevenson Meyner
March 5, 1929-

B. New York City; D. William Edward and Eleanor Bumstead Stevenson; M. Robert Meyner, 1957; Served in U.S. House of Representatives as Democrat-New Jersey, January 3, 1975 to January 3, 1978; 94th through 95th Congress.

Helen Meyner was married to the popular Governor Meyner of New Jersey, and served graciously as the governor's lady for several years before she thought to look toward elective office herself. Though some have characterized the governor's wife role as living in the shadow of her husband, Meyner says that she enjoyed the position. After she was elected congresswoman from New Jersey in 1974, she freely admitted that she felt it was more comfortable campaigning as a wife than as a candidate. "In the beginning, the adjustment to standing on my own and projecting myself to the public was very difficult," she admitted in 1974.

After her husband's service (1953-1961) as governor was over, Helen Meyner stayed in the public eye as a columnist for the *Star-Ledger* in Newark, as a television interviewer, and as a trustee for several organizations including the Newark Museum. She had always been active in civic and political affairs, and had worked as a special assistant in the 1956 presidential campaign of her cousin, Adlai Stevenson. She earned her B.A. degree from Colorado College in 1950, but most of her credentials for political office have come from her practical experience in public life. Her brand of Democratic politics has been clearly liberal, in line with her husband's political views and those of liberal Princeton, where she has resided since 1957. Princeton, however, is not located in her 13th District, which encompasses the river counties of New Jersey and one-half of Morris County, and for this reason the Meyners also kept a residence in Phillipsburg.

Helen Meyner's first try for the 13th District congressional seat was a failure. She lost to a Republican, Joseph Maraziti, by 26,000 votes, possibly because she was a drafted candidate to fill a Democratic vacancy. Her next campaign was harder fought. Again a draft choice, she turned the tables on Maraziti and won by more than 20,000 votes. In her second try she had emphasized the positive factors of being a woman representative. "Women may be more sensitive to education, day care, and environment needs," became an oft-repeated Meyner campaign message.

She was particularly effective in bringing public works money to her district during her two terms, attracting more than $200 million to the 13th District, an amount unmatched by any other New Jersey representative. She also served on the House Select Committee on Aging. But it was International Relations and its Oversight Subcommittee that interested her most. Because she had considerable international background—as a field worker in the American Red Cross in the early 1950s, a guide at the United Nations in New York from 1952 to 1953, and a consultant on consumer affairs to TWA from 1953 to 1956—Meyner had tried for a seat on the House Foreign Affairs Committee, and was appointed to International Relations. The Oversight Subcommittee handles the spectrum of international relations activities from the Peace Corps to the CIA. Helen Meyner, a vocal opponent of continued military aid to Southeast Asia, supported humanitarian assistance administered through international agencies like the Red Cross.

Terse in her assessment of why she lost her third bid for the House to Republican James Courter she quipped, "It appears many of the voters in the 13th feel a woman's place is in the house, and I don't mean in the House of Representatives." A reluctant candidate when she ran, Meyner stated after her 1978 loss that she would never again run for elective office, though public service would remain a major focus of her life. The daughter of an Oberlin College president, the wife of a governor, and a successful politician in her own right—it seems that the public sphere is Helen Meyner's natural habitat.

Selected Writings and Speeches

Many columns in the Newark *Star-Ledger* (1962-1969).

Honors

Honorary degree from Colorado College (1973).

Bibliography

Churchill, Mary. "Helen Meyner Adjusting to a Life in Politics," *The New York Times*, November 17, 1974.

Dworkin, Susan. "Those Freshperson Congresspersons," *Ms.*, April 1975.

Gordon, David. "Meyner Draws on Her Humor to Ease the Defeat," The Sunday Newark *Star-Ledger*, November 12, 1978.

Barbara Ann Mikulski
July 20, 1936-

B. Baltimore, Maryland; D. William and Christine Kutz Mikulski; Single; Served in the U.S. House of Representatives as Democrat-Maryland, January 3, 1977- , 95th Congress- .

Because of Barbara Mikulski's Polish, Catholic, blue-collar background (her parents were in the grocery business in a working class eastside Baltimore neighborhood), many have called her the prototype of a new type of liberal political woman in the United States. She has lived among women of the white lower-middle classes who do not necessarily consider themselves part of the feminist movement, and she is able to speak with some authority about what life is really like for them. "The media have pictured us in the past as sort of Rosie-the-Riveter types, or like the wife in [the film] *Joe*. You wore tacky clothes, liked plastic flowers, read *True Confessions*... and you had an I.Q. of 47. And yet our women aren't like that at all" (*Ms.*, November 1973, p. 72).

At one time she had wanted to be a nun; but instead she turned to the "feminine" profession of social work after becoming interested in the health and consumer problems of Baltimore's impoverished elderly population. She earned an MSW from the University of Maryland in 1965. Together with a lifelong friend, Baltimore's health commissioner, Adele Wilzak, Barbara Mikulski spent her twenties working on projects like REASON (Responding to the Elderly's Ability and Sickness Otherwise Neglected), Narcotics Anonymous, and SECO (Southeast Community Organization). She seized on the issue of ethnic alienation when others were still praising America for being the world's happy melting pot. In the early 1970s Mikulski declared, "America is not a melting pot. It is a sizzling cauldron." That pronouncement, given at the first national conference of the National Center for Urban and Ethnic Affairs, launched the outspoken "outsider's" public career.

Since Mikulski's social activist style of politics was directly opposed to Baltimore's eastside political machine, family and friends were amazed when she announced in 1971 that she had set her sights on the Baltimore City Council. She ran a campaign staffed by family, friends, and volunteers; and she made no payoffs. Yet people were won over by her direct, personal approach. Mikulski's promises to work for the elderly, the neglected, and the have-nots found favor with the First District. Most people agreed that she had "guts," even when they disagreed with her personal politics. When she won a seat to council (odds against her were predicted at 200 to 1 by seasoned politicians), she set about fighting battles for the "little guy," reducing transit fares for the elderly, attempting to establish neighborhood health care facilities, working on plans to assist rape victims, and other issues of egalitarianism that caught her eye. Where issues related to sex and class appeared, Barbara Mikulski was there, also.

In 1973 the Democratic party tapped her to chair the large Commission of Delegate Selection and Party Structure of the Democratic National Committee. This was an appealing assignment for Mikulski, who believes that most Americans do not know how to negotiate the complicated political channels which admit citizens into the core elective process. She states, "You can't guarantee who will be at the convention, but you have to make sure that everyone has a chance."

Mikulski soon emerged as the most colorful Baltimore Council member in recent history; her blunt and witty style of calling issues as she saw them and her notoriety as the serious Democratic reformer of the Mikulski Commission gave her plenty of press. People from her district eagerly awaited the next Mikulski indictment of big government and big business "rip-offs." They could identify with her stories—"I'm out on the highway and stop for oil, pay for it, and 30 miles down the road I find out I'm low on oil and my car doesn't use that much"—and they looked to her to do something about such daily injustices.

In 1977 when she was elected to represent Maryland's Third District, she went to Washington with the eye-opening experience of having run a difficult and losing campaign for the U.S. Senate. In that 1974 campaign she had identified the issues as inflation, unfair taxation, and unemployment. "I picked the issues out of my own guts and experience in my own communities," issues she has tackled in the House along with improved health care for families, and the containment of health costs.

Mikulski is willing to go out on a limb when she feels that the rights of a special issue group are being lost in the bureaucratic shuffle. She frequently expresses anger about programs for women being seen as gifts of the government rather than the just due women have a right to expect. In columnist Ellen Goodman's piece about GI benefits for mothers, Mikulski is quoted as saying, "If motherhood is an occupation which is critically important to society the way we say it is, then there should be a mother's bill of rights." Mikulski will speak out on such issues, but qualifies her statements with pragmatism; she knows Congress would never consider such legislation. On the issue of domestic violence, however, she has scored a notable victory as the force behind the Domestic Violence Prevention and Services Act, which passed overwhelmingly in the House on December 12, 1979. This landmark legislation will channel federal monies into the struggling local shelter programs designed to meet the immediate needs of domestic violence victims.

Mikulski has been identified as one of the more influential practical political theorists in the country. Her idea is simple: to join the various groups in the vast middle class so that average people begin to see that they are fighting a common enemy. "As we move from an economy of affluence to an economy of scarcity, we must be careful that the people who make $5,000 a year are not pitted against those who make $25,000 a year by those who make $900,000," she reminded people often during her lively senatorial campaign. "The two martinis-for-lunch bunch would love for us to fight each other over the resources they have made scarce." Mikulski is a common cause advocate, and many political observers predict that her no-nonsense approach to the issues affecting the majority of ordinary Americans will make her one of the most visible political women in the 1980s.

Selected Writings and Speeches

"Who Speaks for Ethnic America?," *New York Times*, September 29, 1970; "The Mikulski Papers: How We Lost the Election but Won the Campaign," *Ms.*, July 1975.

Barbara Mikulski's papers will be deposited with the Schlesinger Library at Radcliffe College.

Honors

Honorary degrees from Goucher College (1973) and Pratt Institute (1974); "Woman of the Year," by Business and Professional Women's Club Association of Baltimore (1973); Outstanding Alumnus of University of Maryland School of Social Work (1973); of Loyola College (1974); National Citizen of the Year, by the *Buffalo American-Political Eagle* (1974).

Bibliography

Numerous articles in the Baltimore *Evening Sun*.

Carson, Larry. "Barbara Mikulski," [Baltimore] *Evening Sun*, January 15, 1974.

"Fresh Faces Were Not Enough," *Time*, September 23, 1974.

Jones, Carleton. "Barbara, Trumpet of Highlandtown," *Baltimore Sun*, April 17, 1977.

"Mikulski: Queen of the Ethnics," *Newsweek*, November 4, 1974.

"Mr. Van Deerlin's New Recruits," *Broadcasting*, March 14, 1977.

Seifer, Nancy. "Barbara Mikulski and the Blue-Collar Woman," *Ms.*, November 1973.

"Womanpower at the Polls," *Newsweek*, September 23, 1974.

Patsy Takemoto Mink
December 6, 1927-

B. Maui, Hawaii; D. Suematsu and Mitamia Takemoto; M. John Francis Mink, 1951; Served in U.S. House of Representatives as Democrat-Hawaii, January 4, 1965 to January 3, 1977, 89th through 94th Congress.

On the face of it, Patsy Takemoto Mink had many more reasons to fail in politics than to be successful; her gender, her ethnic background, and her youth when she entered the political sphere in Hawaii were only three of her potential liabilities. Mink grew up on Maui, far from Honolulu, the hub of Hawaiian political activity. She attended the University of Hawaii (B.S., 1948) with the intention of going into medicine, but later decided she was of a more philosophical temperament. As she recalls it, her admission to the University of Chicago Law School was a fluke, resulting from the admissions committee's mistaking her for a foreign student and admitting her to the university in order to help fill their quota for foreign students in the first-year class. When she returned to Hawaii in the early 1950s accompanied by husband John Mink, toting her prestigious degree in one arm and her baby daughter, Gwendolyn, in the other, she found that Honolulu law firms did not want her, even though she had the distinction of being the first woman attorney of Japanese descent licensed to practice in the territory. Most refused her because she was the mother of a small child.

A liberationist before Betty Friedan even began to talk about "the feminine mystique," Patsy Mink went into private practice and immediately involved herself in political affairs. Hawaii was mainly old-guard Republican in the 1950s, but Mink and other young professionals found the idea of the Young Democrats of Oahu appealing. She served as the chair for this group for two years, forging valuable political ties in the process. Later she became national vice-president of the Young Democrats of America, representing the group at international conferences such as the Young Political Leaders Conference in Paris. Many political types appeared comfortable with the image she projected of "the bright, pretty, and petite" politico.

In 1956 she made Hawaiian headlines as the first Nisei woman to become a legislator in the territorial house. Her campaign, engineered by her geologist husband, resulted in an easy victory. By 1958, Patsy Mink, strongly involved with the Young Democrats, was making trips to Washington on business, had been admitted to practice before the Supreme Court, and was announcing plans to move from the territorial house into the territorial senate. Though she experienced opposition from the local Democratic powers and other groups with political clout, notably labor, Mink won a seat in the territorial senate. As a senator she sponsored the "Equal Pay for Equal Work" bill, an indication of her growing commitment to legislation that would insure fair labor practices.

There are several ways to state the significance of Patsy Mink's victory in the 1964 congressional election; the youngest member of Congress from the youngest state, the first woman elected from the new state of Hawaii, the first Japanese-American woman elected to Congress. During the late 1960s Representative Mink let it be known that she favored liberal causes, and settled into the routine of Washington politics. Though she was familiar with life in the United States because of her years in Chicago, she faced a grueling schedule of trips back and forth from Washington to her Hawaiian constituency. It is interesting to note how frequently and offhandedly Mink has dismissed what many might consider obstacles to her career. Of the traveling from Washington to Hawaii she has said that she used the time to read; of time constraints due to her responsibilities as a married woman she has declared many times that being a woman politician is no more demanding than being a schoolteacher. Perhaps because of the distance from her constituency, Patsy Mink argued vigorously for a four-year term for representatives.

Mink has always been in the feminist corner of the women's issue, supporting the package of women-related issues including credit, child care, and reproductive freedom. Her committee assignments, Education and Labor, and Interior and Insular Affairs, provided her with frequent forums for liberal positions. She supported Edith Green's Higher Education Act and worked hard for the Elementary and Secondary School Amendment acts. Mink made substantial legislative contributions on behalf of student loans, funding for nonprofit day-care centers, and teachers' sabbatical leaves. Upon her arrival in the Congress, she worked for better economic development programs to benefit the United States Trust Territory of the Pacific and for other U.S. Pacific possessions.

In 1967 she spoke out forcefully against the Vietnam War and the "barbaric" policies of the war that she felt the Johnson administration overlooked. She took a strong stand against punishment of war dissenters. Her position throughout the Vietnam controversy indicted America for spending billions of dollars to escalate a war pitting Asian against Asian, and to her constituency she emphasized the racist underpinnings.

Though Mink's personal philosophy speaks of equal rights for women, her statements about women in politics reveal an optimism and idealism not necessarily reflected in the numbers of women leading active political lives. "The key, the only thing that counts, is whether a woman is genuinely dedicated to the ideal of doing something that will make a difference to her community and to her country. If she has this drive, if she's convinced she can make a contribution, if she's serious and has worked hard and shown the ability to take positions and to stand behind them, to fight for her beliefs, then she cannot fail at an election. I believe this totally" (*Few Are Chosen*, p. 108). Hers has been a career dedicated to providing a role model for women who aspire to public careers, a task she has undertaken through extensive public speaking to women's groups.

On the issue of racism Mink expressed her views in less sanguine terms, probably because of the distinct racial divisions she saw as the major inhibitor of upward mobility in Hawaii, and her own experiences as a student in the United States. "We self-righteously expect all others to admire us for our democracy and our traditions," she told the National Association for Student Affairs at a May 1972 conference in Atlanta. "We are so smug about our superiority, we fail to see our own glaring faults, such as prejudice and poverty amidst affluence."

In 1976 Patsy Mink gave up her seat to campaign for the Senate, but lost in her bid for the Democratic nomination. She was appointed to the State Department position of assistant secretary for Oceans and International Environmental and Scientific Affairs, a position well suited to her Hawaiian background. A 1978 *Ms.* magazine article on political women suggested that Mink's credentials would serve her well if she were named secretary of the Interior because of her work on the Insular Affairs Committee and her understanding of the complex issues of maritime law and sea resources. Mink's persistence and continuing prominence in Hawaiian politics, as well as her double minority identity, assure her reemergence in the 1980s as an influential political woman on the national scene.

Selected Writings and Speeches

"Department Discusses Approach to Environmental Issues," *Department of State Bulletin*, April 18, 1977; "Visions of the Future," *Department of State Bulletin*, October 18, 1977; "Antarctic Resource and Environmental Concerns," *Department of State Bulletin*, April 1978.

A more complete listing of Mink's public speeches may be found in B. Manning, *Index to American Women Speakers* (1980), p. 207.

Honors

Honorary degrees from many colleges and universities, including Lindenwood and Wilson colleges (1965) and Syracuse University (1976); Freedom Fund and Recognition Award, NAACP, Honolulu (1971); Human Rights Award, American Federation of Teachers (1975); National Education Association Award (1977).

Bibliography

In Chamberlin, Hope. *A Minority of Members* (1973).

"For a Troubled Situation ... Try Mink," *Science Digest*, April 1977.

In Lamson, Peggy. *Few Are Chosen* (1968).

"Mrs. Mink Is First Nisei Woman to Become Territorial Legislator," *Honolulu Star-Bulletin*, November 7, 1956.

"Mrs. Mink Will Seek House Seat," *Honolulu Star-Bulletin*, October 2, 1958.

"Political Profiles: The Johnson Years," *Facts on File*, 1976.

Schwindt, Helen Dimos. "All the President's Women," *Ms.*, January 1978.

Walsh, J. "Science at State—Back to Square One," *Science*, May 19, 1978.

Maurine Brown Neuberger
January 9, 1907-

B. Cloverdale, Oregon; D. Walter T. and Ethel Kelty Brown; M. Richard Neuberger, 1945 (widow), Philip Solomon, 1964; Served in U.S. Senate as Democrat-Oregon, January 3, 1961 to January 3, 1967, 87th through 89th Congress.

Maurine Neuberger took over her husband's Senate seat in 1960 after his untimely death, but in many ways she had been serving as co-senator with him since 1954, as he himself had pointed out on numerous occasions. In 1955 she joined him in Washington after having served in the Oregon Legislature from 1951. As her husband's unpaid assistant, Maurine Neuberger attended many functions in his place, answered correspondence, researched legislation, wrote newsletters, and sat in on meetings with constituents when he had schedule conflicts; in short, the Neubergers gave Oregon two senators for the price of one.

Her family came from a small Oregon town where her father was a general practitioner and her mother, a teacher. After she graduated from the University of Oregon (B.A., 1929) she spent more than a decade teaching high school English and working actively in local Democratic politics before meeting Richard Neuberger, whom she married in 1945. The couple became both political and spiritual partners, collaborating together on his campaigns for the state legislature, and working as free-lance journalists to support themselves. In 1951 Maurine served in the Oregon House while Richard served in the state Senate, the first couple to be elected concurrently to both chambers.

Still, Maurine Neuberger hesitated to step into the breach upon her husband's death. Because he had died only a little over one month before filing for the 1960 election, she puzzled over her ability to serve out a full term in the Senate, though she was encouraged to do so by liberals throughout the country. Winning easily in a year when Oregon voters chose Nixon over Kennedy in the presidential contest, Neuberger went to Washington pledging commitment to Oregon voters on liberal issues she knew well, drawing from her experience in the legislature, from her rural background, and from her teaching experience. Medical aid to the elderly, federal aid to education to boost teachers' salaries, and aid to housing were among the cluster of progressive legislative issues she favored. In memory of her husband, a devoted conservationist with whom she had coauthored many articles about Oregon, she promised constituents to work for the Oregon Dunes National Seashore conservation project. When she arrived in Washington as a senator, one of her first legislative coups was to obtain additional money for a 41,000-mile interstate highway construction grant and extension of anti-billboard programs.

As a new member Neuberger received assignments to the Agriculture Committee, the Banking and Currency Committee, and the Special Committee on Aging. Both she and her husband had long believed that the high cost of elections worked against the public's best interests, and she proposed early in her term a bill to place a ceiling on campaign spending. Ironically, she cited lack of funds as a major obstacle to her seeking reelection in 1966, though her marriage to Boston psychiatrist Philip Solomon in 1964 also affected her decision. She had managed to wage a $90,000 election fight in 1960, but figured the 1966 cost at a quarter of a million dollars.

First and foremost a consumerist, before, during, and after her Senate term Neuberger went after the tobacco industry with a vengeance, making national headlines over the issue of cigarette advertising. The surgeon general's warning on each package of cigarettes sold in the United States testifies to her persistence. Both she and her first husband had survived bouts with cancer, and Maurine Neuberger dramatized the need for greater preventive health care by working with the American Cancer Society on cancer prevention and detection campaigns. When she arranged for a mobile diagnostic unit to be stationed outside the Capitol to screen legislators and government workers for chronic diseases, Maurine Neuberger was first in line. While in the Oregon Legislature she tackled the dairy industry, which had lobbied to make the yellow coloring in margarine illegal. To demonstrate the inconvenience caused to homemakers who wanted an aesthetic looking margarine, an aproned Maurine Neuberger, mixing bowl in hand, demonstrated to the Oregon lawmakers just how difficult coloring margarine at home could be. In the late 1970s, 30 years after the margarine controversy and more than a decade after her retirement from the Senate, President Carter tapped her to serve on the President's Consumer Advisory Committee.

Neuberger had a flair for the dramatic during her public life. When she wanted Congress to impose stricter safety standards on the goods of the fabric industry, she staged a well-attended "baby blanket burning" in the Senate. When she modeled a bathing suit at a charity fashion show while her husband was senator, her photograph appeared in every major newspaper across the country. "What do they think a senator's wife wears when she goes swimming?," she quipped to critics when this became an issue during her 1960 campaign.

After her retirement from Congress in 1966, Neuberger taught political science for a time at Radcliffe College. Her second marriage did not last, and she returned to her native Oregon to an athletic outdoor life and local legislative interests, pressing an annual legislative session in Oregon for one. Even in her seventies she kept up the Washington commute, working with President Carter and Esther Peterson on consumer affairs. On many occasions Neuberger averred that she did not miss the Senate grind. "I longed to get back to Oregon. I wanted to spend my later years enjoying life," she stated in a 1977 interview.

Selected Writings and Speeches

"Footnotes on Politics by a Lady Legislator," *New York Times Magazine*, May 27, 1954; *Adventures in Politics; We Go to the Legislature* (1951); "Hazards of Teenage Smoking," *Parents Magazine*, January 1964.

Coauthored and did photography for numerous articles in Oregon periodicals.

The Richard and Maurine Brown Neuberger office files (1954-1966) are held by the Oregon Historical Society, which also holds recorded interviews with Maurine. The papers of Maurine Neuberger reside in the University of Oregon Library, Special Collections.

See B. Manning, *Index to American Women Speakers* (1980), p. 216.

Honors

Past member of board of directors of the United Nations Association.

Bibliography

In Chamberlin, Hope. *A Minority of Members* (1973).

In Engelbarts, Rudolf. *Women in the United States Congress, 1917-1972* (1974).

Hunt, John Clark. "Westways Women: Maurine, Margarine and Cigarettes," *Westways*, November 1975.

Sinovic, Steve. "Ex-Senator Has a New Job," *Oregon Journal*, August 22, 1977.

White, W. S. "Lady from Oregon," *Harpers*, October 1961.

Mary Rose Oakar
March 5, 1940-

B. Cleveland, Ohio; D. Joseph and Margaret Ellison Oakar; Single; Served in U.S. House of Representatives as Democrat-Ohio, January 1977- , 95th Congress- .

Mary Rose Oakar's political coming of age could not be more removed from that of her sister Ohio congresswoman, Frances Payne Bolton, the wealthy Cleveland socialite and philanthropist who served from 1940 to 1969. While Bolton spent her young womanhood as a debutante and voluntary social worker, Oakar worked during her high school and college years as a clerk and a telephone operator. Her education reflects her Catholic roots: Ursuline College (B.A., 1962) and John Carroll University (M.A., 1966). Teaching at Lourdes Academy from 1963 to 1970 and at Cuyahoga Community College until 1975, she became involved in a number of community, civic, and political activities during the 1970s. Her commitment to the Cuyahoga County Democratic party paid off when she was elected to the Cleveland City Council in 1973, a powerful position from which she launched her national political career, moving directly from the City Council into Congress. From her official *curriculum vitae* it appears that wherever community assistance was required, there also was Mary Rose Oakar, as founder and volunteer director of the Near West Side Civic Arts Center in Cleveland during 1970, and as a trustee of numerous organizations, including the Federation for Community Planning, the YWCA, and the Society for Crippled Children.

Much of her backing for the 20th Congressional District seat was a result of her position as Democratic ward leader for Cuyahoga County from 1972 to 1976, and her seat on the Ohio Democratic Central Committee during 1974. Her Catholic working-class background, her single marital status, and her single-minded dedication to her constituents parallel, to a certain extent, the career of Oakar's congressional colleague, Barbara Mikulski of Baltimore. Less flamboyant in her political style than Mikulski, Oakar keeps a low profile in the House, especially on controversial issues.

As a member of the bipartisan Congresswomen's Caucus, Oakar has contributed such women-related legislation as the bill for the Susan B. Anthony dollar, and has supported numerous Caucus agenda items; for example, the enactment of the Federal Employee Flexible and Compressed Work Schedule Act and the Federal Employee Part-time Career Employment Act, the passage of the Displaced Homemakers Assistance Act, the passage of the Rape Victims Privacy Act, and the inclusion of additional considerations to women in the

Humphrey-Hawkins Full Employment Act. All of this legislation seeks to remedy the employment and social discrimination that keeps women in what Congresswoman Patricia Schroeder has termed "the fastest growing poverty group" in the country.

Oakar serves as treasurer of the Congresswomen's Caucus, although as a rule she does not choose a leadership role on women-related legislation, preferring to support the work of her more feminist colleagues on employment and equal rights issues. The problems of cities, of the aged, and of blue-collar workers are her main concern. In addition to her place on the Banking, Finance, and Urban Affairs Committee, she is a member of the Select Committee on Aging, and plays an active role in the Blue Collar Caucus and the Steel Worker's Caucus. These are highly significant areas for the 20th District, and Oakar's previous experience as a Cleveland city councilwoman serves her well. Particularly sensitive to the importance of saving older cities that suffer from a siphoning off of tax resources from center-city to the rapidly expanding suburbs, Oakar worked hard for the Housing and Community Development Act of 1977, legislation that will double funding for Cleveland's inner-city neighborhood preservation projects. Her dedication in working toward legislation that will return federal money to cities won voter endorsement in her second bid for Congress.

Honors

Outstanding Service Award, Office of Economic Opportunity (1973-1975); Community Service Award, American Indian Center of Cleveland (1973); Cuyahoga County Democratic Woman of the Year (1977); Ursuline College Award (1977); Nationalities Service Center Award (1974).

Bibliography

Many references to Oakar in the Cleveland *Press*.

Arnoff, Kathie-Jo. "The Women of the 96th Congress," *AAUW Magazine*, May/June 1979.

Frances Perkins
April 10, 1882-May 15, 1965

B. Boston, Massachusetts; D. Frederick W. and Susan Wight Otis Perkins; M. Paul C. Wilson, 1913; United States Secretary of Labor, March 1933-1944; Chair, U.S. Civil Service Commission, 1946-1953.

When Franklin D. Roosevelt asked Frances Perkins to serve as secretary of Labor in 1933, without doubt his most controversial appointment, she became the first woman to reach Cabinet rank in U.S. history. She helped his administration write the New Deal, shaping such programs as the National

Recovery Act, the Fair Labor Standards Act, and the Social Security Act; and she believed fervently in the Roosevelt philosophy for national recovery during the Depression. "He [FDR] didn't like concentrated responsibility. Agreement with other people who he thought were good, right-minded, and trying to do the right thing by the world was almost as necessary to him as air to breathe," was Perkins' analysis of the president under whom she served for 12 years, the longest term of any Labor secretary in history.

Roosevelt's style of leadership gave Perkins free rein over the Department of Labor, often to the dissatisfaction of labor and political leaders of the day. Wendell Willkie and Robert Moses charged Roosevelt with putting a "lady slummer" into one of the country's most critical posts during a period of massive national unemployment. Though they had no doubts as to her good character and good intentions, they adamantly opposed having a female in the post. Perkins herself preferred to ignore the question of her sex. After all, she could point to years of labor experience—as executive secretary of the New York Consumers' League from 1910 to 1912, as a factory investigator, and as industrial commissioner of the State of New York from 1929 to 1933. In fact, she knew all too well the labor problems of her day. In 1911 she had seen the fire that broke out at the Triangle Shirtwaist Company, in which 146 female workers perished due to the factory's violations of safety regulations. The disaster so haunted her that she personally investigated that incident and the general issue of safety regulations in the workplace, lobbying for legislation to enforce the existing regulations.

By 1912 she was the executive secretary of the New York Commission on Safety. Perkins favored the investigative approach to problem-solving rather than reliance on the reports of subordinates. During her New York years her thorough investigations resulted in many reforms in health and safety regulations for workers, a decreased work week for women (54 hours), and at the same time put her into contact with the important Democratic leaders of her day, among them Franklin D. Roosevelt, Governor Al Smith, and Robert Wagner. These men remembered her later when they looked for strong, outspoken female leadership of programs and commissions that centered on human welfare.

In 1913 Perkins married Paul Caldwell Wilson, a financial analyst also interested in reform government (she later changed her name back to Perkins "to save her husband embarrassment" while she was in public life). After serving for two years as executive director of the New York Council of Organization for War Service, she was appointed by Al Smith to head the State Industrial Commission. In this post she innovated many of the procedural practices that she would later incorporate into the Department of Labor—establishing standards for New York's industrial legislation and issuing monthly statistical summaries of labor participation. Perkins was largely responsible for further reducing the work week for women from 54 to 48 hours. A 48-hour week to her mind would benefit industry, the American family, and hence society-at-large.

As the daughter of a New England factory owner, Perkins grew up in the mill town of Worcester in a privileged environment. Her education was advanced for her day, perhaps because her father fancied himself a classicist and sent his daughter to Mt. Holyoke Seminary, where she majored in the "progressive" curriculum of the sciences. Though she was active in campus politics, a political career at that time occurred neither to her nor to her conservatively Republican parents. Women did not, after all, have the vote when Frances "Fanny" Perkins graduated from Mt. Holyoke in the class of 1902. After doing local charity work with the neighborhood Episcopal Church, she left her parents' home to take a teaching position in Chicago, and from there it was the logical step for her to become involved with Hull House and the settlement house movement. Like many young women of her background and her times, she was drawn toward social work, taking graduate courses in sociology and economics at the University of Pennsylvania and working with the poor in the Philadelphia slums. She was in the vanguard of the educated and dedicated young women of her day who entered graduate school, receiving her master's degree from Columbia University in 1910. Columbia had offered her a fellowship and the opportunities for social work in the city.

Frances Perkins' training and background are everywhere in evidence when tracking her career through the Department of Labor, where she energized the Women's Bureau and the Children's Bureau, concentrating on the people-related issues even when national labor policies appeared to be determined at levels above her. Apparently unconcerned when columnists called her "one of the least important members of the government" and trivialized her contributions toward making life and working conditions more palatable to the ordinary worker, Perkins nevertheless left many of the strike negotiations to her assistant secretary, Edward McGrady. It seems that she was resented most for her inability to bring together the warring CIO and AF of L. Critics derogatorily called her a "social worker" when condemning her style of resolving labor conflicts. As the only woman of her rank in government, she may have thought it the better decision to leave negotiations to McGrady, who eventually became secretary of Labor, rather than to further incite labor leaders.

In 1946 she was appointed by Truman to chair the Civil Service Commission, a position she held until 1953. Until her death in 1965 Frances Perkins remained an active public figure, writing and lecturing, concentrating her energies on the problems of the working class, especially women. The only other woman of her period to capture such public attention was her friend Eleanor Roosevelt. On December 12, 1979, President Carter signed a bill which christened the new Department of Labor Building in her honor—the first federal government building to be named after a woman. The commemorative stamp issued in her honor in 1979 depicts her wearing one of the prim tricorne hats for which she was famous, a pleasant purposeful smile on her lips. One can almost hear her saying, "Being a woman has only bothered me in climbing trees," the only public statement Perkins ever made regarding her sex.

Selected Writings and Speeches

People at Work (1934); *The Roosevelt I Knew* (1946).

Papers of Frances Perkins are held by the Schlesinger Library of Radcliffe College, and by the Franklin D. Roosevelt Library. Tapes and a 5,500-page typescript are housed in Columbia

University's Oral History Collection. Numerous other letters and papers of Perkins can be located using Andrea Hinding's *Women's History Sources* (1979).

A listing of Perkins' public speeches may be found in B. Manning, *Index to American Women Speakers* (1980), pp. 225-27.

Honors

Elizabeth Blackwell Award for outstanding service to mankind, Hobart and William Smith colleges (1962).

Bibliography

In Clapper, Olive Ewing. *Washington Tapestry* (1946).

In Fisher, Dorthea Frances (Canfield). *American Portraits* (1946).

"Lady Returns," *Time*, September 23, 1946.

"Lady Secretary," *Newsweek*, May 24, 1965.

"Last Leaf," *Time*, May 21, 1965.

Martin, George. "How Miss Perkins Learned to Lobby," *American Heritage*, April 1976.

Martin, George. *Madam Secretary, Frances Perkins* (1976).

Mohr, Lillian Holmen. *Frances Perkins: "That Woman in FDR's Cabinet!"* (1979).

In Roosevelt, Eleanor, and L. Hickok. *Ladies of Courage* (1954).

Severn, Bill. *Frances Perkins: A Member of the Cabinet* (1976).

In Vexler, Robert. "Vice-Presidents and Cabinet Members," *Oceana*, vol. 2 (1975).

"Week's Work," *Colliers*, August 24, 1946.

Wyzanski, C. "Madam Secretary: Frances Perkins," *New Republic*, May 22, 1976.

Esther Eggertsen Peterson
December 9, 1906-

B. Provo, Utah; D. Lars and Annie Nielsen Eggertsen; M. Oliver A. Peterson, 1932; Assistant Secretary of Labor, August 17, 1961-1968; Presidential Advisor on Consumer Affairs, 1977- .

A pleasant-looking, blue-eyed Scandinavian woman who wears her hair in a braid wrapped around her head, Esther Peterson's homey looks and personal style belie the vast experience she has had in and around government, as labor organizer and lobbyist, expert in women's labor issues, and consumer advocate. In 1961 she became the highest ranking woman in government as President Kennedy's assistant secretary of Labor. During this same period she served as vice-chair of the President's Commission on the Status of Women, chaired by Eleanor Roosevelt.

The climb to these positions was neither planned nor particularly laborious for Peterson. Following her graduation from Brigham Young University she continued her studies at Columbia, receiving an M.A. in physical education. In 1932 she married Oliver Peterson, a student of domestic labor practices and the international labor movement, who introduced her to the field that would be her vocation. At the time, Esther Peterson was new to New York City, fresh from a Mormon, rural Utah background. She became fascinated with meeting the luminaries of the labor movement and was taken with the problems of the workers themselves. Though she maintained a keen interest in national labor issues, Esther Peterson's primary commitment was that of a full-time homemaker rearing four children. During these early years her dedication to the labor movement was simply an absorbing avocation.

The turning point for Peterson occurred when she volunteered to teach female workers at the Boston YWCA. Her class met regularly on Thursday nights, so she became alarmed when her students failed to show up one evening. When she visited some of the women in their run-down flats, she learned that they were on strike—the "heart-break strike" according to them—because their employers had required them to sew a complicated heart-shaped pocket instead of a square one on each dress they made, with no additional compensation above their usual, meager $1.32 per dozen dresses. From that point on, Peterson worked extensively to improve conditions for women in the garment industry.

She had no problems in getting part-time teaching positions at summer schools for working women, popular during the 1930s, notably the Bryn Mawr Summer School. The special problems of young factory women became her crusade; and she actively sought out promising young women whose educations had been interrupted because of the necessity to work, and found ways to fund their educations. By 1939 Peterson's skill in teaching economic principles to working women was so well known that she was asked to coordinate educational programs for the Amalgamated Clothing Workers of America (ACWA), a post she held until 1945, when she moved on to become the legislative liaison for ACWA in Washington.

Peterson's labor interests broadened when she accompanied her husband to Sweden, where he served as labor attaché in Stockholm. During the years in Sweden (1948-1952) she learned to speak the language so that she could instruct women in the Swedish labor schools. When later her husband was transferred to Brussels (1952-1957) she involved herself with the International Confederation of Free Trade Unions. Her experience in Europe groomed her for the position of legislative representative for the AFL-CIO's industrial union department (1958-1961). " ... I don't know what Senators would do, what people would do, without lobbyists. The main thing is to strengthen the lobby of the people who represent the people's interests." In 1961, President Kennedy asked her to head up the Women's Bureau of the Department of Labor, upgrading the position later that year to assistant secretary of Labor.

Throughout the 1960s and 1970s Peterson insisted that her major interest centered on the human problems of labor as a whole, not merely women's problems. But she conceded that labor issues for women historically have been different from those of men, and that many women had been hampered by protective laws they neither wanted or needed. However, she differed from many feminists on the question of women's labor legislation in her belief that the laws should be flexible enough to accommodate the women who reject so-called protective labor laws, as well as those who want these laws in order to keep their jobs in the face of family contingencies.

Undoubtedly, Peterson is herself a "liberated woman," though she espouses no doctrine of feminism and has never taken an enthusiastic position on ERA. She has long labored, however, for raising minimum wages, since women cluster mainly in the minimum-wage job categories; and she has vigorously advocated measures that give women opportunities to advance in industry. She worried about the "displaced homemakers" before the term had even been described in the sociological literature, and she was sensitive to the problems of reentry women returning to industry after having been absent from the workplace for long periods of time to marry and rear children. When President Kennedy suggested establishing federally funded child-care centers, she hailed this move as "bold and imaginative."

Certainly a political woman, Peterson has worked hard for Democratic causes and candidates, and has a reputation for working well with legislators. She was tapped by President Johnson to split her time at Labor to serve as his presidential assistant for Consumer Affairs at a time when consumer interests were capturing much media attention. During this 1964-1967 political stint, she told interviewers that she worked two-thirds of the time for the president and two-thirds of the time for Labor. Her consumer affairs position became the target for national debate on the plight of the consumer at the hands of advertising and big business. No aspect of consumer concern (or industry concern, for that matter) was too mundane for her vigilant eye. The law requiring manufacturers to sew washing instructions into garments, for example, was one notable result of Peterson's efforts.

She served on the National Committee on Household Employment, and during the Johnson years acted as chair of the President's Commission on Consumer Interests. While she kept active in her numerous commitments to various labor and consumer groups during the Nixon and Ford years, she was no longer acting in an official capacity. President Carter brought Peterson back to the limelight as special assistant for Consumer Affairs in 1977, and with his support she went to Capitol Hill to ask legislators to approve an agency of consumer advocacy. Despite her well-argued proposal, lobby groups, including the U.S. Chamber of Commerce, testified against the establishment of such an agency, calling it unnecessary. To date, the Carter administration has not succeeded in obtaining the legislators' approval.

In the many political and governmental roles Peterson has assumed since the early 1960s (among them co-chair of the Domestic Affairs Task Force and the Democratic Advisory Council of Elected Officials), she has indignantly spoken out against political favoritism in various governmental agencies. Little wonder that she has not achieved great popularity with the many regulatory agencies, which she claims have been traditionally staffed by "cast off party functionaries, well-connected lawyers whose prior careers were marked by single-minded devotion to the interests of the oil companies and other regulated industries." How can such people guard "the public interest as embodied by the Congress in the laws?," she has asked in defending Carter's proposed consumer agency. This is the same question Esther Peterson, people's advocate, has been asking ever since she affiliated herself with working women in the 1930s.

Selected Writings and Speeches

Speech at Democratic Party Platform Hearing, Washington, DC, January 31, 1976, reported in *New York Times*, February 1, 1976; In Lifton, R. J. *The Woman in America* (1964, repr. 1977).

A more complete listing of Peterson's public speeches may be found in B. Manning, *Index to American Women Speakers* (1980), p. 228.

The papers and taped interviews of Esther Peterson are at the Schlesinger Library of Women's History, Radcliffe College. See Andrea Hinding's *Women's History Sources* (1979).

Honors

Honorary degrees from Smith, Simmons, Carnegie Institute of Technology, Northeastern University, University of Michigan, University of Utah, and Temple University, among others.

Bibliography

Christian Science Monitor, February 27, 1961 [Interview].

"Consumer Advocates Struggle to Resuscitate Bill to Create New Consumer Agency: White House Aide Esther Peterson Lobbies Relentlessly," *Wall Street Journal*, October 28, 1977.

"Consumer Staff Ordered in Agencies," *Congressional Quarterly*, January 12, 1980.

In Diamonstein, Barbaralee. *Open Secrets* (1972).

"Government Must Assure Safe Products," *U.S. News and World Report*, December 27, 1976 [Interview].

"Guardian of the Gullible," *Time*, April 29, 1966.

In Kundsin, Ruth B., ed. *Women and Success: The Anatomy of Achievement* (1974).

"Lady Watchdog," *Newsweek*, January 20, 1964.

In Lamson, Peggy. *Few Are Chosen* (1968).

"New Women's Bureau Director," *National Business Woman*, March 1961.

Reilly, Ann M. "White House Consumer Drive: Presidential Assistant Esther Peterson Is a Leader in Consumer Protection," *Dun's Review*, December 1978.

"Richard Lesher, President of U.S. Chamber of Commerce, Attacked Statements by White House Aide Esther Peterson ... in Language Called Sexist by Women," *Wall Street Journal*, May 27, 1977.

"She's Carter's Consumer Activist," *Media Decisions*, June 1977.

Stern, L. "How to Use Your Consumer Clout," *Working Woman*, October 1978.

"Supporters Expect Success This Year for 'Agency of Consumer Advocacy,' " *Salt Lake Tribune*, April 20, 1977.

(Eliza) Jane Pratt
March 5, 1902-August 23, 1965

B. Morven, North Carolina; D. James L. and Lena Little Pratt; Single; Served in U.S. House of Representatives as Democrat-North Carolina, June 3, 1946 to January 3, 1947, 79th Congress.

Women have typically made inroads into the United States Congress by way of one of three circumstances: death of a husband; holding a position of favoritism among male party regulars; or death of a superior. As a faithful administrative assistant to four North Carolina congressmen for 22 years, Pratt ascended the political staircase when Representative William O. Burgin died in April 1946. Because of her knowledge of the Washington political network and the legislative interests of North Carolina's Eighth District, party regulars endorsed Pratt to fill Burgin's vacated seat. So familiar a figure to Eighth District voters was Jane Pratt that the special election in May was essentially perfunctory, and she defeated her opponent, Republican Frank Hulin, by a margin of 20,000 votes, becoming North Carolina's first congresswoman.

During her brief term Pratt served diligently, seldom missing a vote. Though she was informed about the issues, familiar with her constituency, and dedicated, it appears that she was not taken seriously as a legislator. In looking over local press clippings, one finds that Southern journalists employed terms like "charming," "pleasant," and "gracious" when writing about Congresswoman Pratt, choosing to highlight her social skills rather than to profile her legislative victories and ambitions. In one account she was singled out as "one of the Capitol's best-groomed Congressional secretaries." This image of Pratt conflicted somewhat from the reality of her non-stop career, her incessant commuting between Washington and North Carolina, and her stint as a newspaper editor of the *Troy Montgomerian*. When asked about her educational background she confided to an interviewer: "You know I don't have a college degree. When I was at Queens, Charlotte, I meant to study music. Folks said I had a rather fair soprano voice and I had sung in the choir of the Presbyterian churches in Troy and Asheboro. But after papa died, it was necessary for me to give up college and go to work to help mother and the younger children. Since then, I haven't had much time for music."

Political campaigns required then, as they do now, substantial funding, and having been an unmarried secretary for years, at various times helping to support her brothers and sisters, Pratt had limited financial resources. Rather than use her small savings she retired at the end of her term in 1947 to work in various federal agencies (the Department of Agriculture, Library of Congress), taking with her the memories of the day she was sworn into Congress by Speaker Sam Rayburn, and those 22 vigorous years of practical legislative experience. In 1957 she took another administrative assistant's job, this time to Paul Kitchin, representative from Wadesboro, South Carolina, which proved a fine working arrangement until his defeat in 1962. Like her other bosses, Kitchin praised Pratt's tactical sense of the legislative process.

Possibly the ex-congresswoman felt more deeply about her political fortunes than she was willing to publicly declare. She somewhat cryptically assessed the role of the political woman after her retirement from Washington to North Carolina in 1947: "When a campaign ends," she observed, "[women] are too often relegated to their former roles as second-class politicians" (*A Minority of Members*, p. 195).

Bibliography

Many articles in local North Carolina newspapers.

In Chamberlin, Hope. *A Minority of Members* (1973).

Medley, Mary. "The State's New Congresswoman," *The State*, June 15, 1946.

Jeannette Rankin
June 11; 1880-May 18, 1973

B. near Missoula, Montana; D. John and Olive Pickering Rankin; Single; Served in U.S. House of Representatives as Republican-Montana, April 2, 1917 to March 4, 1919, 65th Congress; and January 3, 1941 to January 3, 1943, 77th Congress.

"My father, John Rankin, born Canadian, came to Montana when it was still a territory and settled in Missoula as a builder—architect, logger, sawyer, carpenter. Mother, Olive Pickering, left the relative security of her New Hampshire home and travelled west to become the second school teacher in Missoula. I was born in 1880, the first of seven siblings—Jeannette, Philena, Hattie, Wellington, Mary, Grace, and Edna." In these recollections of suffragist and first United States congresswoman Jeannette Rankin are found the roots of independence and strength which shaped her individualistic approach to politics.

Jeannette Rankin graduated from the University of Montana in her home town of Missoula in 1902. After college, she devoted the next six years of her life to the family, staying at home to help her mother manage the household and the younger children. At the same time she was teaching school and reading widely. The work of Jane Addams came to her attention during this period, and Jeannette was taken with the idea of working with those who had much less in the way of family and financial security than she herself. "I followed her [Jane Addams'] suggestion and entered the New York School of Philanthropy (now the Columbia School of Social Work) in 1908."

After working in Washington State with orphaned children, Jeannette came to realize that though social work might render some immediate assistance to the underprivileged, the triple misfortunes of war, poverty, and lack of education were at the core of these problems, and were the responsibility of the government. "I left social work for suffrage," she recalls. What followed were the grueling years of campaigning for suffrage throughout the United States, a process that tutored Rankin in grass roots political organization; speaking, distributing leaflets, and putting up posters served as preparation for her later political campaigning.

In 1914 Montana granted suffrage. By 1916 Rankin had been elected to Montana's Republican representative-at-large position in the United States Congress, a political step motivated more by her commitment to suffrage than by personal ambition. "We reasoned that the men would find it difficult to vote against the women in their home states when a woman was sitting with them making laws." Rankin introduced the amendment giving women the right to vote; it passed in both houses the next year and became a reality in 1920.

Rankin was not serving in the House when final passage of the amendment was announced. She had voted against a popular war on April 6, 1917, when the House debated the resolution against Germany. Though she had passed in the first roll call vote, on the second go-round she rose and announced, "I want to stand by my country but I cannot vote for war. I vote NO" (*New York Times*, April 7, 1917). In voting her conscience, Rankin realized that as the first woman in Congress, her action would have reverberations for the cause of suffrage in general, and particularly with regard to women in elective office. In 1918 she lost the race for the Senate seat to Thomas J. Walsh. The peace cause became her lifelong labor. Fifty-five years later, she wrote that she had never changed her mind about the 1917 vote: "From 1917 to 1972 I have worked steadily for the cause of world peace: I have lobbied in Congress, worked with the National Council for Prevention of War, and travelled throughout the world to study the effects of the dominance of colonial powers on other peoples."

She worked zealously on Capitol Hill following her 1918 defeat, lobbying for a child labor amendment to be attached to the Sheppard-Towner bill, for consumer legislation, and for pacifist organizations—the Women's Peace Union and the National Council for Prevention of War (of which she became legislative secretary). In 1940 as she gathered support for the First District seat, her campaign slogan struck the familiar chord: "Prepare to the limit for defense, keep our men out of Europe." Ultimately, when she was called upon to stand by that campaign pledge on December 8, 1941, she was the only person in Congress to vote against American involvement in the war with Japan; and in the patriotic fervor that followed no one supported her for standing by her campaign pledge.

Though pacifism and suffrage are the two issues with which Rankin's name is always identified, her legislative record demonstrates her commitment to laws designed to benefit the quality of life for women and children: a bill to allow American women married to foreigners to retain U.S. citizenship, a maternity and infancy bill, an eight-hour work day for women. In her later years, as she vigorously worked for the causes of peace and equal rights for women, she was hailed by second-wave feminists as a hero of the movement. Josephson's biography of Rankin (1974) chronicles the spunky 90-year-old's devotion to politics: "I never left Congress. I was there with Wayne Morse and Ernest Gruening voting against the Tonkin Bay Resolution." Long after she had left office, during the Vietnam War, she led the Jeannette Rankin Brigade, a group of 5,000 women protesting the wars in Southeast Asia, in their 1968 march on Washington, DC.

Throughout her career, Rankin consistently viewed the vote for women as the precursor to one great societal benefit—women as a force for peace. "We did not labor in suffrage just to bring the vote to women," she emphasized in her writing and speaking, "but to allow women to express their opinions and become effective in government. Men and women are like right and left hands; it doesn't make sense not to use both." During the 65th Congress the press had speculated about Rankin's "opportunity for a legislative romance." When she was 91, still unmarried, she told an interviewer, "I've never been married and I haven't had less freedom than a man because of my sex, but because of my ideas."

Selected Speeches and Writings

"What We Women Should Do," *Ladies Home Journal*, August 1917; this is the only original piece that Rankin seems to have written, though she gave many interviews over the years, and has written some brief reminiscences in typescript. The above article urged people to conserve the food supply during World War I.

A listing of Rankin's public speeches may be found in B. Manning, *Index to American Women Speakers* (1980), p. 236.

The Jeannette Rankin Transcript of the Oral History Project, The Bancroft Library of the University of California, Berkeley, is held by the Bancroft Library.

Official papers of Jeannette Rankin are held in several locations because of her affiliation with various peace and suffrage groups. Among the locations: The Montana Historical Society, Helena, Montana (assorted manuscripts, clippings, and files of Montana suffrage activities); University of Illinois, Chicago Circle Campus, Chicago, Illinois (correspondence with Jane Addams and with Florence Kelley). The Schlesinger Library at Radcliffe College, Cambridge, Massachusetts, holds correspondence of Rankin with Harriet Laidlaw, papers of the National Consumers League, with which Rankin was affiliated, and papers of the National Organization for Women, in which Rankin was particularly involved during the New York Regional Conference in January 1971. Files on Rankin exist at the Library of Congress, Archives Division, Washington, DC, which holds the complete papers of the National American Woman Suffrage Association. Manuscript materials on Rankin are held by the National Woman's Party Library in Washington, DC.

Honors

First winner of the Susan B. Anthony Award from the National Organization for Women.

Bibliography

Board, John C. "Jeannette Rankin: The Lady from Montana," *Montana, the Magazine of Western History*, July 1967.

Brownmiller, Susan. "Jeannette Rankin," *New York Times Book Review*, November 3, 1974.

In Chamberlin, Hope. *A Minority of Members* (1973).

"Congresswoman Rankin Returns to the House," *Christian Century*, November 20, 1940.

In Engelbarts, Rudolf. *Women in the United States Congress, 1917-1972* (1974).

Fligelman, B. "First Woman Elected to Congress," *Sunset*, November 1916.

Frappollo, E. "At 91, Jeannette Rankin Is the Feminists' New Heroine," *Life*, March 3, 1972.

In Gruberg, Martin. *Women in American Politics: An Assessment and Sourcebook* (1968).

Harris, Ted Carlton. "Jeannette Rankin: Suffragist, First Woman Elected to Congress and Pacifist" (Ph.D. thesis, University of Georgia, 1972).

Hinckle, W., and M. Hinckle. "History of the Rise of the Unusual Movement for Women Power in the United States, 1961-68," *Ramparts*, February 1968.

"Jeannette of Montana," *Colliers*, April 21, 1917.

Josephson, Hannah Geffen. *Jeannette Rankin: First Lady in Congress: A Biography* (1974).

Rickey, Elinor. *Eminent Women of the West* (1975).

Schaffer, Ronald. "Jeannette Rankin, Progressive-Isolationist" (Ph.D. thesis, Princeton University, 1959).

"Where Are They Now?," *Newsweek*, February 14, 1966.

"Who's Who in the Elections," *Independent Woman*, December 1940.

Winestine, Belle Fligelman. "Mother Was Shocked," *Montana, The Magazine of Western History*, July 1974.

In addition, many articles on Rankin have appeared through the years in the Helena, Montana *Independent*. See especially February 2, 1911; August 30, September 22 and 25, 1912; May 28, October 9 and 10, 1914, for accounts of Rankin's suffrage activities.

Dixy Lee Ray
September 3, 1914-

B. Tacoma, Washington; D. Alvis and Frances Adams Ray; Single; Served as Governor of Washington, January 1977- .

Ray, a marine biologist, may be the most academically credentialed political woman to have held public office in the United States. With advanced degrees from Mills College (M.A., 1938) and Stanford University (Ph.D., 1945), and recognition from learned societies all over the world, she has given the appearance during her relatively short political career of moving easily in a man's world. Indeed, she was named "Maritime Man of the Year" (Seattle, 1967), "Man of the Year" by the State of Israel Bond Organization (1977), and "Man of Science" in an award by the Los Angeles ARCS Foundation (1974). Though a professor of zoology at the University of Washington from 1945 until 1976, Ray spent much of this 30-year period on other prestigious assignments. She served as director of Seattle's Pacific Science Center from

1963 to 1972, and as chairperson of the United States Atomic Energy Commission from 1973 to 1975. Ray briefly joined the Department of State in 1975 as assistant secretary of State for the Bureau of Oceans, International Environmental and Scientific Affairs.

Despite her university affiliation, it is with Washington State's academic community that she has weathered her stormiest times since becoming governor in 1977. Charging that Washington was building a reputation as a "degree-mill state," where faculty tenure protects "the mediocre and incompetent," the Democratic governor was accused by academicians and university administrators of fanning anti-intellectual flames and becoming a prime mover behind the legislative movement to cut the budgets of the state universities. Ray countered that she knew of no competent top managers in Washington's higher education system, hinting that Washington State higher education might be improved by centralization.

Governor Ray's frank method of addressing issues has been popular with other Washingtonians, however. When President Nixon appointed her to chair the Atomic Energy Commission (AEC) in 1972, she admitted that her nomination was due more to the women's liberation movement than to her scientific qualifications. "I was appointed because I was a woman and that's all right with me," she told an interviewer. Immediately she set to work becoming a very active and outspoken chairperson, quickly dispelling notions of her supposed incompetence. Her moderate views on issues of ecology and energy were judged offensive by groups she termed "knee-jerk environmentalists." "Everybody's in favor of resolving the energy crisis and everybody is in favor of preserving the environment. But the people in the Northwest, where the big coal deposits are, don't want their terrain upset; and the people in the Northeast, who need heating fuel the most, don't want an oil port and refineries on their coast, and some of the Nader people don't want any nuclear plants at all generating electric power because of some theoretical dangers," she reasoned in 1974. "I understand these conflicts, but this isn't a perfect world. Somebody—and I mean every one of us—has to make some sacrifices."

Ray appeals to many audiences because, while speaking seriously about energy issues and nuclear power, she uses wit to score her scientific points. In 1976, after her days at AEC were over, she dismissed the nuclear power critics by praising the accomplishments of modern science. "If our tongues were as sensitive as these radiation detectors," she jibed, "we could easily taste one drop of vermouth in five carloads of gin." Pragmatic analysis became her distinctive signature during her five years at AEC, and later her political signature as governor.

Before the energy crisis emerged as the country's chief domestic issue, Ray forecast a disastrous economic situation if alternative energy sources—to her mind, nuclear energy sources—were not developed. At a Middle Western Governor's Conference in 1975, she predicted, "If [oil] imports are cut off, we would have a collapse of our economy. It's the potential crisis that has to be averted by increasing domestic energy supplies."

Ray's lack of patience with mismanagement and bureaucratic bumbling resulted in a short-lived tolerance for her position as assistant secretary for Oceans and International Environmental and Scientific Affairs at the Department of State. She called the State Department "an agency that is never tuned up to do anything. A decision that should take 10 minutes takes 10 days." She concluded from the experience, "I suppose the essence of diplomacy is to avoid taking a final position. People like me should never get involved in an agency like that."

Political pragmatism ruled Ray's declared choice of political party, too. In 1976, after winning the gubernatorial race, she affirmed her belief in the two party system in one breath, and told her audience in the next, "My answer to why did I choose the Democratic Party is that I spent three years in Washington under a Republican administration." Her scorn for bureaucracy jelled during the Washington years, and she espoused a "built-in self-destruct capability" for every agency and office in Washington (*Wall Street Journal*, March 15, 1976).

One point Ray hits hard, whether talking with constituents or with scientists: moderate risk, error, and setback are necessary for progress. Curbing inflation, she insists, requires risk-taking by those in significant positions to turn the economic tide. In a 1980 speech to Scientists and Engineers for Secure Energy, for example, she offered an equation to account for the current state of the economy: "The reality is that zero defects in products plus zero pollution plus zero risk on the job is equivalent to maximum growth of government plus zero economic growth plus runaway inflation."

On the other hand, her endorsement of risk-taking does not imply carelessness, especially where human health and safety are concerned. In 1979 she closed the Hanford nuclear waste disposal site in Washington because improperly packaged waste material was found in trucks bound for the plant. Ray said, "I am ordering the site closed until I can get a guarantee from the Nuclear Regulatory Commission that they will enforce proper packaging. I will not tolerate sloppy procedures." Hanford was reopened only when Ray was satisfied that proper safety measures had been taken. During the June 1980 volcano crisis, citizens praised her decisive management in the face of uncontrollable disaster.

Governor Ray's irreverent attitudes were nurtured in childhood. Her name, derived from the epithet her family gave her, "The Little Dickens," was later shortened to Dixy by the governor herself. She admired Robert E. Lee, so decided to call herself "Dixy Lee Ray." When people question her ecological arguments, she reminds them of her family-owned wilderness area on Fox Island in Puget Sound where she spent all her summers as a girl and which she lists as her permanent home. Her opinions, she states, are based on scientific judgments tempered by the needs of the time, and Ray has an educator's instinct to inform the public about the necessity of balancing environmental and energy imperatives. Perhaps because the energy issue is at the top of the national agenda, an issue that requires leaders with knowledge in both science and politics, Dixy Lee Ray might well be a major political force to be reckoned with should she choose to seek higher public office in the 1980s.

Selected Speeches and Writings

Marine Boring and Fouling Organisms, University of Washington (1959); "An Integrated Approach to Some Problems of Marine Biological Deterioration: Destruction of Wood in Sea Water" (*Marine Biology, Oregon State College Biology Colloquium*, 1959); "Possible Relation between Marine Fungi and Limnoria Attack on Submerged Wood," *Science*, January 9, 1959; *Mainliner*, May 1974 [Interview]; *People*, August 18, 1974 [Interview]; *Los Angeles Times*, May 3,

1974 [Interview]; "And the Pendulum Swings," *Business and Society Review*, Winter 1977-78.

A listing of Ray's public speeches may be found in B. Manning, *Index to American Women Speakers* (1980), p. 237.

Honors

Honorary degrees from over 20 colleges and universities, including Kenyon College (1976), Smith College (1975), University of Maryland (1975), and the University of Alaska (1975); other academic honors include Phi Beta Kappa (1937); Sigma Xi (1940); Guggenheim Fellowship (1952-1953); Danish Royal Society of Natural History (1965); Royal Academy of Science and Engineers, Avel-Axelson Johnson Award, Stockholm, Sweden (1974); Top Ten Most Influential Women in the Nation, *Harper's Bazaar* (1977); Walter H. Zinn Award, sponsored by the American Nuclear Society (1977); Freedom Foundation Award (1978).

Bibliography

Boehm, G. A. W. "Extraordinary First Lady of the AEC," *Reader's Digest*, July 1974.

Chu, D., and W. J. Cook. "Whistling Dixy," *Newsweek*, October 4, 1976.

"Dixy Lee Ray," *San Francisco Examiner and Chronicle: This World*, December 12, 1976.

"Dixy Rocks the Northwest," *Time*, December 12, 1977.

Gillette, R. "Conversation with Dixy Lee Ray," *Science*, July 11, 1975.

Gillette, R. "Ray's Shift to the State Department Will Test Kissinger's Interest in Science," *Science*, November 15, 1974.

Holden, C. "Ray Fed Up, Quits State," *Science*, July 4, 1975.

Libman, Joan. "Woman at the Helm: Dixy Lee Ray's Style," *Wall Street Journal*, December 6, 1977.

Matthews, T. et al. "Governors: New Faces of 1977," *Newsweek*, April 11, 1977.

Miller, Lindsay. *New York Post*, September 9, 1972 [Interview].

Mitzman, Barry. "Governor Aims Her 'Dixyisms' at Higher Education," *The Chronicle of Higher Education*, April 17, 1978.

"Ray Accepting Man of Science Award of Los Angeles Chapter of ARCS Foundation," *Los Angeles Times*, June 25, 1974.

Russell, C. "Profile: Dixy Lee Ray," *BioScience*, September 1974.

Spencer, Colleen. "Frontlines: Dixy Calls Pigs Newsmen," *Mother Jones*, January 1979.

"Washington Award to Governor Ray," *Civil Engineering*, March 1978.

Weckworth, Trudy, and Al McVay, eds. *Dixy: Her First Year as Governor of the State of Washington* (1977).

Patricia Scott Schroeder
July 30, 1940-

B. Portland, Oregon; D. Lee and Bernice Scott; M. James White Schroeder, 1962; Served in U.S. House of Representatives as Democrat-Colorado, January 3, 1973- , 93rd Congress- .

Her heroine is Jeannette Rankin, the first woman elected to Congress whose first vote was against war. She counts her greatest victory in the House the overthrow of the former chairman of the Armed Services Committee, F. Edward Hébert, whom she took to task numerous times in print and in person for his dictatorial manner of running the committee. Challenging the technological imperative she believes shapes the thinking of the Pentagon, the congresswoman from Colorado (the only liberal Democratic woman on Armed Services) has become the conscience of the House Armed Services Committee, consistently needling members on matters of budget and military overkill strategies. "However useless a defense concept, however premature its implementation, however extravagant its cost, an argument to proceed is deemed conclusive on one of two grounds. Either the Russians are doing it and therefore we must do it in order to avoid falling behind, or the Russians are not doing it and therefore we must in order to stay ahead," she has argued repeatedly from her seat on the committee. Her impressive addenda to military authorization bills have outlined the wastes of billions of dollars in defense and recommended substantial cuts.

Being a mother of small children nearly kept Patricia Schroeder out of Congress in 1973. Her maternal responsibilities became a major issue in her first congressional campaign—that, in addition to resistance from Denver political powers who did not want her and organized labor who did not like her. Routinely she began to introduce herself at public gatherings as "the nut you've been hearing about ... the one who keeps her kids in the freezer." Her stellar credentials, lucid speaking style, and sense of humor helped her along. She graduated *magna cum laude* from the University of Minnesota in 1961, and received her law degree from Harvard in 1964. Her professional experiences from 1964 to 1972 included litigation for the National Labor Relations Board in Denver, private practice, and university teaching. Her political and social affiliations (Planned Parenthood, Young Democrats, and the Jefferson County Human Relations Council) were clearly liberal.

Schroeder came to Washington making it clear from the first that she considered being a mother and a legislator to be compatible callings: "I have a brain and a uterus and I use them both," she said in 1973, a witticism she has found occasion enough to repeat during her four terms in the House. Instead of deemphasizing her children's existence, she brought them to the House and toilet-trained daughter Jamie in the Congress during her first term, toting legislative briefs and training pants in the same briefcase. When issues about children and mothers surfaced in the House, Pat Schroeder's children showed up, too, and they frequently visit her office.

She has never soft-pedaled her perception of Washington as the stomping ground for chauvinists all the way from the ranks of the lobbyists to the chairmen of House and Senate committees. In a May 1980 interview Schroeder reflected, "Why do I get up and subject myself to these insensitive people?" She answered her own question in the next breath: "I do it to make a difference." She *has* made a difference, especially on the Armed Services Committee, notoriously politically conservative and fiscally extravagant when it comes to implementing defense contracts for weapons "that can kill people fifteen times over." She successfully maneuvered her way onto the Armed Services Committee in 1973 against the will of Representative Hébert, who took particular delight in reprimanding, lambasting, and insulting Schroeder in Committee. She believes that the Armed Services Committee represents a significant area in which women can effect change since its decisions draw upon about one-half of the national budget and affect the entire national if not world population: "Everyone is always talking about our defense effort in terms of defending women and children, but no one ever asks the women and children what they think." She goes on to say, "As a woman with children I want to be able to say there are other things we can do to protect us than build bases."

Schroeder is sure that her target issues for the 1980s will differ from those on the agendas of many of her male colleagues. "Do you know that women are the fastest growing poverty group in America?," she asks. She cites pension, job, and Social Security discrimination among the major causes of female poverty—problems that can only be remedied by legislation. "My colleagues simply don't understand it," she explains in pointing out why legislation to solve these inequities doesn't move faster. "We are seeing a lot of people dragging their feet on these issues. Look at the backup on ERA, for example."

To her, the Congresswomen's Caucus, which during the 96th Congress for the first time got participation from all congresswomen, represents a considerable gain in lobbying for women-related legislation. Because the caucus invites agency heads and Cabinet officials to meetings to discuss specific problems, Schroeder feels that some gains are being made on issues like credit, women in the military, and job discrimination, even if the pace remains slow. "You have to remember that until we began inviting these people to discuss their agencies and departments with us, many never even considered women's interests." Yet, the Congresswomen's Caucus hasn't done nearly enough to Schroeder's way of thinking. One of the most newsworthy acts of the caucus was sending a delegation of women to Cambodia in 1979 to seek relief for the starving and sick population. "It moved the focus from the political to the humanitarian," the representative concludes from that visit, which resulted in increased food and medical attention for the brutalized Cambodian people.

Nevertheless, Schroeder's views about women working effectively in the highest political echelons fall short of sanguinity. "You can be a little mascot, a trained seal, and the special interest groups will fund your campaign." For the untrainables like Schroeder, the alternative is to be constantly on the dole for campaign monies. The fastest way for a woman to succeed in politics, according to the congresswoman, is "to play the 'sell-out game.' " The money issue looms as a major barrier for Schroeder should she decide to go for a Senate seat. She recalls the unsuccessful attempts made by women to move from House to Senate. "Look at what happened to Mink, Abzug, and Burke," she points out. Clearly she is convinced that women lack the financial backing to make them a viable power in the Senate. Moreover, she believes that it is important for women to establish a power base in the House rather than to lose good women during the course of Senate races.

Another problem she sees as a political woman is the unending personal commitment of time and energy demanded of women even more than of men. "The whole country thinks that you represent them. Since there is no other woman west of the Mississippi in the Congress, I hear from everyone—and get more mail than both Colorado senators." "A woman in politics must resign herself to no days off, no personal time. Sometimes from 4 a.m. to 6 a.m. is my only quiet time during the day." She underscores that for women there is no counterpart to the "political wife." Her husband, Jim Schroeder, whom she met at Harvard Law School, has assisted, even architected, her campaigns, "but he has his own 60-hour week as an attorney in Washington and his own clients." Congresswoman Schroeder freely admits that most of her own salary must go to the airlines in order to pay for the weekly flights to Colorado's First District. Her family travels with her.

Schroeder believes that many women may be discouraged from running for office at the highest levels because of the public debate skills required to move legislation. "Many women lack confidence; maybe this is why you tend to see lawyers seeking political office because you need to feel confident in debating males in public." Debate is a Schroeder long suit. She tends to use a trenchant debate style in dealing with difficult male opponents. When she demanded that the service academies give equal access to women, Virginia representative Dan Daniel chided her: "You're not being really serious about this, are you?" Schroeder replied with insouciance, "No, I'm just here because I didn't have anything better to do this morning, Mr. Daniel." In dealing with the stuff of the House Armed Services Committee—M-16 rifles, ABM systems, the MX missile network, Weteye nerve gas bombs, and other weapons, she frequently reminds the committee of the need for "common sense, good public policy, and plain old-fashioned reasonableness."

She has made her view part of the public record on the issue of the Pentagon's budget, which she believes is in need of careful pruning. According to Schroeder, the Pentagon's lobby on Capitol Hill has traditionally been closed to debate, stacking the deck in favor of greater military expenditures by calling only favorable witnesses to Pentagon proposals to build bigger, more dangerous weapons.

Schroeder is equally concerned about other national issues, predicting alternative forms of energy and the updating of the country's industrial base as the major issues for the 1980s. Hers has long been a voice crying out against bureaucratic bloat in solving major national issues. In 1976 she called for the abolition of the Federal Energy Administration, labeling its growth from "a handful of employees transferred from other agencies into a horde of 3,400, with the highest paid staff in government" a "ridiculous" $440 million waste. To Schroeder, a crucial issue for the 1980s is "asking the rest of the world about bearing the cost of defense—we cannot defend the whole world for everyone." Her membership on the Special NATO Subcommittee of Armed Services accounts for the congresswoman's special sensitivity to the United States' burden for European defense.

On a less global scale, Schroeder has served as a member of the House Post Office and Civil Service Committee. As chair of the Civil Service Subcommittee, she brought the inequities of the federal retirement system to national attention by legislating to correct a system "which prohibits benefits to a divorced spouse, regardless of the length of the marriage, and makes survivors' benefits optional for widows...." She galvanized the energies of the Congresswomen's Caucus to address "the national disgrace that public policy permits women to be thrown out as disposable items after their child-bearing and child-rearing years are over."

Because Pat Schroeder's public style tends to be colorful, even flamboyant, and her personal mien attractive and well-spoken, she commands more press than other political women. This has boomeranged upon occasion; for example, in the well-publicized "Easter bunny suit incident" in China, the congresswoman dressed up briefly in a costume to mark Easter day—a bit of humor that resulted in criticism that she was being "trivial" and "clownish."

Her negative stance in 1980 on the issue of the draft has attracted considerable national attention, perhaps because it has been made into an equal rights responsibilities issue. Schroeder's position: "If you prove to me that the draft is necessary, then I will consider the issue of women being drafted. So far no one has shown me that the draft is necessary." Predictably, Schroeder is the lone person on the Armed Services Committee who takes this approach, though she maintains "there are many others in the House who support my view."

Schroeder is the favored candidate in Denver's First Congressional District election in the fall of 1980. From her statements in print and in private conversation, it appears that establishing a power base in the House via long-term congressional service signals for her a practical strategy for women to bring about legislation that speaks to the needs of society's have-nots. "As it is," states Schroeder, "there are really only a few of us women in Washington truly concerned. We try to make it seem as if there are more of us by being many different places, and by being visible on many different issues."

Increased political participation by women has been a theme Schroeder has sounded since going to Congress. In a 1973 *Christian Science Monitor* interview she affirmed, "The only way we will get a higher quality of life is if everyone participates. Women have been told so often they can spectate and not participate that they have thought they are not capable of participating. But yes; we are."

Selected Speeches and Writings

"A Freshman in the Weapons Club," *Nation*, November 5, 1973; "You Can Do It," *Clout: Womanpower and Politics*, 1974; "The Olympic Boycott," *Rocky Mountain News*, January 30, 1980 [Letter to the Editor]; "Peacemakers" (United Nations speech to honor Elise Boulding, April 23, 1980).

Clippings concerning Pat Schroeder are held by the State Library Commission of Iowa, Des Moines, in the "Iowa Women in Politics" collection.

Bibliography

Many references to Schroeder in the *Rocky Mountain News* and *Denver Post*.

Avery, Pamela. "Hanoi Called Cambodia Key by Schroeder," *Rocky Mountain News*, November 20, 1979.

Barth, Ilene. "Congresswoman Pat Schroeder: She Calls Herself a Troublemaker," *Ms.*, June 1976.

Christian Science Monitor, March 21, 1973 [Interview].

Freed, David. "16-Hour Day Is Normal for Pat Schroeder," *Rocky Mountain News*, October 22, 1979.

Friedman, Norma L. "Patricia Schroeder: Wife, Mother, Congresswoman—She Shows Us How," *Vogue*, November 1978.

House, Karen Elliott. "That's No Pretty Young Thing ... That's Congresswoman Pat Schroeder," *Family Circle*, July 1975.

Kalette, Denise. "A Lady in the House," *Denver Magazine*, October 1979.

Redbook, November 1973 [Interview].

Webb, Marilyn. "Frantic Day in the Life of Representative Pat Schroeder," *Boulder Sunday Camera*, July 9, 1978.

Margaret Chase Smith
December 14, 1897-

B. Skowhegan, Maine; D. George Emery and Carrie Murray Chase; M. Clyde H. Smith, 1930 (widow); Served in U.S. House of Representatives as Republican-Maine, June 10, 1940 to January 3, 1949, 76th through 80th Congress; Served in U.S. Senate as Republican-Maine, January 3, 1949 to January 3, 1973, 81st through 92nd Congress.

One of Margaret Chase Smith's more remarkable traits is her unremarkableness. The former senator's bland style and ordinary mien come through in almost every written portrait of her. For years a powerful figure in the Republican party, she worked long hours, cultivated a common-sense approach in dealing with the issues on the floor of Congress, and held her peace except in rare instances. There are those who say she will be remembered more for her "nay" votes than for the legislation she wrote or commented upon. Seemingly, this strategy went over well with her Maine constituency, whom she served for 9 years in the House and 24 years in the Senate.

Throughout her career Smith stacked up honors by the trunkful, the only nomination for the presidency ever recorded for a woman (1964), and, for the greater part, the respect of Republicans and Democrats alike for being an unassuming level-headed legislator. Toward the end of her fourth term in the Senate, however, many of her colleagues found her exasperating because of her stubborn stand on defense issues and her public scolding of fellow senators. "A club of prima donnas," she called them. She allowed herself but one extraordinary trademark: she always wore a single rose pinned to her lapel. When people referred to her as a "square" for her flag-waving patriotism and rigid notion of duty toward country, Smith was wont to remark that "one of America's greatest needs is for more people who are 'square.' "

She began her distinguished career, after graduating from the local high school in Skowhegan, by working typical small-town jobs: clerk, telephone operator, business manager and office manager at the Maine Telephone Company, and later at the county newspaper and the local waste process company. In short, she did the kinds of routine jobs involving tact and contact that later served her so well when she performed the "thousand thankless party tasks" so necessary for political success. She married Clyde Smith, a man 20 years her senior, in 1930, when he was already firmly established as a successful businessman (president of the Steward Goodwin Company at Bangor) and an undefeatable local politician.

When Clyde Smith was elected to represent Maine's Second District in Congress in 1936, he appointed his wife as his underpaid secretary. Until 1940, when he died, Margaret Chase Smith served her time filing, handling correspondence, researching his speeches and legislation, and baking beans for weekend party functions. It is not difficult to understand why Clyde Smith considered his youthful wife indispensable, nor why he insisted during his last illness that she was the best bet to carry on his liberal Republican tradition in the House should he die. She was elected in June 1940 to complete her husband's unexpired term, and her constituency regularly returned her to Washington thereafter.

While she served in the House, Smith voted Republican on most issues but hardly toed the Republican line. Her committee assignments—Education, Invalid Pensions, and Post Offices—did not allow her the same opportunity to shine that her husband had enjoyed on the more glamorous Labor Committee, but she accepted these assignments with grace and modesty. When she was returned to the 78th Congress she spoke up for a seat on the more prestigious Naval Affairs Committee (later, the Armed Forces Committee), a particularly choice assignment for the representative because of Maine's shipbuilding industry and its almost 3,500 miles of shoreline. Her most memorable legislation on this committee created the WAVES (Women Accepted for Volunteer Emergency Service). Smith suggested that the WAVES be sent overseas for non-combat duties in order to increase the number of men available for combat. To arguments that women should not have to endure such hardships, she replied tersely, "Then we'd better bring all the nurses home" (*A Minority of Members*, p. 142).

Other notably independent actions had to do with labor legislation, an area in which Smith shared the liberal pro-labor views of her deceased husband. Though some Republicans accused her of being a traitor to the GOP for voting against the Smith-Connally bill (an anti-strike piece of legislation which her shipyard workers would have detested), she claimed that the Republican party should not define itself as pro-business, anti-labor. Maine supported her reading of Republican politics on the labor issue and approved her vote to expand Social Security benefits as well.

Though party leadership did not back her when she decided to run for the vacated Senate seat of Senator Wallace White in 1947, Smith won an astounding victory by defeating three male opponents. In rethinking this years later she attributed victory to a vigorous campaign, kept promises, and support from women. She remained the only woman in the Senate while she served, and remains the only woman to have been elected to both the U.S. House and the Senate.

Her years in the Senate followed the same orderly, meticulous pattern of slow and steady dedication to duty that marked the House years. Smith, justifiably proud of her voting record (she hardly missed a vote), maintained that one of the major scandals of the House and Senate was absenteeism. In the early 1970s she complained to her colleagues that the reputation of the Senate was in jeopardy because of "Senate 'moonlighters,' who regard the Senate as strictly secondary to their moneymaking activities in being offered high-paid lecture fees simply because they are Senators. As the Republican dean of the Senate recently said, 'being paid $2,500 for $50 speeches ....' " In her campaigns Smith pointed to her voting record, reminding audiences that she did not have time to ceaselessly campaign since she was efficiently about the business at hand in Washington.

Military preparedness became Smith's big issue over the years, though she waited five years in the Senate before getting a seat on the Armed Services Committee. In the Kennedy years she shocked many observers by advocating that the United States demonstrate "nuclear credibility" to Khrushchev and the Russians during the Cuban missile crisis. Another publicized event involved Smith's unexpected vote against Lewis L. Strauss, the Eisenhower nominee for secretary of Commerce, and later her vote against G. Harrold Carswell, Nixon's controversial nominee for the Supreme Court.

During the early 1970s she scolded America for losing sight of communism's external threat. She indignantly upbraided American foreign policy, which she considered to be hinging upon costly expenditures for the purpose of buying friendship abroad. "We see no real support from our allies in the defense against Communist aggression in Korea and Vietnam—and fat and rich Western European allies we rebuilt with Marshall Plan aid not even carrying their proper share of the NATO that was created and exists for their defense and security," she fumed in a 1971 interview. Margaret Chase Smith's most memorable speech in the Senate occurred on June 1, 1950, when she unleashed her moral indignation on the Senate floor against the forest fire of McCarthyism then sweeping Washington and the entire country. "The American people are sick and tired of being afraid to speak their minds lest they be politically smeared as 'Communists' or 'Fascists' by their opponents." She chastized McCarthy and his ilk as individuals motivated solely by political ambition to exploit "fear, bigotry, ignorance, and intolerance." Though McCarthy's censure by the Senate did not take place until 1954, Smith bore the distinction of first speaking against his abuse of Senate privilege.

Never one to spend much money or time in campaigning, figuring her record spoke plainly for her accomplishments, Smith orchestrated low-key campaigns and won elections by large margins in 1954, 1960, and 1966. In 1972, at the age of 74, Senator Smith met her match in William D. Hathaway. Though Smith's technique of staying off the campaign trail until the very last lap was effective when she was a younger woman, in 1972 the electorate needed the reassurance of the senator's vigor, especially since her opponent was only 48. Then, too, her Maine constituency began to demand more from Smith than an accounting of her faithful voting record. By outlining solutions and programs, Hathaway proved more able to capture the imaginations of Maine voters. Smith came across as somewhat querulous. Throughout her career she had downplayed her gender as a factor in her political career, but as her time in office ran out she began to admit that being a woman in the Senate was an important issue. "I hate to leave where there is no indication another qualified woman is coming in," she confided in a final interview. After leaving office she retired to the hearty climate of her native Skowhegan, Maine.

Selected Speeches and Writings

Gallant Women (1968); *Parade*, July 5, 1970 [Interview]; *Life*, June 19, 1970 [commencement address, Adelphi University]; *U.S. News and World Report*, June 28, 1971 [Interview]; *Declaration of Conscience* (1972); *National Observer*, January 1, 1972 [remarks before the Senate]; "How Margaret Chase Smith Would Monitor the CIA," *Freedom at Issue*, vol. 35, 1976; *Los Angeles Times*, December 26, 1971 [remarks before the Senate].

A more complete listing of Smith's speeches may be found in B. Manning, *Index to American Women Speakers* (1980), pp. 269-71.

Honors

Honorary degrees from more than 50 colleges and universities; one of the Gallup "Four Most Admired Women in the World" (1963); Lieutenant Colonel in U.S. Air Force Reserve (1950-1958).

Bibliography

See *New York Times Index* for numerous references.

In Chamberlin, Hope. *A Minority of Members* (1973).

Donosky, L. "Margaret Chase Smith Still Feisty," *Biography News*, March 1975.

Fleming, Alice. *Senator from Maine: Margaret Chase Smith* (1976).

Grahan, Mary W. "Margaret Chase Smith," *Quarterly Journal of Speech*, vol. 50, no. 4, 1964.

In Lamson, Peggy. *Few Are Chosen* (1968).

Markel, H. "Twenty-Four Hours in the Life of Margaret Chase Smith," *McCall's*, May 1964.

"Mrs. Margaret Chase Smith," *Congressional Quarterly* (special report), January 1964.

In Parshalle, Eve. *Kashmir Bridge-Women* (1965).

Rice, B. "Is the Great Lady from Maine Out of Touch?," *New York Times Magazine*, June 11, 1972.

"Surprising Lady from Maine," *Newsweek*, August 18, 1979.

"Women for President," *U.S. News and World Report*, February 10, 1964.

Virginia Dodd Smith
July 30, 1911-

B. Randolph, Iowa; D. Clifton and Erville Reeves Dodd; M. Haven N. Smith, 1931; Served in U.S. House of Representatives as Republican-Nebraska, January 3, 1975- , 94th Congress- .

Virginia Dodd Smith, who prefers the address Mrs. Haven Smith, has led the kind of professional and publicly involved life that many might characterize as "feminist." But Smith has stated on many occasions that she is not a feminist, simply a woman who sees much to be done for the people in her vast Nebraska Third District. She graduated from the University of Nebraska in 1936, a working, married student. Before her election to Congress, she ran a successful wheat ranch with her husband and served as a board member of the Farm Bureau Federation, a powerful agricultural lobbying group.

Her congressional campaign was interesting for the chauvinist strategy used by her Democratic opponent, who thought that the district, a Republican stronghold, would never send a woman to Congress. He fought her using the slogan, "A woman's place is in the home." Some Smith supporters, the Women's Political Caucus, for example, believed that her election could be jeopardized if she were identified with women-related issues. Accordingly, the Women's Political Caucus did not endorse her for fear of doing more harm than good. During the campaign, however, Smith admitted publicly her support of the ERA and such controversial issues as day-care centers. While staying true to her conservative politics, she did not hide her involvement as a member of the Governor's Commission on the Status of Women from 1964 to 1966.

Nebraska political observers doubted that a woman could be elected in the Third District simply because farm women would not accept her, but in fact the opposite voting behavior appears to have turned the tide in Smith's favor. She won handily on the basis of her impressive credentials—member of the National Livestock and Meat Board (1955-1958), National Commission of Community Health Services (1963-1966), chair of the Presidential Task Force on Rural Development (1969-1971), and a host of other boards and commissions attesting to her interest in the health, welfare, and prosperity of rural workers.

Smith's committee assignments have been many during her three terms: the Interior and Insular Affairs Committee and its subcommittees on National Parks and Recreation, Water and Power Resources; the Committee on Education and Labor and its subcommittees on Manpower, Compensation and Health and Safety, and Post-Secondary Education; and the House Appropriations Committee. As a member of these committees she has displayed considerable initiative in guarding the interests of her district as well as in bringing federal funding to the state. In the area of water projects, a particularly sensitive budgetary area in the 96th Congress, Smith managed to stave off the budget slashers who proposed a $6 million cut from the O'Neill

Unit of the Pick-Sloan Missouri Basin Project, a proposal that would remove federal funding for construction from her district. She argued, "If this soundly conceived, vital project is jeopardized by unnecessary delay for lack of funding, then no public works project, regardless of its merit, will be safe from similar assaults" (*CQ Almanac*, 1979, p. 226). Similarly, she has struggled to maintain funding for medical, nursing, and health training in her state in the face of presidential budget recisions in 1979 and 1980. Her objections to the thrift measures centered on the problems of Nebraska's medically underserved areas. According to Smith, her constituency, covering more than 60 counties and 300 towns, is in need of trained medical personnel, especially specialized nurse-practitioners trained by the programs that are threatened by proposed budget cuts.

Smith's support of further development of the controversial M-X missile system is consistent with her pro-defense views, although she insisted on the ecological provision that the M-X be deployed only on land that is unsuitable for agriculture. Her votes with regard to international programs are often determined by the difficulties faced by America on the domestic front. Why, she asks, should the United States be contributing millions of dollars to the African Development Fund, when a weather station in Valentine, Nebraska must close to save the government less than $10,000 per year? She does not hesitate to state that her constituents oppose all forms of foreign aid, and "Well, it is their money." A $300,000 AID project research grant for the University of Nebraska that she managed to salvage in March 1980 probably will not offend Nebraskans.

Her voting record indicates that she is present for 97% of the votes and that she consistently opposes programs of the administration. Smith takes a solidly Republican stance on major issues as a member of the Republican Policy Committee, which sets the tone for major upcoming legislation. Because she currently serves on the powerful House Appropriations Committee, the control mechanism of the federal purse strings, her conservative voice now has greater political volume than previously. In the 96th Congress Smith joined the Congresswomen's Caucus, mainly because of her interest in legislation to benefit rural women, though the very fact of her conservatism assists in projecting a more unified, less partisan image of the caucus, one that promises more effective coalition efforts for women-related legislation.

Honors

Award of Merit, DAR (1956); Distinguished Service, University of Nebraska, 1956, 1960; Freedom Foundation Award for best public address (1966); International Service Award, Midwest Conference on World Affairs (1970); Woman of Achievement Award, Nebraska Business and Professional Women (1971); Watchdog of Treasury Award (1976); Guardian of Small Business Award (1976).

Bibliography

Arnoff, Kathie-Jo. "The Women of the 96th Congress," *AAUW Magazine*, May/June 1979.

Dworkin, Susan. "These Freshperson Congresspersons," *Ms.*, April 1975.

In Susan J. Tolchin. *Women in Congress* (1976).

Olympia Snowe
February 21, 1947-

B. Augusta, Maine; D. George John and Georgia Goranites Bouchles; M. Peter Snowe, 1969 (widow); Served in U.S. House of Representatives as Republican-Maine, January 3, 1979- , 96th Congress- .

Olympia Snowe captured her first term in the United States House of Representatives at the age of 32, becoming the youngest Republican woman ever elected to the House, as well as its first Greek-American woman. Following her election, one of the congresswoman's first statements called for an end to the powerful congressional seniority system, which in many instances determines control of the committees and the outcome of legislation.

During her first term in office Snowe vocally supported measures to benefit Maine's aging and unemployed population, and decried government waste and bloat, including the exponential growth of the federal civilian work force. Because of the escalating energy crisis in 1979, predicted to worsen during the 1980s, she has championed legislation that speaks to the energy problems of her state, with its bitterly cold winters. Energy is at the top of her constituency's list of concerns, and Snowe's periodic indictments of the Department of Energy in 1979 have stressed governmental mismanagement of the energy situation, especially for the department's failure to independently audit the oil companies. For her part, she has introduced legislation proposing tax credits for the use of wood-burning stoves, and has encouraged her constituents to use public transportation by doing so herself when she is in Maine on her weekend visits.

As a freshman, Olympia Snowe has attracted considerable media attention. Articulate, outspoken, intelligent, attractive, and one of only 16 women when she entered the House, her interviews have been sought by the media, who tapped her in the first week of her term as one of the most promising of the new crop of representatives. Analysts have compared her witty style to that of Clare Boothe Luce, the former Connecticut representative, also a New England Republican.

Snowe rose rapidly to her present position due to tragic circumstances. In 1973 her husband, State Representative Peter Snowe, was killed in a car crash, and she was elected to the Maine House to fill his seat. Reelected in 1974 to represent Auburn for another two-year term, she was effective on the joint standing committees on Election Laws and State Government, as well as on the Reapportionment Committee. In 1976 she moved on to the State Senate, one of two women ever to serve in this body, where she distinguished herself in the health issues area, working on child abuse, clarification of professional and practical nursing credentials, and mental health care facilities as Senate chairperson on the Joint Standing Committee on Health and Institutional Services.

The former Olympia Bouchles is the daughter of the late George Bouchles, a Greek immigrant, and the late Georgia Bouchles, a first generation Greek-American. After their deaths she was reared in Auburn, Maine, by her relatives, James and Mary Goranites. Her interest in politics began at the

University of Maine in Orono, where she earned an undergraduate degree in political science.

Snowe has practiced a "down-home" brand of politics during her first term, reflecting Maine's traditionally conservative and suspicious views of big government. Her weekly reports to constituents are filled with details of the disorderliness of business in the House, of bureaucratic blundering, and of government mismanagement, especially when it concerns the Department of Energy, whose creation in 1979 she adamantly opposed. A member of the Government Operations and Small Business committees, as well as the Select Committee on Aging, Olympia Snowe's diligent efforts and ceaseless campaigning in Maine's Second Congressional District (the largest district east of the Mississippi) have begun to pay off with greater recognition for Maine and for her own political career. At a time when energy is a strategic topic on which to be a constructive critic, she has seized the energy issue as her critical focus.

During the 96th Congress, Snowe joined 34 of her Republican colleagues, including congresswomen Fenwick and Heckler, to vote against the Holt-Gramm Amendment, a measure designed to cut more than $5 billion from social welfare programs such as food stamps and CETA to augment military spending. The issue became one of welfare versus the Pentagon, with many of the more liberal legislators declaring that they were willing to line up to oppose extravagant hikes in military spending if the welfare programs to benefit constituents were at stake.

In a 1979 magazine interview, Snowe spoke confidently of seeing a viable woman presidential candidate during the twentieth century. "Women will rise from local government levels to high state and national positions," and in her analysis, "this experience will help them win public confidence." Into 1980 Olympia Snowe has skillfully worked this formula with demonstrable success.

Selected Speeches and Writings

University of Maine, Machias Commencement Address (May 20, 1979).

Honors

1978 United Press International Survey, one of the 10 most influential women in New England.

Bibliography

"First-Term U.S. Congressmen Viewed," *Christian Science Monitor*, January 4, 1979.

Haberman, Nancy, and Ann Northrop. "The Freshwomen in Congress," *Ms.*, January 1979.

"One of These Women May Be Our First Female President," *People*, September 4, 1979.

Numerous newspaper articles in the local Maine press, including the *Portland, Maine Press Herald, Bangor Daily News, The Lewiston Daily Sun, The Lewiston Evening Journal, The Morning Sentinel*, and others.

Gladys Noon Spellman
March 2, 1918-

B. New York City; D. Henry and Bessie G. Noon; M. Reuben Spellman; Served in U.S. House of Representatives as Democrat-Maryland, January 3, 1975- , 94th Congress- .

In 1972 Gladys Spellman, then the first woman president of the National Association of Counties, saw her future goals "in terms of a seat in Congress, a federal administration job, an executive suite in private industry, or, more locally, the office of the county executive...." By 1974 she was in the running to achieve her first choice—congresswoman from Annapolis and the suburban and rural areas bordering Washington, DC. Spellman came to politics with a strong interest in educational issues and a background as a schoolteacher and strong supporter of the PTA. On the surface her credentials appear to be in the traditional mold of suburban wife and mother during the 1940s and 1950s. As a young mother, for example, she raised quite a ruckus with the County Board of Commissioners when she came before them, four-year-old in tow, to demand kindergartens for local children. A striking feature about her preparation for public life, however, is the depth and breadth of her civil commitment.

Her voting record since she came to Congress has been a progressive one, speaking eloquently of her commitment to women-related issues. Although her own career pattern centered around the birth and rearing of her three children, as a member of Prince Georges County Council in Maryland during the 1970s Spellman initiated much progressive, women-related legislation directed to the needs of working women with children, single women, and sexually assaulted and battered women. It was her idea to experiment with a program of flexitime in Prince Georges County government, one that allowed employees to architect their personal schedules according to their needs, an especially sensitive plan to the needs of working couples with children and to single-parent families. In Congress, through her Post Office and Civil Service Committee assignments, she worked on a flexitime bill for federal employees.

With regard to such incendiary issues as abortion, Spellman tends to speak more conservatively. "Personally, I don't know what to think about abortion; I don't have any positive answers. I do support the Supreme Court decision and I would vote against legislation that, by withholding funds, would limit the rights of certain women to have abortions," she stated in a 1975 interview (*Ms.*, April 1975, p. 79). But abortion remains an unpopular issue in her district, and she has taken a position of caution; she does not see "abortion as a viable alternative to family planning."

As a member of the Congresswomen's Caucus, she heads up the ERA task force. "Men don't relate to the special needs of women," Spellman has said when speaking about the special function of the Congresswomen's Caucus in pushing legislation through to undo laws that discriminate against women. She herself nurtured a significant piece of legislation through committee that assures retirement benefits for divorced spouses of federal employees, a law originally proposed by Colorado legislator Patricia Schroeder. Since

Spellman's constituency in Maryland's Fifth District is composed of many federal employees who live just outside Washington, this protection for spouses was especially important.

Though remedying domestic legislation as it applies to women has been a first priority with the caucus, the congresswomen have interpreted their role as one of visible humanitarian commitment abroad. When the congresswomen sent a delegation to visit Cambodia in the fall of 1979, Spellman stated in her press release a concern for the children of the world: "For, as with all wars, it is the children who are suffering. And, as with all wars, it is the children of Cambodia who are least responsible."

Spellman has been a popular colleague in the House. In 1974 her peers elected her vice-chairman of the congressional freshman class. During the 94th Congress she initiated several new House rules and procedures to help undermine or streamline (depending on one's point of view) the seniority system, a protocol much to the disadvantage of women, who were more than likely newcomers to the House. She championed moves to open up congressional meetings to the public, a reflection of her consumerist stance characteristic of her Prince Georges County days: "I am still convinced that politics should belong to the people, and that we should not have a few kingmakers and a few bosses who dictate."

In the 96th Congress Spellman began her third term on the House Committee on Banking, Finance, and Urban Affairs, and on three of its subcommittees: General Oversight and Renegotiation, Housing and Community Development, and Consumer Affairs. Her service to community and to consumers in her pre-Congress days documents her excellent preparation for congressional committee assignments. She served on the Maryland State Comprehensive Health Planning Advisory Council, and chaired, among other groups, the board of trustees of Prince Georges General Hospital, the Washington Suburban Transit Commission, and the Regional Planning Board during her committee-filled days of local government and civic service through the 1960s and 1970s. She once compared her political career to "a love affair with local government." As the first woman on the Prince Georges Board of Commissioners, and ultimately its board chairman after 12 years of service, Gladys Spellman learned how to adeptly maneuver in the male-dominated political world, a skill that has served her well in Congress.

She has long considered herself privileged to be able to give her life to public service, crediting her husband, who supplied her with "the advantage of being a kept woman." "I have a husband who provides the food, and sees to it that I have enough money to put some clothes on my back and have a shelter over my head," she explained in one interview. For her, government exists to help ordinary people solve problems, and her role is one of easing the process along. The federal revenue-sharing program and the Equal Credit Opportunity Act amendments now stand as legislation she helped to shape, legislation of which she is particularly proud. No one who has seen Gladys Spellman in action doubts that the extensive local political experience she brought with her has contributed to her effectiveness in Washington.

Bibliography

Many bibliographical references to Spellman in the *Baltimore Sun* index.

Arnoff, Kathie-Jo. "The Women of the 96th Congress," *AAUW Magazine*, May/June 1979.

Cosstick, Vicky. "Bipartisanship Helping Women," *New Directions for Women*, Autumn 1979.

Dworkin, S. "These Freshperson Congresspersons," *Ms.*, April 1975.

Lewthwaite, Gilbert A. "Prince Georges County's Gladys Spellman to Be First Woman to Head National Group," *Baltimore Sun*, June 26, 1972.

Patterson, S. M. "Political Update: From Maryland with Promise (and Reservations)," *Ms.*, April 1975.

Radcliffe, Donnie. "Rushing on the Hill," *The Washington Post*, December 6, 1978.

Nancy Stevenson
June 8, 1928-

B. New Rochelle, New York; D. William Bryant and Ferdinanda Legare Backer; M. Norman Williams Stevenson, 1956; Served as Lieutenant Governor of South Carolina, January 1979- .

Nancy Stevenson, who in biographical sketches lists herself as a writer, has not "written a word" since she was elected lieutenant governor in 1978, the first woman-held statewide elective office in South Carolina. Stevenson grew up in Charleston. After graduating from Smith College in 1949, she travelled to Sweden and later got a job with the *New York Herald Tribune.* When her marriage to Scandinavian diplomat Olav Moltkae-Hansen ended in divorce in 1954, she returned with her children to Charleston, where she became an editorial assistant for the *South Carolina Medical Journal*, edited by her stepfather, Dr. Joseph I. Waring. During this same period Stevenson co-authored three novels with Patricia Robinson. She married attorney Norman Williams Stevenson in 1956.

In tracking her activities during the sixties and seventies, it appears that Stevenson's political career emerged from her involvement in community affairs. From 1965 to 1969 she served as vice president of the South Carolina Historic Society; from 1970-1974 as secretary and treasurer of the College of Charleston Foundation. She co-chaired the Save Charleston Foundation and served as president of the Footlight Players in the Dock Street Theater during 1973-1974. In 1974 Stevenson was elected to the South Carolina House of Representatives, where she served on the Education and House Ways and Means committees until November 7, 1978, when she was elected lieutenant governor.

Stevenson's speeches indicate a strong commitment to women in general and to the improvement of the national profile of women in political office.

"We have been able to vote for 57 years now," she stated in a 1979 address to professional women. "They [women] comprise 53% of all registered voters in the United States. Yet they hold only 7% of all political offices in this country and most of these offices are lower level positions that don't pay at all or pay next to nothing." She cites the inability to raise large sums of money as women's greatest liability in running for political office. She is an outspoken critic of military weakness. "We are no longer in the position of the strongest nation in the world," she stated in a 1979 address to college students. "We are no longer able to negotiate or conduct our foreign economic policies from a position of total strength."

Concerned with how the government can respond more readily to the needs of ordinary citizens, Lieutenant Governor Stevenson developed a telephone assistance program to assist South Carolinians in locating the state-provided benefits and services for which they are eligible. This program, PAL, has proved successful, and the lieutenant governor hopes to pioneer further outreach efforts from her office.

Selected Speeches and Writings

Under the collective pen names Margaret Duval and Daria Macomber, Stevenson has co-authored three novels: *Return to Octavia* (1964); *A Clearing in the Fog* (1970); *Savage Summer* (1976); "Assets and Liabilities of Women Running for Political Office," Camden Business and Professional Women's Club (March 12, 1979); "Women in the World Today," American Business Women of Greer (July 24, 1979); "Role of Government," University of South Carolina Graduation Exercises (August 18, 1979).

Honors

"1976 Bicentennial Career Woman of the Year," selected by the Trident Business and Professional Women of Greater Charleston; *Ms.* magazine (January 1980) selected her as an outstanding woman of the 1980s in "Women to Watch in the 80's."

Bibliography

Surratt, Clark. "The Lieutenant Governor," *The State Magazine* (Charleston, SC), September 30, 1979.

Leonor Kretzer Sullivan
August 21, 1903-

B. St. Louis, Missouri; D. Frederick William and Eleanor Jostrand Kretzer; M. John B. Sullivan, 1941 (widow); Served in U.S. House of Representatives as Democrat-Missouri, January 3, 1953 to January 3, 1977, 83rd through 94th Congress.

In 1970 Leonor Kretzer Sullivan placed in the *Congressional Record* some unique correspondence about a national problem she felt was getting little or no attention from the federal government. The short life of a pair of panty hose, according to the representative, was a national scandal; further, the National Science Foundation refused to help with the problem. "Millions of American women would like to see the nation which can dress men in the garments necessary to withstand the hostile environment of the moon help women to get through a day without a bag, sag, wrinkle or tear in an expensive and frequently essential article of wearing apparel here on earth." Was she joking? Absolutely not.

Consumer advocate Sullivan, during her 24 years in Congress, often noted that the American woman deserved better products than the marketplace provided, including pure, nontoxic drugs, cosmetics, and foods. Lipstick, hair colorings, and a host of "feminine" products did not escape her critical consumerist's examination. Most importantly, she raised consumer consciousness about the importance of food and drug inspection by tackling the industries head-on, continually reminding people that her approach to legislation began "with a woman's viewpoint." The first bill Sullivan introduced called on the Food and Drug Administration (FDA) to change factory inspection laws so that inspectors would be allowed to enter food, drug, and cosmetic plants at any time during the working day without previous notification. To Sullivan, the policy of an unannounced visit was critical: "If anybody knows company is coming, they're certainly going to clean up and be ready." Later she took on cyclamates, barbiturates, and the poultry inspection process. But her most stunning victory was the Consumer Protection Act of 1968.

She considered her woman's eye view on the world to be a unique congressional asset because "woman do most of the buying, women use most of the products made for the home." In her opinion, many congresswomen felt it to be politically threatening to associate themselves with women's issues, and many congressmen overlooked consumer interests because they were simply ignorant of many substances commonly used in the home. Due to Sullivan's watchdogging, coal tar dyes used in coloring everything from oranges to lipsticks were banned in the 1960s.

Sullivan might well have arrived in Congress by the time-honored route of inheriting the congressional seat of her husband, who had died in 1951 while serving his fourth term. Like Margaret Chase Smith, she had worked as her husband's administrative assistant. But the St. Louis Democratic party regulars selected another candidate, who lost the election to Republican Claude Bakewell. In 1952 she was able to convince those in control to let her run — and this time she defeated Bakewell.

Sullivan's entry into the formal political world was not easy. She had considerable trepidation about speaking to groups, a fear she finally conquered by attending public speaking classes; and because the Democratic party was not enthusiastic about her candidacy, their coffers were not as available to her as they might have been for her husband. After losing the nomination to Bakewell, Sullivan had signed on as an administrative assistant with Representative Leonard Irving of Missouri's Fourth District in order to finance the following year's primary campaign. Certainly she was not afraid or ashamed of office work; before her marriage she had been involved in demonstrating office machines and later was a teacher of office machine operators.

Throughout her career, Leonor Sullivan espoused strong views about women's rights and women's role in society. Believing that most women prefer to give their adult lives to marriage and family, she never advocated the expanded participation of women in politics. Rather, she candidly admitted that it was a good thing to have a "sprinkling of women" in the Congress. When she was first on the ballot in St. Louis' Third District she ran under the name "Mrs. John B. Sullivan," and, in fact, used this term of address in her correspondence throughout her Washington years. Though she was the first in Congress to call herself a congress*woman*, when the Equal Rights Amendment came up for vote, she opposed it, arguing that it would rip the fabric of American family life and undermine the protective labor laws that she viewed as beneficial to women. Furthermore, Sullivan argued, "[ERA] would make it impossible for our courts to punish a deserting father for failure to at least provide support for his children," a position that put her under feminist fire. She once said, "I do not think that wives and mothers should have equal responsibility with men to support their families."

On the other hand, Sullivan for years worked to gain equal pay for equal work and to banish job discrimination. She often encouraged women to be firm in claiming their just rights and privileges on the job, and "not let men decide their futures." She was surprised to find that other women in Congress often tried to steer clear of "women's issues," for she wanted to be known as a congresswoman who championed issues in which women took direct interest. "A woman with a woman's viewpoint is of more value than when she forgets she's a woman and begins to act like a man," she often said.

Though her own assignments were the House Banking and Currency Committee (she became chairwoman of its Consumer Affairs Subcommittee and ranking member of its Subcommittee on Housing) and the Merchant Marine and Fisheries Committee, Sullivan was an especially persistent spokeswoman for the food stamp program. During the 86th Congress Democratic members rallied around this program in an unusual show of unity. To Sullivan, the food stamp program was "a food utilization program, rather than a welfare program." During the Nixon administration she accused the Department of Agriculture of insensitivity, maintaining that food stamps offered low-income families assistance in "the most effective and the most dignified and the most humane and intelligent manner."

Sullivan's propensity for self-effacement and hard work was legend over the years. Respected by her congressional peers as a diligent student of issues and of legislation, she also received recognition from supporters for her distinguished committee work. In 1974 maritime labor unions and business interests who lauded her efforts as chair of the House Merchant Marine and Fisheries Committee (from 1973 to her retirement) commissioned her portrait to be painted and hung in the committee hearing room. Sullivan's even manner of handling disagreements with colleagues was no more in evidence than on the evening of the unveiling of the portrait. A gala to commemorate the unveiling was attended by President Gerald Ford and many political luminaries. Ironically, this event (September 24, 1974) occurred when the power of her committee stood in jeopardy due to a proposed House reorganization plan. Sullivan, who had vigorously fought to revive the waning fortunes of the Merchant Marine, graciously thanked everyone for coming, including representatives Albert and Bolling, the prime movers behind the vote to strip her committee of most of its authority. But she did not miss the opportunity to announce firmly and cheerfully her intention to fight the good fight against this "bad reform" on the House floor.

Sullivan retired from public life in 1977. The only woman ever elected to Congress from Missouri admitted that Washington politics had become "frustrating" because of the bloated bureaucracy in the areas most interesting to her—education, welfare, Medicare, housing, and consumerism.

Selected Speeches and Writings

"Excerpt from Debate," *Congressional Digest*, June 1964; "Citizen's Role in Furthering Consumer Interests," *Vital Speeches*, June 1, 1966; "Excerpt from Debate," *Congressional Digest*, March 1968; "Sullivan, Flood Fear Panama Giveaway," *Human Events*, March 1, 1975.

A more complete listing of Sullivan's public speeches may be found in B. Manning, *Index to American Women Speakers* (1980), p. 285.

Bibliography

Many articles in the *St. Louis Post-Dispatch*.

Bowes, David B. "Pressure Put On Administration to Junk Food Stamp Program," *St. Louis Post-Dispatch*, April 29, 1969.

In Chamberlin, Hope. *A Minority of Members* (1973).

"Consumerism's 12 Shakers and Doers," *Sales Management*, July 15, 1969.

In Engelbarts, Rudolf. *Women in the United States Congress, 1917-1972* (1974).

"New Faces," *Newsweek*, October 28, 1968.

Political Profiles: The Johnson Years (1976).

Women's Bureau. *Women of the 88th Congress* (1963).

Women's Bureau. *Women of the 84th Congress* (1955).

Lurleen Burns Wallace
September 19, 1926-May 7, 1968

B. Tuscaloosa, Alabama; D. Henry Morgan and Estelle Burroughs Burns; M. George Wallace, 1943; Served as Governor of Alabama, January 16, 1967 to May 7, 1968.

In spite of her triumph at the polls in 1966, Lurleen Wallace, Alabama's first woman governor, will always be remembered as the "political wife" of George Wallace. Because Alabama law prevented him from seeking a consecutive term, the ambitious Governor Wallace persuaded Lurleen to run in his place. Though it seems she had no political aspirations for herself, and had never sought public office before the 1966 campaign, she scored overwhelming victories over seasoned political men in the Democratic primary and in the general election. According to political analysts in the state, most of the electorate realized that a vote for Lurleen was a vote for George, and that George Wallace would maintain control of the state while waiting for his next opportunity to seek office. In his press statement preceding the campaign, George Wallace made this clear: "If my wife is elected, we are frank and honest to say that I shall be by her side and shall make the policies and decisions affecting the next administration." National columnists and commentators labelled George Wallace's motives in fostering his wife's candidacy "greedy" and "self-interested."

During the campaign, Lurleen Wallace carefully reminded voters that her election would insure the continuation of her husband's legislative program for the state. George Wallace followed Lurleen to the podium at each campaign gathering, articulating exactly what that program would be—mainly keeping undesirable elements out of Alabama, including "socialists," "beatniks," and of course the federal government, which had pushed Governor George Wallace up to "the schoolhouse door."

Indeed, when George Wallace was sworn in as governor of Alabama on January 14, 1963, he had pledged, "Segregation now, segregation tomorrow and segregation forever." His term as governor had been marked by civil rights demonstrations and mass arrests, and he was "beginning to tire of agitators, integrationists, and others who seek to destroy law and order in Alabama." In September 1963 the battle raged on; all Southern schools had been successfully integrated except for those in Alabama. Governor Wallace pitted his state troopers against the National Guard, who had been ordered to reopen the schools. Bombings and riots continued, and in 1965 Martin Luther King led the famous march from Selma to Montgomery.

This was the violent legacy that Lurleen Wallace inherited as her husband's successor. Since she rubber-stamped almost everything her husband did or said, it can be assumed that she was in sympathy with his views. She did, however, avoid the racial issue in campaign speeches, using the slogan "Stand Up for Alabama." Many posters simply read "Vote for Wallace," failing to inform the electorate that Lurleen was the Wallace for whom they were casting their ballots.

An interesting sidelight of Lurleen Wallace's campaign was the bogus candidacy of another woman, Delores Price, who reportedly was paid to enter the race by supporters of former governor John Patterson. Delores Price appeared with her husband, "Shorty" Price, at political gatherings around Alabama, aping the Wallaces' campaign strategy, which featured the husband and wife appearance. Eventually the Price team dropped out, but the point they were trying to make lingered on.

Lurleen had little preparation for the life she was to lead as politician's wife and governor. Her formal education ended with business college, and at the time of her marriage she was a clerk in a variety store. Before 1966, her participation in state affairs had been limited to the social sphere, but even social functions seemed difficult for her to manage. Understandably, she was shy and uneasy in public, preferring to let her husband run the show. During her campaign, she limited her speeches to three minutes. Although it is impossible to know for sure, the speeches Lurleen read to the public during her short time in office reportedly came from the mind and pen of her husband. Requesting funds for state troopers in order to resist integration, the cut-off of funding for institutions like Tuskegee Institute, that had demonstrated for civil rights, and repressive measures against blacks and civil rights activists were all familiar George Wallace standards. Lurleen Wallace's inaugural speech was perhaps her most succinct political statement. In it she railed against outside forces which she saw as hostile to Alabama—China, Cuba, Russia, and Washington—and promised continued resistance to integration efforts in state schools.

In June 1967, Lurleen Wallace entered the M. D. Anderson Hospital and Tumor Institute in Houston, Texas, for the removal of a cancerous tumor. George Wallace effectively took over all functions after his wife's hospitalization while she remained in residence to sign official documents. Much of her time during the final months was spent with her children and parents. With her death, Lieutenant Governor Albert Brewer, a Wallace loyalist, assumed the governor's post.

Although Lurleen Wallace was never considered a major political figure, she should be remembered for her significant contributions to Alabama state hospitals; in June 1967 the legislature approved overwhelmingly her request to increase the funding for such institutions. Considering the constraints of her position and her deteriorating health, this stands as a commendable contribution.

Selected Speeches and Writings

The official papers of Lurleen Wallace are to be found in the Civil Archives Division of the State of Alabama Department of Archives and History, Montgomery, Alabama. A good deal of material on Lurleen Wallace is housed with the George Wallace papers, now at the University of Alabama in Birmingham Library.

Bibliography

Frady, M. "Governor and Mr. Wallace," *Atlantic*, August 1967.

"From Defiance to Detente," *Time*, January 27, 1967.

"Gallant Charade," *Newsweek*, May 20, 1968.

Jenkins, Ray. *Christian Science Monitor*, April 1, 1967.

Jenkins, Ray. "Queen of Alabama and the Prince Consort," *New York Times Magazine*, May 21, 1967.

National Review, May 21, 1968 [Obituary].

"Political Complications," *Newsweek*, July 17, 1967.

"Wallaces: More Clues to '68 Plans," *U.S. News and World Report*, January 30, 1967.

Wolman, H. "Mrs. Governor Faces the Feds," *Commonweal*, May 5, 1967.

Sarah Ragle Weddington
February 5, 1945-

B. Abilene, Texas; D. Doyle and Lena Catherine Ragle; Single; Served as Assistant to the President, August 1979- .

When Sarah Weddington was selected one of the 10 best Texas legislators in the state house in 1975, her award read, "To the Honorable Sarah Weddington for HIS outstanding service." Though Weddington's personality seems to be such that she accepts such incidents with equanimity rather than bitterness, it taught her, she said later, "that we had work ahead of us five years ago, and we have work ahead of us today."

At the time Weddington was appointed to President Carter's senior White House staff as special assistant in charge of women-related issues, she had already spent more than 10 years steadily climbing the state and national political peaks. She graduated from the University of Texas School of Law in 1967 at age 23, and at 26 had successfully argued a landmark abortion case before the Supreme Court, which resulted in the upset of the majority of the country's antiabortion laws. During 1970 and 1971 she was assistant city attorney in Fort Worth, her springboard into state politics. While in private practice specializing in family law from 1971 to 1977, Weddington served as a state legislator from Travis County, working hard for women's issues and establishing a reputation for overall legislative excellence. "As one of the handful of women legislators," she recalls, "I stood out in the crowd, so I worked doubly hard to make sure that I did my legislative homework."

During her third term she left the Texas House for Washington as a member of the Department of Agriculture's legal staff. Her reputation for managerial excellence, legal skill, and an appetite for ceaseless work took her to the highest ranking attorney's spot at Agriculture, a position in which she had 350 people reporting to her, most of whom were lawyers. During 1977 she gained international political experience as a delegate to the North Atlantic Treaty Alliance in Denmark, followed by a tour of the People's Republic of China sponsored by the National Committee on United States-China Relations.

Weddington, for all her political ambition and success, comes across to audiences as "mild-mannered." A Texas journalist attributes her success to the public image she projects of propriety, serenity, and dignity. "As she sails forth with her lovely manners, wearing stockings and heels, her hair in a bun, her pearls in place, her posture erect (she is rumored to have slouched once in the early 1950s), she can de-fang even the Solid Rock League" (*Ms.*, January 1979). The Solid Rock League is an antiabortion group in Houston, typical of the many antiabortion, anti-ERA groups with which Weddington must deal on a daily basis in her position as special assistant to President Carter. Her chief responsibilities are to brief the president on women-related issues and to interpret to the public Carter's achievements and policies in this area. Credit, domestic violence, employment, ERA, displaced homemakers, minority women, and welfare are all issues of concern to Sarah Weddington.

Because she sees herself as a transcriber of Carter's policies rather than as a policymaker, Weddington treads carefully in her public statements about abortion. Though feminist groups and Carter himself are aware of her personal stand, her office issues statements about the Carter administration's "proposed improvements in family planning and infertility services."

Speaking at public events all over the country (National League of Women Voters, Coalition of Labor Union Women, YWCA International, National League of United Latin American Citizens Conference, for example), Weddington attempts to galvanize support for the president by underscoring his efforts on behalf of ERA, and his appointments of women to important judicial positions, Cabinet-level jobs, agency heads, and ambassadorial posts. Publications that come out of Weddington's office, like *Women in Government: Your Guide to More Than 400 Top Women in the Federal Government*, speak of Carter's commitment to bringing women into visible governmental positions, and serve to highlight the effectiveness of the Interdepartmental Task Force on Women, which Carter created and Weddington chairs. This task force also publishes the "good news" on women in a newsletter entitled *White House News on Women*. The idea behind the task force is to draw on the ideas and skills of both male and female policy and staff representatives from the major federal agencies, who will study seven major issues affecting women—inflation, taxes, occupational desegregation, retirement and welfare, federal employment, IWY (International Women's Year) coordinating/monitoring, and, finally, federal statistics and regulations.

Weddington's visibility is widely in evidence as she serves as the president's domestic and foreign ambassador on the global issues affecting women. In 1980 she served as the White House representative for planning the United Nations Mid-Decade Conference on Women in Copenhagen, and sponsored the OECD (Organization for Economic Cooperation and Development) proposal to hold the Women and Employment Conference in Paris.

When she accepted the post at the White House, Weddington stipulated that she be considered part of Carter's senior staff and report directly to the president. Carter agreed to the bargain from the outset, and Weddington has expressed publicly her satisfaction with their arrangement. Photographs portray the special assistant working closely with the president and other senior government officials on policy issues affecting women. By mid-1980, a year that saw three women in Cabinet-level positions, Weddington was able to report in one of her frequent speeches, "Part of my job in advising the President on women's issues includes assessing what has been accomplished and then looking ahead. An important and exciting change that I perceive is the new recognition that women are moving into the mainstream of our national life, and a new acceptance of that movement."

Selected Speeches and Writings

"The Record of Jimmy Carter on Women's Issues" (prepared by the Interdepartmental Task Force on Women, January 1980); Address to 1980 Women in Business Conference (Chicago, IL, March 13, 1980); Address to Mid-Decade Regional Conference on Women (Dallas, TX, March 14, 1980); "Working Women in the '80s," at Texas Women's Career Day (Fort Worth, TX, March 14, 1980); "The American Family Album, 1980," at the Women's Legislative Exchange (Harrisburg, PA, March 18, 1980); "Address to Communications Workers of America Legislative-Political Conference (Washington, DC, March 25, 1980).

Honors

One of Texas' 10 best legislators, by *Texas Monthly* magazine (1975); one of America's 50 outstanding young leaders, by *Time* (1979); "10 Women of the Future," by *Ladies Home Journal* (1979); Women's Equity Action League Elizabeth Boyer Award (1979); Honoree of Texas State AAUW Endowed Fellowship (1979); Business and Professional Women Award for Outstanding Women in National Government (1978); honorary doctorates from Hamilton College (1979) and McMurray College (1979).

Bibliography

Doyle, Judy. "The Weddington Style," [Orlando, FL] *Sentinel Star* (People section), October 22, 1979.

Ivins, Molly. "Sarah Weddington," *Ms.*, January 1979.

Stern, Linda. "Sarah Weddington: Advocate with Clout," *Working Women*, February 1980.

In U.S. Congress. Senate. Committee on the Judiciary. Subcommittee on Constitutional Amendments. *Abortion*. Part 4. 93rd Congress, 2nd Session. Washington, DC, 1974-1976, pp. 297-304.

"Women in Government: Will We Rise to the Challenge?," *Ladies Home Journal*, Fall 1979.

Jessica (Judy) McCullough Weis
July 8, 1901-May 1, 1963

B. Chicago, Illinois; D. Charles H. and Jessie Martin McCullough; M. Charles W. Weis, Jr., 1921; Served in U.S. House of Representatives as Republican-New York, January 3, 1959 to January 3, 1963, 86th through 87th Congress.

Jessica McCullough Weis, club woman extraordinaire, entered politics by way of the Junior League (vice-president of Rochester chapter in 1935) and the Chatterbox Club (which she founded in Rochester in 1923). Her reputation and ultimately her political influence illustrate the effect of volunteerism on the fortunes of political women.

With her finishing school background (Miss Wright's School in Bryn Mawr, 1916; Mme. Rieffel's French School in New York City, 1916-1917), and her father's and husband's powerful connections, Jessica Weis presented the stable and monied Republican image that had worked well for Clare Boothe Luce. She possessed the money, the time, and the energy to be where the political action was in the Republican party. Certainly Weis did not abandon club work; in 1940 she served as vice-president of the politically powerful National Federation of Women's Clubs. Between her Chatterbox days and her arrival in Washington as a congresswoman in 1959, she performed well the heavy-duty political spadework necessary for cultivating a receptive constituency, in her case, New York's 38th District.

For nearly 20 years before her congressional debut Weis had labored in the Monroe County Republican Committee, first to rid the land of Roosevelt and his New Dealers, and later to ready the country for a Dewey-Warren ticket. Dewey's campaign brought her the distinction of being the first woman ever appointed to the position of associate campaign manager in a national campaign. Eventually her man did make it to the White House, and President Eisenhower, remembering her energetic efforts on his behalf, appointed her in 1954 to the national advisory board of the Federal Civil Defense Administration. After that, the prestigious political assignments leap-frogged Weis into increasingly visible positions: she served at the State Department's request as an American adviser on the Inter-American Commission of Women, and undertook a major planning role for the 1956 Republican Convention in San Francisco, a natural assignment for this veteran of GOP conventions from 1940 on.

When Kenneth Keating vacated his House seat to run for the United States Senate, Weis announced her candidacy and took to the highway in one of the nation's first van campaigns, winning over the predominantly blue-collar industrial and agricultural workers, a tactic that resulted in a decisive victory over her Democratic opponent, Alphonse L. Cassetti. A staunch Eisenhower supporter, Weis not surprisingly embraced the conservative positions of the Eisenhower administration; she was a strong supporter of the draft, and took every public opportunity to vote "no" to "the spenders" who advocated a raft of public works—from new power projects by the TVA to bills that would allow more available money for veterans' housing.

Judy Weis, a shrewd campaigner, neither preached nor practiced active feminism. She supported the principle of civic contributions by women, and if that should put them into public office-holding positions, so much the better. As one of the persons responsible for the restoration of Susan B. Anthony's Rochester home, she was in attendance at the annual festivities honoring the suffragist, where she delivered positive messages concerning women's participation in the public sphere.

Weis probably could have stayed on in Congress for a third term. Her diligent service and reputation as a deliverer on promises made her popular in the 38th District. A strong advocate of advanced technology, she was a member of the House committee, Science and Aeronautics, in its infancy, a time when the country stood behind costly space exploration. Not long after returning to Congress for a second term, however, she discovered she had terminal cancer. Weis died in May 1963.

Selected Speeches and Writings

Papers of Jessica Weis, located at the Women's Archives, The Schlesinger Library, Radcliffe College, include her official congressional papers, 1958-1962, correspondence to Mamie Eisenhower, Oveta Culp Hobby, Kenneth Keating, Dwight Eisenhower, and Richard Nixon, among others, two letters from Weis' husband, and several undated speeches.

Bibliography

Many articles about Weis listed in *New York Times Index, 1958-1963* and the *Rochester Democrat and Chronicle*, covering the years 1937-1962.

"Jessica Weis Not to Seek Re-election," *New York Times*, June 15, 1962.

New York Times, May 2, 1963 [obituary].

"Republicans Substitute Mrs. Weis for Representative Keating," *New York Times*, September 11, 1958.

"Salute to Three Freshmen," *National Business Woman*, February 1959.

"She Is Elected," *New York Times*, November 5, 1958.

Anne Wexler
February 10, 1930-

B. *New York City; D. Leon Ralph and Edith Rau Levy; M. Joseph D. Duffey, 1974; Served as Assistant to the President of the United States, May 1, 1978- .*

As assistant to the president and a member of Carter's senior staff, Wexler's major responsibility has been to serve as a liaison between the president and the public on key presidential issues. According to Wexler, her task has three phases—"first, in developing policy and drafting of legislation for priority issues; second, in the development of strategy to carry out those policies and to get them through the Congress; and third, in building an increasing base of support for those issues as they work their way through the legislative process from the subcommittee level through final passage." Wexler's work as a midwife to presidential policy has involved her in birthing programs to handle inflation, hospital cost containment, energy, and urban policy, among other issues. She has described her job as "a combination of consultation, negotiation, participation, persuasion, patience, and follow-up." Because Washington has a proliferation of well-paid, well-informed lobbyists representing almost every view on the legislative spectrum, the president's staff must constantly expand its public relations to gain support for those priority issues the president wishes Congress to act upon. Wexler's position of orchestrating the support systems is by definition political. Journalist Dom Bonafede has phrased it well: "To Anne Wexler, all the world is a potential lobbyist."

Anne Wexler was generally viewed as the successor of Midge Costanza. Costanza, who had been a former vice mayor of Rochester, New York, had made what some Georgian aides considered "outspoken and tactless" errors, interpreting her job as that of liaison for women's causes rather than for Carter's policies to the public-at-large. Costanza's resignation paved the way for Wexler to move into the president's inner circle, where her rank and salary reflect her role as Carter's senior assistant. Wexler also has an interest in women-related issues; she had served as chairperson of the President's Task Force on Women Business Owners when she was at the Commerce Department as deputy under secretary.

Prior to her Commerce Department appointment, Wexler was associate publisher of *Rolling Stone* magazine, working on the corporate diversification, promotion, and circulation aspects of the rock music and arts periodical. Her educational background includes a B.A. in history from Skidmore College (1950), and the John F. Kennedy School of Government, Harvard University (1973) as a Fellow of the Institute of Politics. In 1970, she was director of the Voting Rights Project for Common Cause.

Anne Wexler possesses wide-ranging political experience from having served on numerous Democratic party committees and task forces during the late sixties and early seventies: the Connecticut McCarthy for President Committee (co-chair); the Carter/Mondale campaign's National Steering Committee (and as floor leader for Jimmy Carter at the 1976 Democratic National Convention); chief consultant to the Commission on Party Structure and Delegate Selection from 1969-1972; the National Democratic Committee's Education and Training Council; and many more assignments working through the Democratic Party in her home state of Connecticut. Her politics might best be labelled as liberal.

Wexler's operation in the White House rests upon her considerable skills to galvanize special interest groups behind an issue dear to the White House, and to convince them that their support is of special importance to the president. The briefings on legislative issues orchestrated by her, often with Carter and his top aides as speakers, are of paramount importance in developing support for presidential programs. During 1980, an election year, much of this work will be directed toward Carter's reelection. Although not elected to her position, Wexler's job, along with those of Sarah Weddington (women's issues) and Esther Peterson (consumers' issues), has been designed to cultivate and cater to special constituencies. As she remarked at a Washington Press Club speech in 1978, her job cannot help but be a political one: "Because of the changing nature of Washington, we in the Carter administration have a rare opportunity to combine the best of the old with the best of the new. We don't reject interest group politics; instead, we consult with a larger number of more representative groups. We don't reject smoke-filled rooms, but we do insist that those rooms be large, and that they be filled with people who were never before invited into them."

Selected Speeches and Writings

Remarks by Anne Wexler, Assistant to the President, to the Washington Press Club (October 19, 1973); "White House and Congress: Why the Troubles?," *U.S. News and World Report*, June 18, 1979.

Honors

Outstanding Alumna Award from Skidmore College (1972); "100 Women of Our Time," *Harper's Bazaar* (1971).

Bibliography

Bonafede, Dom. "Carter's Recent Staff Shakeup May Be More of a Shakedown," *National Journal*, June 17, 1978.

Corrigan, Richard. "Chalk One Up for the President's Energy Lobbyists," *National Journal*, September 30, 1978.

"Wexler Fills the Vacuum," *Time*, February 5, 1979.

Bibliography

Political Women:
The Literature

The standard sources in their various editions and ongoing forms have been consulted in shaping these biographical profiles: *Who's Who in America, Contemporary Biography, Biographical Index,* the *New York Times Biographical Index, Facts on File,* the *Congressional Quarterly Almanac, Who's Who in American Politics, Biographical Directory of American Congress, Congressional Quarterly Weekly Report,* and other Congressional Quarterly Inc. guides, the *Official Congressional Directory,* and the *New York Times Obituary Index.* The bibliography included here moves beyond these standard biographical reference sources to more specialized monographs, periodicals, archives, and services that have political women as their primary focus.

At the outset, it is important to note that this bibliography, like the profiles themselves, concentrates on the literature about traditional two-party participation in American politics rather than the significant body of literature about political activists—women who have contributed to socialism, political radicalism, anarchist movements, and the like.

Rather, the bibliography offered here traces the literature along five main paths: major, recent women-related reference materials important to consult for biographical materials and bibliographic citations to American political women; significant historical books and articles outlining the major issues of the late nineteenth and early twentieth century suffrage movement in the United States; books and periodicals chronicling the achievements of contemporary political women and attitudes toward their participation held by the society-at-large; contemporary studies dealing with the second wave of feminism (1962 on) and its impact on contemporary women in politics; and finally, essays and books examining the very structure of the existing political science literature and its research bias in the study of motivation and participation of women in the political process. As a convenience to the reader, listings of selected dissertations, particularly relevant women-related periodicals, indexing services and their access cues, and selected libraries and organizations pertinent to political women appear here.

Because many of the bibliographic references listed here lead users to the important pre-1970s books and periodical articles on political women, this survey of the literature is deliberately brief and keyed to major studies that do not surface, for the most part, in the bibliographies and tools cited in the reference portion of the bibliography. Literature about specific political women appears after each profile in the main body of the book and does not receive attention in this general bibliography, except in the case of collected biographies. Effort has been made to include published works that are accessible to the user in most academic libraries and in reference departments of libraries, or through the use of interlibrary loan, rather than to identify difficult-to-find report literature often available only in mimeograph form. Scholarly sources in the journal literature take precedence over popular periodical articles for obvious reasons.

Readers should be aware of feminist scholarship's role in redefining the entire area of women's political attitudes and participation. Though it is important to be familiar with the existing theory and basic concepts of political science literature (and some of those classic men-as-norm, women-as-deviant studies are listed), the new feminist political science research emphasizes personal communications and interactions among women and members of political groups, which often account for women's participation or nonparticipation. Review essays (for example, Boals, 1975) will assist the reader in understanding this approach.

The Equal Rights Amendment (ERA) has emerged as one of the major political considerations of our time, as crucial to women in politics during the 1970s and 1980s as suffrage was to political (though unenfranchised) women during the early part of this century. Thus, information sources about ERA are given here because they reflect upon this major political and social movement so closely aligned with the women's liberation movement and its impact on the political lives of women in the United States.

In order to tap the most current scholarly sources of political science periodical literature, extensive use was made of data base searches (including computer files of *Public Affairs Information Service, America: History and Life,* and *Political Science Abstracts*), along with manual searches of abstracting, indexing, and current awareness sources. Unpublished bibliographies and conference papers produced another valuable mine of sources to be sifted and weighed for their appropriateness, although these sources are deliberately scarce in the bibliography itself.

As in all other areas of women-related research, sources on minority women range from scarce to nonexistent. Although one can find, fairly easily, the work by and about specific minority political women, studies relating to the experiences of these women as a political group are overshadowed by the work focusing on female political elites—women who conform to the white, middle-class, well-educated group typical of male political elites as well.

Major Reference Materials on Political Women:
Biographical reference, bibliographies, guides to archives, and who's who materials

Arthur and Elizabeth Schlesinger Library on the History of Women in America. *The Arthur and Elizabeth Schlesinger Library on the History of America, the Manuscript Inventories and the Catalogs of Manuscripts, Books, and Pictures.* Boston: G. K. Hall, 1973. 3 vols.

This superb collection developed originally out of the Women's Rights Collection, a 1943 gift of the papers of approximately 100 suffrage memorabilia donated by Maud Wood Park, herself an active suffragist. Manuscripts represent the core of the collection, which has grown considerably since this inventory was printed, although books, periodicals, and pamphlets are included as well. Historical research on America's political women begins here.

Biographical Directory of the Governors of the United States, 1789-1978. Edited by Robert Sobel and John Raimo. Westport, CT: Meckler Books, a division of Microform Review, 1978. 4 vols.

This reference book contains little about women, since few of them have been elected to gubernatorial positions. However, the introductory essay is illuminating for its documentation of women's absence in the political sphere.

California. Equal Rights Amendment Project. *The Equal Rights Amendment: A Bibliographic Study.* Westport, CT: Greenwood Press, 1976.

This is an invaluable guide to difficult-to-access information about ERA buried in newsletters, House and Senate hearings, debates and reports, and other government publications. Much material from the Herstory collection (previously without decent subject access) shows up here, as well as newspaper coverage of the ERA in the nation's major newspapers. Indexing is by author and organization. Throughout, the explanatory notes are first-rate. This tool provides a starting point for any ERA research.

Cardinale, Susan. *Special Issues of Serials about Women, 1965-1975.* CPL Exchange Bibliography Series, no. 995. Monticello, IL: Council of Planning Librarians, 1976.

Check this bibliography on scholarly and popular special issues of periodicals for materials on political women. For more recent special issues relating to women and politics, see the *Canadian Newsletter of Research on Women* (vol. 7, no. 1, March 1978).

Common Women Collective. *Women in U.S. History: An Annotated Bibliography.* Cambridge, MA: The Collective, 1976.

For materials related to radical women's political movements in the United States, including anarchists, communists, socialists, lesbians, and Chicanas, this offers material on class, race, and sex not likely to be found in treatments of more traditional sources on women politicians working within the system.

Davis, Lenwood G. *The Black Woman in American Society: A Selected Annotated Bibliography.* Boston: G. K. Hall, 1975.
Davis covers many aspects of black women's participation in society as a whole. Of special interest is his listing of elected officials. See also Davis' *Black Women in the Cities, 1872-1975: A Bibliography of Published Works on the Life and Achievements of Black Women in Cities in the United States,* 2nd ed. CPL Exchange Bibliography Series, no. 751-752. Monticello, IL: Council of Planning Librarians, 1975.

Engelbarts, Rudolf. *Women in the United States Congress, 1917-1972: Their Accomplishments; With Bibliographies.* Littleton, CO: Libraries Unlimited, 1974.
The format of this reference book allows the reader brief biographical glimpses of congresswomen, as well as bibliographies for each subject. See also Hope Chamberlin's *A Minority of Members: Women in the U.S. Congress.* New York: Praeger Publishers, 1973.

Haber, Barbara. *Women in America: A Guide to Books, 1963-1975.* Boston: G. K. Hall, 1978.
Haber's gracefully written, carefully selected annotations provide a guided tour to the best and most provocative works on the women's movement, politics, and history. As curator of printed books at Radcliffe's Arthur and Elizabeth Schlesinger Library, she knows the sources.

Harrison, Cynthia E., ed. *Women in American History: A Bibliography.* Clio Bibliography Series, no. 5. Santa Barbara, CA: ABC-Clio, 1979.
A stunning bibliography of 3,395 abstracts, culled primarily from volumes 1-14 (1964-1977) of *America: History and Life* (AHL). Many entries on political women, political theory, and political participation.

Hinding, Andrea, ed. *Women's History Sources: A Guide to Archives and Manuscript Collections in the United States.* New York: Bowker, 1979. 2 vols.
Primary-source material is essential in tracing the political experiences of women. This guide to archival and manuscript material relevant to women describes more than 18,000 collections in 1,600-plus repositories throughout the United States. Index entries lead the user to collections on political activists, political clubs, politicians, and practical politics as well as to specific women by surname. No archival source is all-inclusive, but Hinding provides an excellent search strategy for mining special collections on political women.

Hughes, Marija Matich. *The Sexual Barrier: Legal, Medical, Economic, and Social Aspects of Sex Discrimination.* Enl. and rev. ed. Washington: Hughes Press, 1977.
An annotated list of 8,000 items concerned with women's rights, this bibliography is invaluable for its coverage of long-standing legal and political women-related issues—employment and ERA—as well as new issues: aging,

child care tax deductions, credit, political clout, Social Security, and the draft. Though the bibliography is international in scope, the excellent arrangement and indexing will lead users quickly to important U.S. periodical, monographic, report, and document literature.

Jacques Cattell Press, eds. *Who's Who in American Politics, Seventh Edition 1979-1980.* New York: R. R. Bowker, 1980.

The standard who's who source for all politicians. See previous editions for deceased politicians and those who are no longer active.

James, Edward T., et al., eds. *Notable American Women, 1607-1950: A Biographical Dictionary.* Cambridge, MA: Belknap Press of Harvard University Press, 1971. 3 vols.

Because very few women were in the mainstream of American politics before 1950, this definitive biographical source on American women is better for historical work on abolitionists and suffragists than for finding material on congresswomen. A new edition is expected in the early 1980s.

Kirkpatrick, Meredith. *Women in Public Service: A Selective Bibliography.* CPL Exchange Bibliography Series, no. 1465. Monticello, IL: Council of Planning Librarians, 1978.

Similar in scope and arrangement to other CPL bibliographies, Kirkpatrick is worth consulting for 1970s citations to political women.

Krichmar, Albert. *The Women's Rights Movement in the United States, 1848-1970: A Bibliography and Source Book.* Metuchen, NJ: Scarecrow Press, 1972.

Bringing together all types of significant literature related to the women's rights movement, Krichmar's bibliography is a helpful source on legislative issues, ERA, the Federal Women's Bureau, and specific legislators. See Krichmar, *The Women's Movement in the Seventies* (1977) for 8,600 more citations of the literature from 1970 to 1976. Krichmar's 1977 effort is international, but its coverage of U.S. legal and political issues remains the strong point of the project.

Levenson, Rosaline. *Women in Government and Politics: A Bibliography of American and Foreign Sources.* CPL Exchange Bibliography Series, no. 491. Monticello, IL: Council of Planning Librarians, 1973.

An unannotated bibliography, this source is organized into four major sections: Bibliographies and Indexes; Women in Government; Women in Politics (U.S.); Women in Government and Politics in Other Countries. Emphasis on materials from 1940-1970. Definitely a selective work.

Levitt, Morris. *Women's Role in American Politics.* CPL Exchange Bibliography Series, no. 446. Monticello, IL: Council of Planning Librarians, 1973.

Another CPL bibliography, usually accessible in libraries subscribing to the series. Consult for the offerings of pre-1970s material.

Oakes, Elizabeth, and Kathleen Sheldon. *Guide to Social Science Resources in Women's Studies.* Santa Barbara, CA: ABC-Clio, 1978.

Much good material on the American women's movement and political women surfaces in this small but excellent feminist bibliography. Not restricted to American materials.

Rutgers University, New Brunswick, NJ: Center for the American Woman and Politics. *Women in Public Office: A Biographical Directory and Statistical Analysis.* New York: Bowker, 1976.

This important biographical source identifies 13,000 local, state, and federal women public officeholders in a geographically arranged directory. The statistical essay draws upon data analysis by the Eagleton Institute. The second edition (Scarecrow Press, 1978) updates and expands the earlier profiles and offers the first analysis of nationwide data comparing the political views of male and female officeholders. Essential.

Sapiro, Virginia. *A Guide to Published Works on Women and Politics.* Ann Arbor, MI: Institute for Social Research, University of Michigan, 1975.

Sapiro compiled this 81-page pamphlet for university teachers of political science seeking reliable literature about women in politics.

Schlachter, Gail, and Donna Belli. *The Changing Role of Women in America: A Selected Annotated Bibliography of Reference Sources.* CPL Exchange Bibliography Series, no. 931. Monticello, IL: Council of Planning Librarians, 1975.

Schlachter and Belli are reliable guides to the principal sources on women's changing roles—sources such as dictionaries, encyclopedias, handbooks, statistical compilations, documents, biographical sources, directories, and major bibliographies up to 1974. See also Schlachter's *Minorities and Women: A Guide to Reference Literature in the Social Sciences.* Los Angeles: Reference Service, 1977.

Stanwick, Kathy, and Christine Li. *The Political Participation of Women in the United States: A Selected Bibliography, 1950-1976.* Metuchen, NJ: Scarecrow Press, 1977.

This updating and expansion of Stanwick and Li's *Women and American Politics: A Selected Bibliography, 1965-1974* includes over 1,500 references to published and unpublished works from 1950 to 1976 on American women's political participation at all levels of society. The authors are staff members of the Center for the American Woman and the Study of Politics, Eagleton Institute of Politics, Rutgers University. Topics include women holding elective and appointive offices; voting patterns of women; biographies and autobiographies of political women.

Stineman, Esther. *Women's Studies: A Recommended Core Bibliography.* Littleton, CO: Libraries Unlimited, 1979.

The 1,800 carefully annotated entries in Stineman will lead users to citations on the women's movement and its political implications, basic reference bibliographies, and sociological works. Chapters on law, politics, and history will be particularly useful for those tracing women's place in American politics.

United States. Bureau of the Census. *A Statistical Portrait of Women in the United States.* Washington, DC: U.S. Department of Commerce, Bureau of the Census. For sale by Superintendent of Documents, U.S. Government Printing Office, 1976.

The chapter on voting and public office holding yields much on political women.

Historical Treatments: Women in American politics and suffrage

Antell, Joan B. "The Suffrage Movement." *Current History* 70 (1976): 203-205, 231-32.

A good outline of woman suffrage nationally and locally for the period 1848-1920, with reference to Congress and the Supreme Court.

Buhle, Mari Jo, and Paul Buhle. *The Concise History of Woman Suffrage from the Classic Work of Stanton, Anthony, Gage and Harper.* Urbana: University of Illinois Press, 1978.

This is the condensation of Elizabeth Cady Stanton's *History of Woman Suffrage, 1850-1902*, published originally 1881-1922 (Arno reprint, 1969). Originally six volumes.

Chafe, William Henry. *The American Woman: Her Changing Social, Economic and Political Roles, 1920-1970.* New York: Oxford University Press, 1972.

Chafe's important book grows out of his analysis of 1920s political movements.

Cook, Blanche, ed. *Crystal Eastman on Women and Revolution.* New York: Oxford University Press, 1978.

Crystal Eastman stands out as one of the most activist political women of the century.

Cott, Nancy. *Roots of Bitterness: Documents of the Social History of American Women.* New York: E. P. Dutton, 1972.

This is an important collection of primary-source documents on the history of American women from colonial times to the beginning of the twentieth century, including diary, biographical and autobiographical selections, as well as other documents touching upon women and politics in American history.

Elshtain, Jean Bethke. "Moral Woman and Immoral Man: A Consideration of the Public-Private Split and Its Political Ramifications." *Politics and Society* 4 (1974): 453-73.

Cites Aristotle and Machiavelli as sources nineteenth and twentieth century suffragists used in their arguments that women's superior morality would purify politics. Elshtain shows that these ideologies were grounded in a middle-class righteousness that in itself is sexist, classist, and racist.

Flexner, Eleanor. *Century of Struggle: The Woman's Rights Movement in the United States.* Rev. ed. Cambridge, MA: Belknap Press of Harvard University Press, 1975.
Apart from Flexner's meticulous research and documentation, the chief merit of the book is the way it situates the history of the suffrage movement within a broader framework of the social history of the period.

Gluck, Sherna, ed. *From Parlor to Prison: Five American Suffragists Talk about Their Lives.* New York: Random House, 1976.
Oral history.

Johnson, Dorothy E. "Organized Women as Lobbyists in the 1920's." *Capitol Studies* 1 (1972): 41-58.
Women's organizations closed ranks after the ratification of the 19th Amendment in 1921, and called themselves the Women's Joint Congressional Committee. WJCC became the lobbying unit for women-related legislation from 1920-1929.

Kerber, Linda. "The Republican Mother: Women and the Enlightenment—An American Perspective." *American Quarterly* 28 (Summer 1976): 187-205.
Traces the political roles of the foremothers of the Republic who were active politically despite their not having citizenship.

Lane, Ann. *Mary Ritter Beard: A Sourcebook.* New York: Schocken Books, 1977.
Section I of Beard's writings, "Political Activism—The Early Years," includes "Mothercraft," "Votes for Working Women," and "The Legislative Influence of Unenfranchised Women." Mary Beard was perhaps the most important feminist historian activist America has ever known, and her political theories provide the scaffolding for an informed discussion of contemporary women in politics.

Lansing, Marjorie. "Political Change for the American Woman." In Iglitzin, Lynne B., and Ruth Ross, eds. *Women in the World.* Santa Barbara, CA: ABC-Clio, 1976, pp. 175-81.
A study of women's political participation from the days of suffragism to the 1970s. Before 1920 the feminist movement was active, but went into a period of dormancy from the 1920s to the 1960s.

Levitt, Morris. "The Political Role of American Women." *Journal of Human Relations* 15 (1967): 23-35.
A psychological survey examining women's lack of political participation from 1920 to 1964.

Masel-Walters, Lynne. "Their Rights and Nothing More: A History of *The Revolution* 1868-70." *Journalism Quarterly* 53 (1976): 242-51.

Elizabeth Cady Stanton and Susan B. Anthony published the controversial periodical *The Revolution*, a chronicle of the suffrage movement for 30 years.

Mohr, James C. *Abortion in America: The Origins and Evolution of National Policy.* New York: Oxford University Press, 1978.

Primarily a historical study of the subject, Mohr traces the various interest groups that have impacted the abortion movement as a political cause since the 1800s.

Morgan, David. *Suffragists and Democrats: The Politics of Women's Suffrage in America.* East Lansing: Michigan State University Press, 1972.

Morgan confines his study of women's suffrage in the United States to the final years of the battle, 1916 to 1920, "when it had become a source of political dispute among the politicians."

Nolen, Anita Lonnes. "The Feminine Presence: Women's Papers in the Manuscript Division." *Quarterly Journal of the Library of Congress* 32 (1975): 348-65.

The Manuscript Division of the Library of Congress has collected the papers of women whose roles were mainly as observers—first ladies and other women in the social mainstream of Washington.

Republican Party. National Committee, 1960-1964. *The History of Women in Republican Conventions and Women in the Republican National Committee.* Comp. by Josephine L. Good. Washington, DC: 1963.

Stanton, Elizabeth Cady. *Eighty Years or More.* London: Fisher and Unwin, 1898. Reprint. New York: Schocken Books, 1976.
Autobiography.

Stucker, John. "Women's Political Role." *Current History* 70 (1976): 211-14, 232-33.

Outlines women's escalating political participation from 1830 to the 1970s.

Werner, Emmy E. "Women in Congress: 1917-1964." *Western Political Quarterly* 19 (1966): 16-30.

Demographic data and analysis on 70 women who served from 1917 to 1964.

Wills, Garry. "Feminists and Other Useful Fanatics." *Mankind* 6 (1977): 9-10, 42-44.

What can you expect from an article that appears in *Mankind*? Wills analyzes the failure of movements that do not zealously pursue their ends using radical means. Radicalism, he claims, was the only way that feminists were able to win suffrage. If men hadn't felt that granting the vote would nip the radical element in the suffrage movement, they would not have given in to the suffrage "fanatics."

Young, Louise M. "Women's Place in American Politics: The Historical Perspective." *Journal of Politics* 38 (August 1976): 295-335.

Young traces the roles of American women in political life back to Anne Hutchinson in 1634. Feminist leaders since the seventeenth century have emphasized the societal good that comes when women are politically active. Abigail Adams and Mercy Otis Warren in the early nineteenth century and Jane Addams and Carrie Chapman Catt in the latter part of the nineteenth century are positive examples of those women who have made powerful political statements.

Contemporary Women in Politics, Current Voting Studies, and Political Issues Relating to Women

Abzug, Bella S., and Cynthia Edgar. "Women and Politics: The Struggle for Representation." *Massachusetts Review* 13 (1972): 17-24.

The authors point to the sexual and cultural biases which exclude not only women but all disadvantaged and minority groups. They suggest that women's participation in politics involves larger issues than the women's movement; and that in fact their participation would assure a truly representative and responsive government for all Americans.

American Politics Quarterly (July 1977).
A special issue devoted to women and American politics.

Amundsen, Kirsten. *A New Look at the Silent Majority: Women and American Democracy.* Englewood Cliffs, NJ: Prentice-Hall, 1977.

In this updated version of the author's 1971 study, *The Silenced Majority*, Amundsen surveys discrimination against women in the labor market and in politics, concluding that changes made in recent years have been superficial.

Amundsen, Kirsten. *The Silenced Majority: Women and American Democracy.* Englewood Cliffs, NJ: Prentice-Hall, 1971.

Asks the question, "Why do American women have no political power?" and explores American myths that contribute to women's political powerlessness.

Andersen, Kristi. "Working Women and Political Participation, 1952-1972." *American Journal of Political Science* 19 (1975): 439-53.

Andersen traces the increasing involvement of working women in political activities. The 1972 election marked a change in women's participation, with both feminists and working-class women actively involved.

Beck, Melinda. "Sisterhood at City Hall." *Newsweek*, April 16, 1979, p. 48.
Jane Byrne, Dianne Feinstein, Margaret Hance, Isabella Cannon, Patience Latting, and Janet Gray Hayes are the women mayors analyzed.

Bellush, Jewel. "Women and Political Power: It's about Time." *National Civic Review* 66 (1977): 186-88.

If women are to realize their rightful due in the American political scheme, they must have power. To gain power they need training. Bellush writes about the Women's Political Training Center, which teaches women the nitty-gritty of becoming organizers, lobbyists, and candidates.

Boneparth, Ellen. "Women in Campaigns: From Lickin' and Stickin' to Strategy." *American Politics Quarterly* 5 (July 1977): 289-300.

An analysis of a California campaign in 1974, with attention to the backgrounds and tasks performed by females, and their perceptions of male and female roles in the campaign. When females were the candidates, women generally held higher leadership positions in the campaign. Women talked of sex discrimination in the campaigns and their inability to confront this discrimination in the context of the campaign work. Data were generated by interviews and mail surveys.

Bryant, Anita. *The Anita Bryant Story: The Survival of Our Nation's Families and the Threat of Militant Homosexuality.* Old Tappan, NJ: Revell, 1977.

A study of the intersection of politics and social issues by the woman who led the crusade to repeal the homosexual rights ordinance of Dade County.

Bryce, Harrington J., and Alan E. Warrick. "Black Women in Elective Offices." *Black Scholar* 6 (1974).

Not surprisingly, 1973 statistics indicate few women and fewer black women occupying elective offices.

Buchanan, Christopher. "Why Aren't There More Women in Congress?" *Congressional Quarterly Weekly Report*, August 12, 1978, pp. 2108-10.

A precis of the social, economic, and political reasons that exclude many women from more active political participation.

Bullock, Charles S., and Patricia Lee Findley Heys. "Recruitment of Women for Congress: A Research Note." *Western Political Quarterly* 25 (1972): 416-23.

The conclusions based on secondary sources indicate that women who have come to office as widows serving out their husbands terms are less likely to maintain a lasting commitment to a political career than women who have sought political office on their own. The latter group also tends to seek re-election more often than the widowed group.

Butler, Filiberti, and Dorothy Gray. *Everywoman's Guide to Political Awareness.* Millbrae, CA: Les Femmes, 1976.

Calkin, Homer. *Women in the Department of State: Their Role in American Foreign Affairs.* Washington, DC: U.S. Department of State, 1979.

This definitive analysis and listing of women in the State Department supersedes Calkin's 1977 study, *Women in American Foreign Affairs*. The information appears in no other printed source, and is an invaluable profile of women's invisibility in the Department of State until the 1970s.

Chamberlin, Hope. *A Minority of Members: Women in the United States Congress.* New York: Praeger, 1973.
Sprightly profiles and a very helpful appendix listing women in Congress, 1917-1973.

Colon, Frank T. "The Elected Woman." *Social Studies* 56 (1967): 256-61.
Focuses on the societal biases that keep women out of major offices at the federal level—male bias, the conflicts of job and family duties, and the necessity for mobility to be where the job is. No bibliographies.

Costantini, Edmond, and Kenneth H. Craik. "Women as Politicians: The Social Background, Personality, and Political Careers of Female Party Leaders." *Journal of Social Issues* 28 (1972): 217-36.
Beware of possible authorial bias.

Costello, Mary. "Women Voters." *Editorial Reports on the Women's Movement.* Washington, DC: *Congressional Quarterly* (1973), pp. 105-124.
Costello writes a state-of-the-art report on women holding elective office during the early 1970s, including an overview of the National Women's Political Caucus.

Darcy, R., and Sarah Schramm. "When Women Run against Men." *Public Opinion Quarterly* 41 (Spring 1977): 1-12.
What are the advantages of being a woman candidate running against a man? The major connection between sex and success seems to be that women are more likely to be nominated in Democratic districts. If a woman is nominated in a Democratic district, and if she is not running against a male incumbent, sex appears to have little effect on her defeat or success.

Diamond, Irene. *Sex Roles in the State House.* New Haven, CT: Yale University Press, 1977.
Explores the effect of competition on sex discrimination at the state level of politics. Diamond explains in her preface that the major hypothesis that she seeks to "develop and test—that sex differentiation decreases as competition for political office increases—relates to the sexes in politics in contemporary America. State legislatures are the particular focus because this is the one political arena where the question of sex differences can be examined in a systematic and quantitative fashion." Diamond uses aggregate data, survey data, and personal interviews in her analysis of where women are elected to the legislature, sex differences between male and female legislators, and possibilities for change.

Dubeck, Paula J. "Women and Access to Political Office: A Comparison of Female and Male State Legislators." *Sociological Quarterly* 17 (1976): 42-52.
Dubeck's study sampled the political fortunes of female state legislators against those of males, using variables of education, marital status,

occupation, age, beginning of political career, tenure, and occupation. The study found that political success for both men and women hinged on the social characteristics that define success in other societal endeavors.

Farney, Dennis. "Uphill Race: Women Still Facing Many Hurdles in Drive for Seats in Congress." *Wall Street Journal*, October 11, 1978.

Ferree, Myra Marx. "A Woman for President? Changing Responses: 1958-1972." *Public Opinion Quarterly*, no. 28 (Fall 1974), pp. 390-99.

Prejudice against the notion of a woman for president remained firm until 1972, which witnessed a 13% reduction in prejudice mainly because women themselves frequently responded positively to the idea of a woman president.

Frankovic, Kathleen A. "Sex and Voting in the U.S. House of Representatives, 1961-1975." *American Politics Quarterly* 5 (July 1977): 315-30.

Gehlen, Frieda L. "Women in Congress." *Trans-action* 6 (1969): 36-40.

Examines the collegial patterns of women in Congress, especially with regard to the formation of power networks. Though chairing committees is a matter of seniority rather than sex, women seem to be assigned to the less prestigious committees, and hence are cut off from power sources in many cases. An interesting article because it predates the Congresswomen's Caucus.

Gelb, Joyce, and Marian Lief Palley. "Women and Interest Group Politics: A Case Study of the Equal Credit Opportunity Act." *American Politics Quarterly* 5 (July 1977): 331-52.

Demonstrates that women acceptable to political elites (professionals who patiently manipulate the existing political system) can successfully achieve their ends through the traditional political process. The fight for the Equal Credit Act of 1974 supports the thesis that "elitist America gives power to those already within the system."

Githens, Marianne, and Jewel C. Prestage, eds. *A Portrait of Marginality: The Political Behavior of the American Woman.* New York: David McKay, 1977.

As the title suggests, women, especially black women, have problems getting into active politics.

Githens, Marianne, and Jewel Prestage. "Women State Legislators: Styles and Priorities." *Policy Studies Journal* 7 (Winter 1978): 264-70.

Gruberg, Martin. *Women in American Politics: An Assessment and Sourcebook.* Oshkosh, WI: Academia Press, 1968.

Helpful for material up to 1967, Gruberg's journalistic work looks at "the Achievement of American Women in Politics since 1920," including such issues as their indirect influence on politics and their political powerlessness. Gruberg supplies lists and biographies in his sourcebook, "Women in Government since 1920."

Hansen, Susan B. et al. "Women's Political Participation and Policy Preferences." *Social Science Quarterly* 56 (1976): 576-90.

Focusing on 1968 to 1972, the authors attempt to correlate policy changes in American government and party politics with the increasingly active political participation of women.

Henry, Keith S. "The Black Political Tradition in New York: A Conjunction of Political Cultures." *Journal of Black Studies* 7 (1977): 455-84.

Discusses political experiences of West Indians who were imported to the New York setting, where their skill in oratory served them well. While native black women made strides in politics fairly early, this is not true of native black men.

"How Carter Will Pick All Those Federal Judges: An Emphasis Is on Merit, But Is Politics Out? Blacks, Women Have the Edge." *Business Week*, December 4, 1978, pp. 100+.

Popular treatment.

Hyatt, James C. "Women: A So-so Year in Politics." *Wall Street Journal*, October 21, 1976, p. 24.

Popular treatment.

"In More Big Cities, It's 'Her Honor, the Mayor.' " *U.S. News and World Report*, July 16, 1979, p. 52.

Popular treatment.

Jaquette, Jane, comp. *Women in Politics*. New York: Wiley, 1974.

"Politics" in Jaquette includes experiences outside of the structured two-party American system. Among the essays: "The Making of the Apolitical Woman: Femininity and Sex-Stereotyping in Girls" (Lynn B. Iglitzin); "Women and Political Socialization: Considerations of the Impact of Motherhood" (Cornelia B. Flora and Naomi Lynn); and "Ideology and the Law: Sexism and Supreme Court Decisions" (Susan Kaufman Purcell). The work of major feminist political scientists appears in this anthology.

Jaquith, Cindy. "Where Is the Women's Political Caucus Going?" *International Socialist Review* 33 (1972): 4-7.

Outlines National Organization for Women (NOW) political strategies, with focus on caucus leaders Abzug, Chisholm, and Friedan.

Jennings, M. Kent, and Norman Thomas. "Men and Women in Party Elites: Social Roles and Political Resources." *Midwest Journal of Political Science* 12 (1968): 469-97.

Data for the study were generated from Michigan delegates to the 1964 Democratic and Republican conventions. Predictably, male delegates appeared to have more clout due to their political experiences. Career women's roles paralleled more closely the roles of males in the party elite than those of homemakers.

Johnson, Marilyn, and Kathy Stanwick. *Profile of Women Holding Office.* New Brunswick, NJ: Center for the American Woman and Politics. Eagleton Institute of Politics. Rutgers—the State University, 1976.

The authors compiled data on women serving in elective offices throughout the nation in this first summary and statistical analysis of political women.

Kelly, Rita Mae, and Mary Boutilier. *The Making of Political Women: A Study of Socialization and Role Conflict.* Chicago, IL: Nelson-Hall, 1977.

Portraits of 36 political women (including Eleanor Roosevelt and Shirley Chisholm) suggest that if women are not encouraged to act as public individuals, they will see little change in the sexual arrangements that now exist in politics.

King, Mae C. "The Politics of Sexual Stereotypes." *Black Scholar* 4 (1973): 12-23.

Suggests that black women can have little power in a racist system weaned on stereotypes defining black females.

Kirkpatrick, Jeanne J. *The New Presidential Elite: Men and Women in National Politics.* New York: Russell Sage, 1976.

Commissioned by the Center for the American Woman in Politics at Rutgers University, this book seeks to assess the validity of the hypothesis that women running for higher office face obstacles that differ in degree and/or kind from their male counterparts. Data are based on interviews and questionnaires gathered from the 50 women state senators and representatives selected for their diversity to attend a conference on women and politics in 1972. Kirkpatrick analyzes the four hypothetical constraints often used to explain women's low profile on the political scene: psychological constraints, cultural constraints, role constraints, and male conspiracy to exclude them. She also discusses political styles that characterize the women in this study.

Kirkpatrick, Jeanne J. *Political Women.* New York: Basic Books, 1974.

The Center for the American Woman and Politics of the Eagleton Institute of Politics at Rutgers sponsored this important study of congressional women.

Krusche, Earl R. "Level of Optimism as Related to Female Political Behavior." *Social Science* 41 (1966): 67-75.

Not surprisingly, this study found that women who face the future with optimism and confidence appear more likely to involve themselves actively in politics than their more pessimistic sisters.

Lamson, Peggy. *Few Are Chosen: American Women in Political Life Today.* Boston: Houghton Mifflin, 1968.

Lively profiles of Frances Bolton (congresswoman); Esther Peterson (labor); Martha Griffiths (congresswoman); Patsy Mink (congresswoman); Constance Motley (federal judge); Ann Uccello (mayor); Eugenie Anderson (diplomat); Margaret Chase Smith (senator); Margaret Heckler (congresswoman); Ella T. Grasso (governor).

Lamson, Peggy. *In the Vanguard: Six American Women in Public Life.* Boston: Houghton Mifflin, 1979.

"In the end my selection was entirely subjective. Each of the women who appears on these pages had strong appeal.... I knew none of them personally before I sought their participation, I admired them all as public figures." Portraits of Millicent Fenwick (congresswoman); Juanita Kreps (Commerce); Elizabeth Holtzman (congresswoman); Elaine Noble (Massachusetts House); Eleanor Holmes Norton (Equal Opportunity Commission); Rose Bird (California Supreme Court).

Lee, Marcia Manning. "Why Few Women Hold Public Office: Democracy and Sexual Roles." *Political Science Quarterly* 91 (Summer 1976): 297-314.

According to Lee, few women have held public office, and few will until responsibilities for child care are more equally distributed. Ironically, because women's assigned roles are restricting, they need to have a greater voice in public policy-making as elected officials.

Littwin, Susan. "Escaping from the Chauvinist Cellar: Except in the Black Precincts, Women Are Not Doing Very Well Breaking into Elective Office in California." *California Journal* 9 (May 1978): 148-50.

Louis Harris and Associates. *The 1972 American Women's Opinion Poll: A Survey of the Attitude of Women on Their Roles in Politics and the Economy.* New York: Louis Harris, 1972.

Lynn, Naomi B., and Cornelia B. Flora. "Motherhood and Political Participation: The Changing Sense of Self." *Journal of Political and Military Sociology* 1 (1973): 91-104.

According to Lynn and Flora, women's political participation is determined to some degree by their mothers' attitudes. Data were generated using mothers and non-mothers as compared to the University of Michigan, Survey Research Center's study of the American electorate (1968).

McBee, Mary L., and Kathryn A. Blake, eds. *The American Woman: Who Will She Be?* Beverly Hills, CA: Glencoe Press; London: Collier-Macmillan, 1974.

The 11 articles include contributions by Patsy Mink and Juanita Kreps.

McCourt, Kathleen. *Working-Class Women and Grass-Roots Politics.* Bloomington: Indiana University Press, 1977.

The views in this study reveal the politics of white working-class women from Chicago's southwest side. Interviews cover such subjects as women's attitudes toward the local and national political system, and their own participation in politics. Essential for an understanding of women who often feel that the political system passes them by.

McGrath, Wilma E., and John W. Soule. "Rocking the Cradle or Rocking the Boat: Women at the 1972 Democratic National Convention." *Social Science Quarterly* 55 (1974): 141-50.
Demonstrates women delegates' awareness of sex discrimination and the women's movement.

Margolis, Diane Rothbard. "The Invisible Hands: Sex Roles and the Division of Labor in Two Local Political Parties." *Social Problems* 26 (Feb. 1979): 314-24.

Meisol, Patricia. "Women in Politics—Increasing in Numbers, but Not on the Hill." *National Journal*, July 15, 1978, pp. 1128-31.

Mend, Michael R. et al. "Dynamics of Attitude Formation Regarding Women in Politics." *Experimental Study of Politics* 5 (August 1976): 25-39.
The authors argue that the election of Governor Ella Grasso of Connecticut; Mayor Janet Gray Hayes of San Jose, California; and Chief Justice Susie Sharp of North Carolina, along with 18 women members of the U.S. House, indicates that in 1974 women were playing an increasingly important role in American politics. In attitude surveys the study found that "If she performs only adequately—and is compared with a similarly performing male—a woman's disadvantages will be noticed and she will be rewarded accordingly. But, if we are talking of two truly outstanding performances, the male will collect the reward."

Milwaukee County Welfare Rights Organization. *Welfare Mothers Speak Out: We Ain't Gonna Shuffle Anymore.* New York: Norton, 1972.
An important political statement by members of a group not ordinarily considered to wield political clout, this volume examines the sociology of welfare and gives a forum for the views of welfare mothers. A concrete proposal for a Guaranteed Adequate Income Plan devised by the National Welfare Rights Organization suggests that welfare mothers have significant claims on an unresponsive political system.

Ralph Nader Congress Report. *Citizens Look at Congress.* Washington: Grossman, 1972-1974.
Each report in this series, separately authored and researched, yields excellent resource material on the congresswoman-subject. Biographical material is supplemented by an analysis of the congresswoman's voting record, committee work, interest group ratings, and records of key floor and committee votes. Write directly to Grossman if unlocatable through interlibrary loan.

Richardson, James T., and Sandie Fox Wightman. "Religion and Voting on Abortion Reform: A Follow-up Study." *Journal for the Scientific Study of Religion* 14 (1975): 159-65.
The results of a study on how religious affiliation affects the voting behavior of legislators.

Roosevelt, Eleanor, and Lorena B. Hickok. *Ladies of Courage.* New York: E. P. Putnam, 1954.

With the revival of interest in Eleanor Roosevelt and her co-author, Lorena B. Hickok, this book becomes important once again. Hickok profiles the political career of Eleanor Roosevelt. The segment "How to Break into Politics" provides stimulating comparative reading for contemporary political analysis of women, and the roads by which they gain access to power.

St. John, Jacqueline. "Women's Legislative Issues." *Vital Speeches*, June 15, 1972.

Schreiber, E. M. "Education and Change in American Opinions on a Woman for President." *Public Opinion Quarterly* 42 (Summer 1978): 171-82.

"Score Card of Gains, Losses for Women in Politics: Female Candidates Are Finding It Tough These Days To Get into Congress, but They're Winning Big in Local and State Races." *U.S. News and World Report*, August 21, 1978.

Shabad, Goldie, and Kristi Andersen. "Candidate Evaluations by Men and Women." *Public Opinion Quarterly* 43 (Spring 1979): 18.

Smalley, Hazel C. "Black Women Legislators Answer Questions." *Black Politician* 2 (1971): 4-45.
In this article black women holding elective office disaffiliate themselves from women's movement issues and concentrate on problems of employment, law enforcement, drugs, and housing.

Stone, Betsey. "Women and the '72 Elections." *International Socialist Review* 33 (1972): 14-19, 39.
The 1972 presidential candidates demonstrated a lack of sensitivity to women's issues, as observed by the Socialist Workers Party and the National Women's Political Caucus.

Stucker, John. "Women's Political Role." *Current History* 70 (May 1976): 211-14.
Women have only recently (1970s) come into their own as politicians and skillful lobbyists in their own behalf. The analysis here suggests that even after gaining the right to vote in 1920, many women failed to take advantage of the franchise. According to the author, as women expand their legislative agenda beyond education and social welfare, they will gain even greater political power. As it is, women's groups have organized in sophisticated political ways to end public and private discrimination.

Tolchin, Susan J. *Women in Congress, 1917-1977*. Washington, DC: U.S. Government Printing Office, 1976.
This handy 112-page booklet contains useful little portraits of congressional women; a photograph accompanies each biography. The booklet was written and printed "for the use of the Joint Committee on Arrangements for the Commemoration of the Bicentennial."

Tolchin, Susan J., and Martin Tolchin. *Clout: Womanpower and Politics.* New York: Coward, McCann & Geoghegan, 1974.

The authors believe that politics is open to women's contributions because of the major political and social upheavals of the 1970s: the women's movement, Watergate, and the peace movement. Among the many recognizable names the Tolchins invoke are Bella Abzug, Sissy Farenthold, Shirley MacLaine, Gloria Steinem, and Patricia Schroeder. Schroeder's speech on campaigning, "You Can Do It," and "Tips for Running for Public Office," from the Office of Women's Activities of the Democratic National Committee, suggest the practical formula and tone of the Tolchins' analysis of mainstream politics.

Van Hightower, Nikki. "The Recruitment of Women for Public Office." *American Politics Quarterly* 5 (July 1977): 301-314.

This study focuses on 60 women candidates running in New York City and Long Island in 1972, with attention to their recruitment. The party directly recruited 54% of the women. Most women (70%) became involved in politics during their adult years, many of them through civic and mass movement activities. Women candidates are characterized as being white, native born, monied, well-educated, and upwardly mobile.

Volgy, Thomas J., and Sandra S. Volgy. "Women and Politics: Political Correlates of Sex-Role Acceptance." *Social Science Quarterly* 55 (1975): 967-74.

The data presented here indicate that women who reject traditional sex-role values tend to be more active in politics.

"What [Else] the 94th Congress Might [or Might Not] Do?" *Ms.*, March 1975.

Women's History Research Center. *Women's History Research Center Microfilms.* See "Herstory" and "Law."

Excellent material about contemporary women in politics. This microfilmed collection of documents, held by many libraries, provides important and generally inaccessible information "gathered from mass, alternative, and professional publications" during the sixties and up to the mid-seventies. The original collection for the law materials resides at the University of Wyoming, while the original periodical collection is at Northwestern University. Contact the Women's History Research Center, 2325 Oak, Berkeley, CA 94708 for locations of the microfilm collections and reel guides.

Equal Rights Amendment, Contemporary Feminism, Social and Political Theory

Brady, David, and Kent L. Tedin. "Ladies in Pink: Religion and Political Ideology in the Anti-ERA Movement." *Social Science Quarterly* 56 (1976): 564-75.

Brady and Tedin profile anti-ERA activists. Using 1975 data, they identify anti-feminist origins. Religious backgrounds and political ideology figure into the stance taken by opponents of equal rights.

Brown, Barbara A. et al. *Women's Rights and the Law.* New York: Praeger, 1977.
A good source on the Equal Rights Amendment and its legal implications.

Chafe, William H. "Feminism in the 1970s." *Dissent* 21 (1974): 508-518.

Cummings, Bernice, and Victoria Schuck. *Women Organizing: An Anthology.* Metuchen, NJ: Scarecrow, 1979.
Many articles of contemporary interest, ranging from local to national-level politics. Among the articles: "The Women's Movement and the Four Black Congresswomen"; "The League of Women Voters and Political Power"; "Exploring the Relationship between Female Candidacies and the Women's Movement"; and "Women as Voluntary Political Activists: A Review of Recent Empirical Research."

Evans, Sara. *Personal Politics: The Roots of Women's Liberation in the Civil Rights Movement and the New Left.* New York: Random House, 1979.

Fox, Robin, and Lionel Tiger. *The Imperial Animal.* New York: Holt, Rinehart and Winston, 1971.
Tiger's *Men and Groups* (1969) provided the groundwork for this analysis of male bonding. Females form bonds with each other outside of the male hierarchy, and can often influence the status patterns of males. However, females in all complex political systems (prehistoric human as well as prehuman primate) are not welcomed into male hierarchies. The implications for political women are manifest. Tiger and Fox conclude that it may be necessary to pass laws "that compel boards of directors to have female members, or female quotas in the legislatures, before the greater participation [by women], which would obviously be to everyone's benefit, could be effected."

Ginsburg, Ruth Bader. "The Need for the Equal Rights Amendment." *American Bar Association Journal* 59 (1973): 1013-1019.

Hershey, Marjorie Randon. "The Politics of Androgyny? Sex Roles and Attitudes toward Women in Politics." *American Politics Quarterly* 5 (July 1977): 261-87.
Using the Bem Sex Role Inventory, the author studied how undergraduates rate their own sex role attitudes and correlated these attitudes with students' political views. Males and females who score high on the masculine scale expressed a keener interest in politics. Hershey found that the students with more flexible sex role attitudes expressed greater interest in women's liberation and more positive attitudes toward women in politics.

Iglitzin, Lynne. "Political Education and Sexual Liberation." *Politics and Society* 2 (1972): 241-54.
According to Iglitzin, women's liberation has challenged women to participate more fully as they see a necessity to contribute to policy-making that directly affects them.

Janeway, Elizabeth. *Man's World, Woman's Place.* New York: Dell Publishing, 1971.

Janeway's eloquent and scholarly exploration of social mythology, of the social system that creates the mythology, and of the definitions of women's roles takes issue with arguments of prominent social scientists such as David McClelland and Erik Erikson, who rationalize that societal health is contingent upon the split between man's "outer space" and woman's "inner space." According to Janeway, any discussion of woman's place as wife, housewife, and mother must take into account history, values, and facts. The author calls for an understanding of the tremendous emotional power of myth in order to meet real crises and shifts in the social order.

Lavine, T. Z. "Ideas of Revolution in the Women's Movement." *American Behavioral Scientist* 20 (March/April 1977): 535-66.

A technical discussion of the contemporary women's liberation movement beginning in 1964. The author sees the concept of negative identity as an overriding one among the feminists.

Mezey, Susan Gluck. "Support for Women's Rights Policy: An Analysis of Local Politicians." *American Politics Quarterly* 6 (October 1978): 485-97.

Mezey's study is an example of the new feminist political science. Her analysis uses a "feminist policy index" to measure whether men and women differ from each other in political behavior, testing a sample of 50 male and 50 female Connecticut politicians during the 1976-1977 political year. The study reveals attitudes about sex roles and women's rights, and reflects a women's studies perspective.

Miller, Margaret I., and Helene Linker. "Equal Rights Amendment in California and Utah." *Society* 11 (1974): 40-53.

Compares and contrasts strategies used in California and Utah, which resulted in California's successful campaign and Utah's failure to pass ERA.

Novack, George. "The Reradicalization of American Politics." *International Socialist Review* 35 (1974): 4-11.

A review of radical movements of the 1970s, with the focus on feminist and minority movements.

Reid, Inez Smith. "Can We Overcome the Traumatic Sixties?" *Essence* 10 (June 1979): 67.

Black women found themselves in a peculiar position in the 1960s. When white women gave birth to the women's movement out of the experiences in the civil rights movement, black women found themselves alienated from feminists whose political priorities were different from their own.

Thom, Mary. "New Lease on Life for the ERA? The Case for Extension." *Ms.*, May 1978, pp. 56, 78, 80.

United States. Congress. Senate. Committee on the Judiciary. Subcommittee on the Constitution. *Equal Rights Amendment Extension.* Hearings,

Ninety-fifth Congress, 2nd Session. S.J. Res. 134. U.S. Government, 1979.

United States. National Commission on the Observance of International Women's Year. *The Spirit of Houston: The First National Women's Conference: An Official Report to the President, the Congress, and the People of the United States.* Washington, DC: Superintendent of Documents, March 1978.
Final report.

United States. National Commission on the Observance of International Women's Year, 1975. " ... To Form a More Perfect Union...." *Justice for American Women: Report of the National Commission on the Observance of International Women's Year.* Washington, DC: Department of State, 1976.
Prepared as a report to the president and to the people of the United States, parts I, II, and III discuss barriers keeping women from full participation in American life: Full Partnership for the Homemaker; Mass Media; ERA; The Creative Woman; Money for Culture and Research; Power Brokers; Strong Laws—Weak Enforcement; Women and the Workplace; Indian Problems; Reproductive Freedom; Parents and Children; Where Women Are Heading; The Third Century. Part IV lists the members of the commission, while part V contains the findings and recommendations of its working committees. Useful reference material and original research authorized by the commission are summarized in part VI.

Wohl, Lisa Cronin. "Toward a Mass Feminist Movement." *International Socialist Review* 32 (1971): 19-23, 57-66.
Discusses a major cluster of feminist issues—political participation, child care, marriage, and abortion.

Wohl, Lisa Cronin. "White Gloves and Combat Boots: The Fight for ERA." *Civil Liberties Review* 1 (1974): 77-86.
According to Wohl, the signals indicate that ERA may be a tougher battle than suffrage was.

Political Science on Women:
Critiques of the Literature

Boals, Kay. "Review Essay: Political Science." *Signs: Journal of Women in Culture and Society* 1 (1975): 161-74.
A feminist state-of-the-art essay on the expanded knowledge about women in politics. Women elected before 1972 reflect the dominant culture, while women elected after 1972 do not conform to narrow definitions of sex roles, and often have high political aspirations. According to Boals, male-researched analyses of women's political participation are often biased, using male behavior as the norm and female behavior as deviant. A bibliography accompanies the critique of the literature.

Bourque, Susan C., and Jean Grossholtz. "Politics an Unnatural Practice: Political Science Looks at Female Participation." *Politics and Society* 4 (1974): 225-66.

Explores stereotypes of political women and suggests that political science literature may contribute to this negative image.

Goot, Murray, and Elizabeth Anne Reid. *Women and Voting Studies: Mindless Matrons or Sexist Scientism?* Beverly Hills, CA: Sage Publications, 1975.

This 44-page paper begins with the assumption that the political science literature is rife with sexist assumptions about women's political participation as voter and vote-getter, with specific examples of prejudice and biased research design drawn from political scientists' writings.

Jaquette, Jane S. "Political Science." *Signs: Journal of Women in Culture and Society* 2 (1976): 147-64.

To promote feminist scholarship in political science it is necessary to reexamine the existing corpus of knowledge. Jaquette calls for a study of personal interactions in small political groups, especially with regard to nonverbal communications. Feminist political scientists are caught in a double-bind. On the one hand, they know that female participation is different in quality and more private than that of males; yet feminist researchers are often criticized for taking a "trivial" approach to political science.

Mitchell, Joyce M., and Rachel R. Starr. "A Regional Approach for Analyzing the Recruitment of Academic Women." *American Behavioral Scientist* 15 (1971): 183-205.

The authors prove male dominance in graduate programs of political science. The article suggests that negative images of political women may be due to male-biased research.

Ogden, Susan. "Courses on Women in Politics." *Teaching Political Science* 4 (1977): 145-62.

Ogden offers pedagogical insights into teaching "women in politics" at the university level. She also outlines the problems, mainly due to the male-center approach of the predominantly male discipline of political science.

Orum, Anthony M. et al. "Sex, Socialization, and Politics." *American Sociological Review* 39 (1974): 197-209.

The article suggests that political scientists use three approaches to explain the differences in political behavior between men and women: situational, structural, and socialization. The authors find little evidence that political socialization is a valid approach.

Palley, Marian Lief. "Women and the Study of Public Policy." *Policy Studies Journal* 4 (Spring 1976): 288-96.

The author notes that sociologists and anthropologists rather than political scientists have been responsible for research on women in society. Very little work has been undertaken in the area of political policy analysis. Instead, treatments of women in politics have been biographical or deal with the role of women in groups. According to Palley, political scientists have their work cut out for them if they begin examining the effect of political actions on women and women's impact upon political policy-making.

Shanley, Mary L., and Victoria Schuck. "In Search of Political Women." *Social Science Quarterly* 55 (1974): 632-44.
The authors take a historiographic and feminist view of the writings of political scientists on women from 1903 to 1974, and offer some conclusions about women's treatment in the political science literature.

Selected 1970s Dissertations: Women in Politics

Banthin, Joanne Marie. "The New York State Women's Political Caucus: A Case Study in Organizational Behavior." University of Michigan, 1973. *Dissertation Abstracts International*, vol. 35, no. 1, 527-A.

Blahna, Loretta J. "The Rhetoric of the Equal Rights Amendment." University of Kansas, 1973. *Dissertation Abstracts International*, vol. 34, no. 12, 7909-A.

Camhi, Jane Jerome. "Women against Women: American Antisuffragism 1880-1920." Tufts University, 1973.

Dunkle, Debora Ellen. "Women and Politics: The Political Role Expectations of Adolescent Females." State University of New York, 1974. *Dissertation Abstracts International*, vol. 35, no. 10, 6770-A.

Elshtain, Jean Bethke. "Women and Politics: A Theoretical Analysis." Brandeis University, 1973. *Dissertation Abstracts International*, vol. 34, no. 7, 4343-A.

Fails, Eleanor V. "The American Congresswoman from 1950-1970: A Study in Role Perception." Loyola University of Chicago, 1974. *Dissertation Abstracts International*, vol. 35, no. 2, 1235-A.

Feagans, Janet. "Female Political Elites: Case Studies of Female Legislators." Howard University, 1972. *Dissertation Abstracts International*, vol. 35, no. 6, 3826-A.

Lee, Marcia Manning. "The Participation of Women in Suburban Politics: A Study of the Influence of Women as Compared to Men in Suburban Governmental Decision-Making." Tufts University, 1973.

Merritt, Sharyne Ann. "Political Women and Political Men: Sex Differences in Motivations and Adaptations of Elected Local Political Office." Case Western Reserve University, 1975. *Dissertation Abstracts International*, vol. 36, no. 9, 6283-A.

Morrison, Glenda Eileen. "Women's Participation in the 1928 Presidential Election." University of Kansas, 1978. *Dissertation Abstracts International*, vol. 39, no. 7, 4449-4450-A.

Nelson, Marjory. "Ladies in the Street: A Sociological Analysis of the National Women's Party, 1910-1930." State University of New York, 1976. *Dissertation Abstracts International*, vol. 37, no. 6, 3926-A.

Paget, Karen Maxine Eggert. "A Woman in Politics: Change in Role Perception." University of Colorado, 1975. *Dissertation Abstracts International*, vol. 36, no. 5, 3095-3096-A.

Smith, Kathryn Sladek. "The Characteristics and Motivations of American Women Who Seek Positions of Political Leadership." New School of Social Research, 1976. *Dissertation Abstracts International*, vol. 37, no. 2, 1203-1204-A.

Stucker, John Joseph. "The Impact of Woman Suffrage on Patterns of Voter Participation in the United States: Quasi-Experimental and Real-Time Analyses, 1890-1920." University of Michigan, 1973.

Taliaferro, James Hubert, Jr. "The Emergence of the Political Female Character as Revealed in Selected American Plays from 1762 to 1860." New York University, 1976. *Dissertation Abstracts International*, vol. 37, no. 9, 5448-5449-A.

Van Hightower, Nikki. "The Politics of Female Socialization." New York University, 1974. *Dissertation Abstracts International*, vol. 35, no. 10, 6772-6773-A.

General Indexes and Abstracting Services:
Subject headings related to women in politics

ACCESS: Supplementary Index to Periodicals
  Use: Women—Equal Rights

Advance Bibliography of Contents
  Use: Political Science and Government

Business Periodicals Index
  Use: Women in Politics

Current Index to Journals in Education
  Use: Abortion, Day Care, Equal Opportunity

Education Index
Use: Women—History
Women—Equal Rights

Essay and General Literature Index
Use: Personal names, e.g., Jordan, Chisholm
Woman
Women
Sex Discrimination against Women

Index to Legal Periodicals
Use: Abortion
Married Women
Credit
Equal Protection

Index to Periodical Articles by and about Negroes
Use: Women in Politics

International Bibliography of the Social Sciences: Economics
Use: Women
Employment—Women

International Bibliography of the Social Sciences: Political Science
Use: Women in Politics

Reader's Guide to Periodical Literature
Use: Personal names, e.g., Jordan, Chisholm
Women—Employment
Women—Equal Rights
Women—Politics

Sociological Abstracts
Use: Women
Women in Politics

Resource List on Women in Politics: Organizations and Libraries

Bancroft Library
Regional Oral History Office
University of California
Berkeley, CA 94270
"California Political Leaders, 1920-1970," in Women in Politics Oral History Project. The idea behind this project is to document women's active participation in politics between the passage of the Nineteenth Amendment

and the 1960s women's movement. For bound holdings of material, write to the above address.

Center for the American Women and Politics
Eagleton Institute
Rutgers University
New Brunswick, NJ 08901

Center for Women in Government
CDSC, GSPA, SUNY Albany
Draper Hall 302
1400 Washington Avenue
Albany, NY 12222

Congresswomen's Caucus
Congress of the United States
House of Representatives
Washington, DC 20515

Joint Center for Political Studies
Suite 926, Woodward Building
1426 H Street, NW
Washington, DC 20005

League of Women Voters
1730 M Street, NW
Washington, DC 20036

National Women's Education Fund
1532 16th Street, NW
Washington, DC 20036

National Women's Political Caucus
1411 K Street, NW
Washington, DC 20005

Northwestern University Library
Special Collections, Women's History Periodicals Collection
Evanston, IL 60201

NOW Action Center
425 13th Street, NW, Room 1001
Washington, DC 20004

The Schlesinger Library
Radcliffe College
3 James Street
Cambridge, MA 02138
   The Schlesinger Library presently houses papers of Dorothy McCullough Lee, Jeannette Rankin, Edith Nourse Rogers, Jessica Weis, and Esther

Peterson. Prominent political women, for example, congresswomen Elizabeth Holtzman and Barbara Mikulski, have promised papers to the Schlesinger Library. In addition, the library holds papers of various Democratic and Republican national committeewomen, and heads of the Women's Bureau. Tape recordings of interviews with political women included in Peggy Lamson's *Few Are Chosen* (1968) are also housed here.

Sophia Smith Collection (Women's History Archives)
Smith College
Northampton, MA 01063

State Historical Society of Wisconsin
University of Wisconsin
Madison, WI 53706
 The State Historical Society of Wisconsin holds one of the largest collections of women's movement newsletters and periodicals of any library in the United States. Women's suffrage periodicals include *The Revolution* and *The New Era*, while modern movement papers include *Off Our Backs, Women in Action*, and the 850 titles in the *Herstory* microfilm collections based on the Women's History Library periodicals collection (now housed in Northwestern University's special collections).

Women and Politics
2900 M Street, NW
Washington, DC 20007

Women's Action Alliance
370 Lexington Avenue, Room 600
New York, NY 10017

Women's Equity Action League
805 15th Street, NW, Suite 822
Washington, DC 20005

Women's History Research Center
2325 Oak Street
Berkeley, CA 94708

Serial Publications Featuring
Women's History, Feminist Theory, and Politics

Chrysalis
(1977 to date)
1727 N. Spring Street
Los Angeles, CA 90012

Feminist Studies
(Summer 1972 to date)
c/o Women's Studies Program
University of Maryland
College Park, MD 20742

FRONTIERS: A Journal of Women Studies
(1975 to date)
University of Colorado
Boulder, CO 80309

Ms. Magazine
(September 1972 to date)
123 Garden Street
Marion, OH 43302

Signs: Journal of Women in Culture and Society
(Autumn 1975 to date)
University of Chicago Press
5801 Ellis Avenue
Chicago, IL 60637

Women and Politics
(1980)
The Haworth Press
149 Fifth Avenue
New York, NY 10010

Women Studies Abstracts
(Winter 1972 to date)
Rush Publishing Company
P.O. Box 1
Rush, NY 14543

Appendix I
Women of the Congress 1917-1980

Hazel Abel
U.S. Senate
Republican — Nebraska
November 8, 1954 to
December 31, 1954
83rd Congress

Bella S. Abzug
U.S. House of Representatives
Democrat — New York
January 21, 1971 to January 3, 1977
92nd through 94th Congresses

Maryon Allen
U.S. Senate
Democrat — Alabama
1978 to January 3, 1979
95th Congress

Elizabeth Andrews
U.S. House of Representatives
Democrat — Alabama
April 10, 1972 to January 3, 1973
92nd Congress

Irene Baker
U.S. House of Representatives
Republican — Tennessee
March 19, 1964 to January 3, 1965
88th Congress

Iris Blitch
U.S. House of Representatives
Democrat — Georgia
January 5, 1955 to January 3, 1963
84th through 87th Congresses

Corinne (Lindy) Boggs
U.S. House of Representatives
Democrat — Louisiana
March 27, 1973-
93rd Congress-

Veronica Boland
U.S. House of Representatives
Democrat — Pennsylvania
November 19, 1942 to
January 3, 1943
77th Congress

Frances Payne Bolton
U.S. House of Representatives
Republican — Ohio
March 5, 1940 to January 3, 1969
76th through 90th Congresses

Reva Beck Bosone
U.S. House of Representatives
Democrat — Utah
January 3, 1949 to January 3, 1953
81st through 82nd Congresses

Marilyn Lloyd Bouquard
U.S. House of Representatives
Democrat — Tennessee
January 3, 1975-
94th Congress-

Eva Bowring
U.S. Senate
Republican — Nebraska
April 26, 1954 to November 8, 1954
83rd Congress

Vera Buchanan
U.S. House of Representatives
Democrat — Pennsylvania
August 1, 1951 to November 26, 1955
82nd through 84th Congresses

Yvonne Braithwaite Burke
U.S. House of Representatives
Democrat — California
January 3, 1973 to January 3, 1979
93rd through 95th Congresses

Beverly Byron
U.S. House of Representatives
Democrat—Maryland
January 3, 1979-
96th Congress-

Katharine Byron
U.S. House of Representatives
Democrat—Maryland
July 11, 1941 to January 3, 1943
77th Congress

Hattie Caraway
U.S. Senate
Democrat—Arkansas
December 8, 1931 to January 3, 1945
72nd through 78th Congresses

Shirley Chisholm
U.S. House of Representatives
Democrat—New York
January 3, 1969-
91st Congress-

Marguerite Church
U.S. House of Representatives
Republican—Illinois
January 3, 1951 to January 3, 1963
82nd through 87th Congresses

Marian Clarke
U.S. House of Representatives
Republican—New York
January 3, 1934 to January 3, 1935
73rd Congress

Cardiss Collins
U.S. House of Representatives
Democrat—Illinois
June 7, 1973-
93rd Congress-

Emily Taft Douglas
U.S. House of Representatives
Democrat—Illinois
January 3, 1945 to January 3, 1947
79th Congress

Helen Gahagan Douglas
U.S. House of Representatives
Democrat—California
January 3, 1945 to January 3, 1951
79th through 81st Congresses

Florence Dwyer
U.S. House of Representatives
Republican—New Jersey
January 3, 1957 to January 3, 1973
85th through 92nd Congresses

Elaine Edwards
U.S. Senate
Democrat—Louisiana
August 7, 1972 to January 3, 1973
92nd Congress

Willa Eslick
U.S. House of Representatives
Democrat—Tennessee
December 5, 1932 to March 4, 1933
72nd Congress

Mary Elizabeth Farrington
U.S. House of Representatives
Republican—Hawaii
August 4, 1954 to January 3, 1957
83rd through 84th Congresses

Rebecca Latimer Felton
U.S. Senate
Democrat—Georgia
November 21, 1922 to
November 22, 1922
67th Congress
(Filled vacancy caused by Senator Thomas Watson's death; the next day she gave up the seat to Senator Walter George, the elected candidate for the vacancy.)

Millicent Hammond Fenwick
U.S. House of Representatives
Republican—New Jersey
January 3, 1975-
94th Congress-

Geraldine A. Ferraro
U.S. House of Representatives
Democrat—New York
January 3, 1979-
96th Congress-

Elizabeth Gasque
U.S. House of Representatives
Democrat—South Carolina
September 13, 1938 to
January 3, 1939
(Not sworn in)

Florence Gibbs
U.S. House of Representatives
Democrat—Georgia
October 3, 1940 to January 3, 1941
76th Congress

Kathryn Granahan
U.S. House of Representatives
Democrat—Pennsylvania
January 3, 1957 to January 3, 1963
84th through 87th Congresses

Ella Grasso
U.S. House of Representatives
Democrat—Connecticut
January 21, 1971 to January 3, 1975
92nd through 93rd Congresses

Dixie Bibb Graves
U.S. Senate
Democrat—Alabama
August 20, 1937 to January 10, 1938
75th Congress

Edith Green
U.S. House of Representatives
Democrat—Oregon
January 5, 1955 to January 3, 1975
84th through 93rd Congresses

Isabella Greenway
U.S. House of Representatives
Democrat—Arizona
January 3, 1934 to January 3, 1937
73rd through 74th Congresses

Martha W. Griffiths
U.S. House of Representatives
Democrat—Michigan
January 5, 1955 to January 3, 1975
84th through 93rd Congresses

Julia Butler Hansen
U.S. House of Representatives
Democrat—Washington
January 3, 1961 to January 3, 1975
86th through 93rd Congresses

Cecil Harden
U.S. House of Representatives
Republican—Indiana
January 3, 1949 to January 3, 1959
81st through 85th Congresses

Margaret Heckler
U.S. House of Representatives
Republican—Massachusetts
January 10, 1967-
90th Congress-

Marjorie S. Holt
U.S. House of Representatives
Republican—Maryland
January 3, 1973-
93rd Congress-

Elizabeth Holtzman
U.S. House of Representatives
Democrat—New York
January 3, 1973-
93rd Congress-

Nan Wood Honeyman
U.S. House of Representatives
Democrat—Oregon
January 5, 1937 to January 3, 1939
75th Congress

Winnifred Mason Huck
U.S. House of Representatives
Republican—Illinois
November 20, 1922 to March 3, 1923
67th Congress

Muriel Humphrey
U.S. Senate
Democrat—Minnesota
January 26, 1978 to January 3, 1979
95th Congress

Virginia Jenckes
U.S. House of Representatives
Democrat — Indiana
March 9, 1933 to January 3, 1939
73rd through 75th Congresses

Barbara C. Jordan
U.S. House of Representatives
Democrat — Texas
January 3, 1973 to January 3, 1978
93rd through 95th Congresses

Florence Prag Kahn
U.S. House of Representatives
Republican — California
March 4, 1925 to January 3, 1937
69th through 74th Congresses

Nancy Landon Kassebaum
U.S. Senate
Republican — Kansas
January 3, 1979-
96th Congress-

Elizabeth Kee
U.S. House of Representatives
Democrat — West Virginia
July 26, 1951 to January 3, 1965
82nd through 88th Congresses

Edna Kelly
U.S. House of Representatives
Democrat — New York
November 8, 1949 to January 3, 1969
81st through 90th Congresses

Martha Keys
U.S. House of Representatives
Democrat — Kansas
January 3, 1975 to January 3, 1978
94th through 95th Congresses

Coya Knutson
U.S. House of Representatives
Democrat — Minnesota
January 5, 1955 to January 3, 1959
84th through 85th Congresses

Katherine Langley
U.S. House of Representatives
Republican — Kentucky
December 5, 1927 to March 4, 1931
70th through 71st Congresses

Rose Long
U.S. Senate
Democrat — Louisiana
February 10, 1936 to January 3, 1937
74th Congress

Clare Boothe Luce
U.S. House of Representatives
Republican — Connecticut
January 6, 1943 to January 3, 1947
78th through 79th Congresses

Georgia Lusk
U.S. House of Representatives
Democrat — New Mexico
January 3, 1947 to January 3, 1949
80th Congress

Kathryn O'Loughlin McCarthy
U.S. House of Representatives
Democrat — Kansas
March 9, 1933 to January 3, 1935
73rd Congress

Ruth Hanna McCormick
U.S. House of Representatives
Republican — Illinois
April 15, 1929 to March 4, 1931
71st Congress

Clara McMillan
U.S. House of Representatives
Democrat — South Carolina
January 3, 1940 to January 3, 1941
76th Congress

Helen Douglas Mankin
U.S. House of Representatives
Democrat — Georgia
February 25, 1946 to January 3, 1947
79th Congress

Catherine May (Bedell)
U.S. House of Representatives
Republican—Washington
January 7, 1959 to January 3, 1971
86th through 91st Congresses

Helen Meyner
U.S. House of Representatives
Democrat—New Jersey
January 3, 1975 to January 3, 1978
94th through 95th Congresses

Barbara Mikulski
U.S. House of Representatives
Democrat—Maryland
January 3, 1977-
95th Congress-

Patsy Mink
U.S. House of Representatives
Democrat—Hawaii
January 4, 1965 to January 3, 1977
89th through 94th Congresses

Maurine Neuberger
U.S. Senate
Democrat—Oregon
January 3, 1961 to January 3, 1967
87th through 89th Congresses

Mae Ella Nolan
U.S. House of Representatives
Republican—California
February 2, 1923 to March 4, 1925
67th through 68th Congresses

Catherine D. Norell
U.S. House of Representatives
Democrat—Arkansas
April 25, 1961 to January 3, 1963
87th Congress

Mary Teresa Norton
U.S. House of Representatives
Democrat—New Jersey
December 7, 1925 to January 3, 1951
69th through 81st Congresses

Mary Rose Oakar
U.S. House of Representatives
Democrat—Ohio
January 3, 1977-
95th Congress-

Caroline O'Day
U.S. House of Representatives
Democrat—New York
January 3, 1935 to January 3, 1943
74th through 77th Congresses

Pearl Oldfield
U.S. House of Representatives
Democrat—Arkansas
January 11, 1929 to March 4, 1931
70th through 71st Congresses

Ruth Bryan Owen (Rohde)
U.S. House of Representatives
Democrat—Florida
April 15, 1929 to March 4, 1933
71st through 72nd Congresses

Shirley N. Pettis
U.S. House of Representatives
Republican—California
May 6, 1975 to January 3, 1978
94th through 95th Congresses

Gracie Pfost
U.S. House of Representatives
Democrat—Idaho
January 3, 1953 to January 3, 1963
83rd through 87th Congresses

Eliza Jane Pratt
U.S. House of Representatives
Democrat—North Carolina
June 3, 1946 to January 3, 1947
79th Congress

Ruth Baker Sears Pratt
U.S. House of Representatives
Republican—New York
April 15, 1929 to March 3, 1933
71st through 72nd Congresses

Gladys Pyle
U.S. Senate
Republican—South Dakota
November 8, 1938 to
January 3, 1939
(Not sworn in)

Jeannette Rankin
U.S. House of Representatives
Republican—Montana
April 2, 1917 to March 4, 1919
January 3, 1941 to January 3, 1943
65th and 77th Congresses

Louise Goff Reece
U.S. House of Representatives
Republican—Tennessee
May 23, 1961 to January 3, 1963
87th Congress

Charlotte Reid
U.S. House of Representatives
Republican—Illinois
January 9, 1963 to October 7, 1971
88th through 92nd Congresses

Corinne Riley
U.S. House of Representatives
Democrat—South Carolina
April 12, 1962 to January 3, 1963
87th Congress

Alice Mary Robertson
U.S. House of Representatives
Republican—Oklahoma
April 11, 1921 to March 4, 1923
67th Congress

Edith Nourse Rogers
U.S. House of Representatives
Republican—Massachusetts
December 7, 1925 to
September 10, 1960
69th through 86th Congresses

Katharine St. George
U.S. House of Representatives
Republican—New York
January 3, 1947 to January 3, 1965
80th through 88th Congresses

Patricia Scott Schroeder
U.S. House of Representatives
Democrat—Colorado
January 3, 1973-
93rd Congress-

Edna Simpson
U.S. House of Representatives
Republican—New York
January 7, 1959 to January 3, 1961
86th Congress

Margaret Chase Smith
U.S. House of Representatives
Republican—Maine
June 10, 1940 to January 3, 1949
76th through 80th Congresses

U.S. Senate
Republican—Maine
January 3, 1949 to January 3, 1973
81st through 92nd Congresses

Virginia Dodd Smith
U.S. House of Representatives
Republican—Nebraska
January 3, 1975-
94th Congress-

Olympia Snowe
U.S. House of Representatives
Republican—Maine
January 3, 1979-
96th Congress-

Gladys Noon Spellman
U.S. House of Representatives
Democrat—Maryland
January 3, 1975-
94th Congress-

Winifred Stanley
U.S. House of Representatives
Republican—New York
January 6, 1943 to January 3, 1945
78th Congress

Leonor Kretzer Sullivan
U.S. House of Representatives
Democrat—Missouri
January 3, 1953 to January 3, 1977
83rd through 94th Congresses

Jessie Sumner
U.S. House of Representatives
Republican—Illinois
January 3, 1939 to January 3, 1947
76th through 79th Congresses

Lera Thomas
U.S. House of Representatives
Democrat—Texas
March 30, 1966 to January 3, 1967
89th Congress

Ruth Thompson
U.S. House of Representatives
Republican—Michigan
January 3, 1951 to January 3, 1957
82nd through 84th Congresses

Jessica Weis
U.S. House of Representatives
Republican—New York
January 3, 1959 to January 3, 1963
86th through 87th Congresses

Effiegene Wingo
U.S. House of Representatives
Democrat—Arkansas
December 1, 1930 to March 4, 1933
71st through 72nd Congresses

Chase Going Woodhouse
U.S. House of Representatives
Democrat—Connecticut
January 3, 1945 to January 3, 1947
January 3, 1949 to January 3, 1951
79th and 81st Congresses

Appendix II
Women Ambassadors of the United States Currently Serving (Spring 1980)

Ann Cox Chambers
Ambassador
American Embassy
Brussels, Belgium

Joan M. Clark
Ambassador
American Embassy
Valletta, Malta

Anne Forrester Holloway
Ambassador
American Embassy
Bamako, Mali

Mari-Luci Jaramillo
Ambassador
American Embassy
Tegucigalpa, Honduras

Marilyn P. Johnson
Ambassador
American Embassy
Lomé, Togo

Geri M. Joseph
Ambassador
American Embassy
The Hague, Netherlands

Anne Clark Martindell
Ambassador
American Embassy
Wellington, New Zealand

Mary C. Neville
Deputy Mission Director
U.S. – AID/SANA
United States Embassy
Sana, Yemen

Barbara Newell
Ambassador
United States Permanent Representative to the United Nations Educational, Scientific and Cultural Organization
American Embassy
Paris, France

Nancy Ostrander
Ambassador
American Embassy
Paramaribo, Surinam

Nancy V. Rawls
Ambassador
American Embassy
Abidjan, Ivory Coast

Sally Shelton
Ambassador
American Embassy
Barbados, Grenada

Mabel M. Smythe
Ambassador
American Embassy
Yaoundé, Cameroon

Appendix III
Women Chiefs of Mission (COM)
1933-1980

Eugenie Moore Anderson
Denmark
October 1949 to January 1953

Bulgaria
May 1962 to December 1964
Fourth Woman COM (Ambassador)
Political Appointment

Anne L. Armstrong
United Kingdom
January 1976 to March 1977
Eighteenth Woman COM
  (Ambassador)
Political Appointment

Shirley Temple Black
Ghana
September 1974 to July 1976
Sixteenth Woman COM
  (Ambassador)
Political Appointment

Patricia M. Byrne
Mali
October 1976 to October 1979

Burma
December 1979-
Twenty-first Woman COM
  (Ambassador)
Career Diplomat

Ann Cox Chambers
Belgium
May 1977-
Twenty-third Woman COM
  (Ambassador)
Political Appointment

Joan M. Clark
Malta
March 1979-
Thirtieth Woman COM
  (Ambassador)
Career Diplomat

Betty Crites Dillon
Permanent Representative to International Civil Aviation Organization (Montreal)
November 1971 to November 1977
Twelfth Woman COM (Minister)
Political Appointment

Eileen Donovan
Barbados
July 1969 to August 1974
Eleventh Woman COM
  (Ambassador)
Career Diplomat

Ruth L. Farkas
Luxembourg
March 1973 to May 1976
Fourteenth Woman COM
  (Ambassador)
Political Appointment

Rosemary L. Ginn
Luxembourg
May 1976 to June 1977
Twentieth Woman COM
  (Ambassador)
Political Appointment

Florence Jaffray Harriman
Norway
May 1937 to April 1940
Second Woman COM (Minister)
Political Appointment

Patricia Roberts Harris
Luxembourg
June 1965 to September 1967
Ninth Woman COM (Ambassador)
Political Appointment

Anne Forrester Holloway
Mali
November 1979-
Thirty-third Woman COM
 (Ambassador)
Political Appointment

Mari-Luci Jaramillo
Honduras
September 1977-
Twenty-sixth Woman COM
 (Ambassador)
Political Appointment

Marilyn P. Johnson
Togo
October 1978-
Twenty-ninth Woman COM
 (Ambassador)
Career Diplomat

Geri M. Joseph
The Netherlands
July 1978-
Twenty-eighth Woman COM
 (Ambassador)
Political Appointment

Carol Laise
Nepal
September 1966 to June 1973
Tenth Woman COM (Ambassador)
Career Diplomat

Clare Boothe Luce
Italy
March 1953 to December 1956
Sixth Woman COM (Ambassador)
Political Appointment

Anne Clark Martindell
New Zealand
July 1979-
Thirty-second Woman COM
 (Ambassador)
Political Appointment

Marquita M. Maytag
Nepal
March 1976 to April 1977
Nineteenth Woman COM
 (Ambassador)
Political Appointment

Perle Mesta
Luxembourg
July 1949 to April 1953
Third Woman COM (Minister)
Political Appointment

Mary S. Olmsted
Papua New Guinea
November 1975 to September 1979
Solomon Islands
July 1978 to September 1979
Seventeenth Woman COM
 (Ambassador)
Career Diplomat

Nancy Ostrander
Surinam
June 1978-
Twenty-seventh Woman COM
 (Ambassador)
Career Diplomat

Ruth Bryan Owen
Denmark
April 1933 to June 1936
First Woman COM (Minister)
Political Appointment

Nancy Rawls
Togo
February 1974 to August 1976
Fifteenth Woman COM
　(Ambassador)

Ivory Coast
December 1979-
Career Diplomat

Rozanne L. Ridgway
Finland
May 1977 to February 1980
Twenty-fourth Woman COM
　(Ambassador)
Career Diplomat

Sally Angela Shelton
Barbados, Grenada and Dominica
May 1979-
Thirty-first Woman COM
　(Ambassador)
Political Appointment

Mabel M. Smythe
United Republic of the Cameroon
May 1977-
Twenty-fifth Woman COM
　(Ambassador)
Political Appointment

Margaret Joy Tibbetts
Norway
July 1964 to May 1969
Eighth Woman COM (Ambassador)
Career Diplomat

Melissa F. Wells
Guinea-Bissau and the Cape
　Verde Islands
October 1976 to March 1977
Twenty-second Woman COM
　(Ambassador)
Career Diplomat

Katherine Elkus White
Denmark
April 1964 to September 1968
Seventh Woman COM (Ambassador)
Political Appointment

Jean M. Wilkowski
Zambia
June 1972 to April 1976
Thirteenth Woman COM
　(Ambassador)
Career Diplomat

Francis E. Willis
Switzerland
July 1953 to May 1957

Norway
May 1957 to March 1961

Ceylon
March 1961 to September 1964
Fifth Woman COM (Ambassador)
Career Diplomat

Appendix IV
Women Currently Serving as Federal Judges

U.S. District Court

Susan Black
Middle District
Florida

Patricia Boyle
Eastern District
Michigan

Ellen Burns
District Court
Connecticut

Orinda Evans
Northern District
Georgia

Joyce Hens Green
District Court
District of Columbia

June Green
District Court
District of Columbia

Shirley Jones
District Court
District of Columbia

Mary Johnson Lowe
Southern District
New York

Gabrielle McDonald
Southern District
Texas

Constance Baker Motley
Southern District
New York

Mariana Pfaelzer
Central District
California

Sylvia Rambo
Middle District
Pennsylvania

Mary Anne Richey
District Court
Arizona

Mary Lou Robinson
Northern District
Arizona

Elsijane Trimble Roy
Eastern and Western District
Arkansas

Norma Shapiro
Eastern District
Pennsylvania

Zita Weinshienk
District Court
Colorado

Veronica Wicker
Eastern District
Louisiana

Rya Zobel
District Court
Massachusetts

Source: National Women's Political Caucus, 1980

U.S. Circuit Court

Betty Fletcher
Ninth Circuit
Washington

Amalya Kearse
Second Circuit
New York

Cornelia Kennedy
Sixth Circuit
Michigan

Phyllis Kravitch
Fifth Circuit
Georgia

Carolyn Randall
Fifth Circuit
Texas

Mary Schroeder
Ninth Circuit
Arizona

Delores Sloviter
Third Circuit
Pennsylvania

Patricia Wald
District of Columbia Circuit

Source: National Women's Political Caucus, 1980

Appendix V
Women Currently Serving in Government in Key Departmental, Agency, and White House Positions (Spring 1980)

[Because shifts in government positions are frequent, the following list is arranged alphabetically by office holder rather than by departments. Complete departmental and agency listings of women in key positions are available from individual departments and agencies or from the White House, Office on Women, Washington, DC 20500.]

Bess Abell
Executive Assistant to Mrs. Mondale
Office of the Vice President

Veronica M. Ahern
Director of International Affairs
Department of Commerce

Jodie T. Allen
Deputy Assistant Secretary for Policy, Evaluation and Research
Department of Labor

Anita F. Alpern
Assistant Commissioner, Planning and Research
Internal Revenue Service
Department of the Treasury

Bette B. Anderson
Under Secretary
Department of the Treasury

E. Vernice Anderson
Executive Secretary
National Science Board
National Science Foundation

Elizabeth Anderson
Executive Director
Carcinogen Assessment Group
Environmental Protection Agency

Virginia M. Armstrong
Director of Personnel
Department of Health, Education and Welfare

Evelyn L. Attix
Executive Officer
National Heart, Lung and Blood Institute
Department of Health, Education and Welfare

Margaret Ayres
Chief Counsel, Urban Mass Transportation Administration
Department of Transportation

Hope Babcock
Deputy Assistant Secretary
Energy and Minerals
Department of Interior

Barbara A. Bailar
Associate Director for Statistical Standards and Methodology
Bureau of the Census
Department of Commerce

Elizabeth E. Bailey
Member
Civil Aeronautics Board

Appendix V — Women Currently Serving in Government in Key Positions

Dorthea Baker
Administrative Law Judge
Department of Agriculture

Barbara Bankoff
Special Assistant to the
  Administrator
Environmental Protection Agency

Patricia Y. Bario
Deputy Press Secretary
The White House

Nancy Barrett
Deputy Assistant Secretary for
  Policy, Evaluation and Research
Department of Labor

Joan B. Barriage
Chief Flight Standards Division
Great Lakes Division
Federal Aviation Agency

Mary P. Bass
Inspector General
Department of Commerce

Delores Battle
Director, Office of Employment
  and Training
Department of Labor

Mary E. T. Beach
Associate Director (Small Business
  Policy and International Corporate
  Finance)
Division of Corporation Finance
Securities and Exchange Commission

Caryl S. Bernstein
Vice President for Insurance
Overseas Private Investment
  Corporation

Joan Z. Bernstein
General Counsel
Department of Health, Education
  and Welfare

Eula Bingham
Assistant Secretary for Occupational
  Safety and Health
Department of Labor

Kay Bitterman
Coordinator, Office of Food for
  Peace, AID
Department of State

Beate Bloch
Associate Solicitor for Division of
  Labor-Management Laws
Department of Labor

Julia Chang Bloch
Deputy Director
Office of African Affairs
International Communication
  Agency

Betty Bolden
Deputy Director of Personnel
  Management
Department of Labor

Carol A. Bonosaro
Assistant Staff Director for Program
  Planning and Evaluation
United States Commission on
  Civil Rights

Edna A. Boorady
AID Mission Director
Department of State

Barbara A. Boyes
Assistant Commissioner for Survey
  Design
Bureau of Labor Statistics
Department of Labor

Marilyn Bracken
Deputy Assistant Administrator for
  Program Integration and
  Information
Office of Toxic Substances
Environmental Protection Agency

June Brown
Inspector General
Department of Interior

Mary Lou Burg
Commissioner
Copyright Royalty Tribunal

Beatrice Burgoon
Director, Office of Labor-
  Management Relations Service
Department of Labor

Dillon K. Burke
Senior Staff Economist for Money
  and Finance
Council of Economic Advisors

Julia Burks
BNC Director — Courses
International Communication
  Agency

Goler T. Butcher
Assistant Administrator for AID —
  Bureau for Africa
Department of State

Carolyn K. Buttolph
Director, Systems Planning Division
Internal Revenue Service
Department of the Treasury

Isabelle R. Cappello
Administrative Law Judge
Interstate Commerce Commission

M. Kathleen Carpenter
Deputy Assistant Secretary of
  Defense, Equal Opportunity
Department of Defense

Mary Carter
Director, Southern Region Research
  Center
Science and Education
  Administration

Lois A. Chatham
Director, Division of Special Treat-
  ment and Rehabilitation Programs
Department of Health, Education
  and Welfare
National Institute of Alcohol Abuse

Antonia Handler Chayes
Under Secretary of the Air Force
(Manpower, Reserve Affairs and
  Installations)
Department of the Air Force

Nancy Chisholm
Director, Economic Market Analysis
  Division
Policy Development and Research
Department of Housing and Urban
  Development

Deborah Christie
Director, Mobility Forces Division
Department of Defense

Barbara A. Clark
Director, Bureau of Domestic
  Aviation
Civil Aeronautics Board

Eloise E. Clark
Assistant Director for Biological,
  Behavioral, and Social Sciences
National Science Foundation

Carin A. Clauss
Solicitor
Department of Labor

Joan B. Claybrook
Administrator of National Highway
  Traffic Safety Administration
Department of Transportation

Sarah W. Clements
Deputy for Materiel Acquisition
Department of the Army

Ruth C. Clusen
Assistant Secretary for Environment
Department of Energy

Appendix V — Women Currently Serving in Government in Key Positions

Barbara Coleman
Associate Administrator
Food and Nutrition Service
Department of Agriculture

Roxanne Barton Conlin
U.S. Attorney
Southern District of Iowa
Department of Justice

Michele B. Corash
General Counsel
Environmental Protection Agency

Nina W. Cornell
Chief, Office Plans and Policy
Federal Communications
    Commission

Mary E. Corning
Assistant Director for International
    Programs
Department of Health, Education
    and Welfare
National Library of Medicine

Leonora Cross
Director, Editorial and Publications
    Management
Department of Health, Education
    and Welfare
Division of Public Affairs

Angeliki Cutchis
Director, Tactical Air Analyses
Department of Defense

Alice Daniel
Assistant Attorney General
Civil Division
Department of Justice

Patsy A. Danner
Co-Chair
Ozarks Regional Commission

Joan M. Davenport
Assistant Secretary, Energy and
    Minerals
Department of Interior

Evelyn T. Davidson
Superintendent
United States Mint

Karen Davis
Deputy Assistant Secretary for
    Planning and Evaluation Health
Department of Health, Education
    and Welfare

Lynn E. Davis
Deputy Assistant Secretary of
    Defense for Policy Plans and
    NSC Affairs
Department of Defense

Ruth M. Davis
Deputy Under Secretary of Defense
    for Research and Advanced
    Technology
Department of Defense

Patricia M. Derian
Assistant Secretary for Human
    Rights and Humanitarian Affairs
Department of State

Edith Jones Dobelle
Staff Director
The White House

Christine S. Dodson
Staff Secretary
National Security Council

Virginia M. Dondy
Deputy Special Assistant to the
    Secretary and Deputy Secretary of
    Defense
Department of Defense

Patricia K. Drew
Deputy Advocate of the
    Advisory Council
Small Business Administration

B. Sue Dueitt
Deputy for Human Systems
    and Resources
Office of Assistant Secretary of
    the Army
Department of Defense

208 / Appendix V — Women Currently Serving in Government in Key Positions

Constance Dupre
Associate General Counsel
Legal Division
Equal Employment Opportunity
 Commission

Jane M. Edmisten
Deputy General Counsel
Merit Systems Protection Board

Rollee H. Efros
Assistant General Counsel
General Government Matters
General Accounting Office

Marie D. Eldridge
Administrator, National Center for
 Education Statistics
Department of Health, Education
 and Welfare

Anne M. Elledge
Director, Office of Personnel Policy
 and Communications
Department of Health, Education
 and Welfare

Kathryn Elliott
Director of Public Affairs
National Endowment for the
 Humanities

M. Diane Elliott
Assistant Director, Office of
 Legislative Affairs
Community Services Administration

Nancy Halliday Ely
Assistant Legal Adviser for African
 Affairs
Department of State

Joyce Evans
Assistant General Counsel
Office of Personnel Management

Rita I. Fair
Executive Assistant to the Chair
Federal Home Loan Bank Board

Kathleen Mathea Falco
Assistant Secretary of State
International Narcotics Matters
Department of State

Lucy A. Falcone
Deputy Assistant Secretary for
 Domestic Economic Policy
 Coordination
Department of Commerce

Francesta Farmer
Director, Office of Interagency
 Coordination
Equal Employment Opportunity
 Commission

Betty J. Farwell
Director of Real Estate
Office of the Chief of Engineers
Department of the Army

Ellen Feingold
Director of Civil Rights
Department of Transportation

Florence Fiori
Director, Bureau of Health Facilities
 Financing, Compliance and
 Conversion
Department of Health, Education
 and Welfare

Kathryn N. Folger
Legislative Management Officer
Office of Congressional Affairs
Department of State

Carol T. Foreman
Assistant Secretary for Food and
 Consumer Services
Department of Agriculture

Susan Foster
Deputy Under Secretary of
 Intergovernmental Affairs
Department of Health, Education
 and Welfare

Appendix V — Women Currently Serving in Government in Key Positions / 209

Charlotte Frank
Director of Office Field Services
Equal Opportunity Commission

Arvonne Fraser
Coordinator, Office of Women in
   Development, AID
Department of State

Frankie Freeman
Inspector General
Community Services Administration

Margaret Freeston
Deputy General Counsel
Consumer Product Safety
   Commission

Jennifer Froistad
Director
Development Education Peace Corps

Ellen Frost
Deputy Assistant Secretary of
   Defense for International
   Economic Affairs
Department of Defense

Catherine H. Furlong
Senior Statistician
Council of Economic Advisors

Monica Gallagher
Associate Solicitor for Plan
   Benefits Security
Department of Labor

Angelina Garcia
Director, Office of Personnel
   Services
International Communication
   Agency

Frances Garcia
Commissioner
Copyright Royalty Tribunal

Nancy Garrett
Associate Director, Administration
National Parks Service
Department of Interior

Anne J. Geary
Assistant Director, Division of
   Consumer Affairs
Federal Reserve System

Katherine B. Gillman
Senior Staff Member
Oceans and International
   Environment
Council of Environmental Quality

Caroline Davis Gleiter
Assistant Staff Director for Program
   and Policy Review
United States Commission on
   Civil Rights

Jennie Goicoechea
Administrative Law Judge
National Labor Relations Board

Cynthia Graae
Assistant Staff Director for
   Federal Evaluation
United States Commission on
   Civil Rights

Andrea Diane Graham
Assistant Director for Affirmative
   Employment Programs
Office of Personnel Management

Sally H. Greenberg
Associate Director for Executive
   Personnel and Management
   Development
Office of Personnel Management

Mary Greenwood
Associate Deputy Director for
   Extension
Department of Agriculture

Stella Hackel
Director
Bureau of the Mint

Tila Maria de Hancock
Assistant to the Secretary for
   International Affairs
Department of Health, Education
   and Welfare

210 / Appendix V — Women Currently Serving in Government in Key Positions

Ruth S. Hanft
Acting Deputy Assistant Secretary for Health Research, Statistics, and Technology
Department of Health, Education and Welfare

Gladys Chang Keith Hardy
Deputy Director for Management
National Institute for Education
Department of Health, Education and Welfare

Elizabeth J. Harper
Deputy Assistant Secretary for Visa Services
Bureau of Consular Affairs
Department of State

Donna R. Harrigan
Regional Director, Chicago
Small Business Administration

Gail Harrison
Assistant to the Vice President for Issues and Development and Domestic Policy
The White House

Janet O. Hart
Director, Division of Consumer Affairs
Federal Reserve System

Madeline Hastings
Director, Office of Existing and Moderate Rehabilitation House
Department of Health, Education and Welfare

Barbara Heller
Deputy Under Secretary
Department of Interior

Alexis M. Herman
Director of Women's Bureau
Department of Labor

Allison B. Herrick
Associate Assistant Administrator for Program and Policy
Office of Planning and Budget AID

Ruth R. Hess
Director, Budget Policy and Procedures Division
Department of the Navy

Laurabeth H. Hicks
Director, Division of Secondary Occupational Planning
Department of Health, Education and Welfare

Mary N. Hilton
Deputy Director, Women's Bureau
Department of Labor

Mary Elizabeth Hoinkes
Assistant Legal Adviser for Oceans, Environment and Scientific Affairs
Department of State

Joan Hollenbach
Chief Counsel
Occupational Safety and Health Review Commission

Sheila S. Hollis
Director, Office of Enforcement
Department of Energy

Susan Holloway
Special Assistant for Administration
Office of the Vice President
The White House

Helena Howe
Director, Community College Unit
Department of Health, Education and Welfare

Mary Finch Hoyt
Press Secretary and East Wing Coordinator
The White House

Appendix V — Women Currently Serving in Government in Key Positions / 211

Ann H. Hughes
Deputy Director, Office of International Trade Policy
Department of Commerce

Merna Hurd
Director, Water Planning Division
Environmental Protection Agency

Perdita Huston
Regional Director for Northern Africa, Near East Asia and Pacific
Peace Corps

Alice Stone Ilchman
Associate Director for Educational and Cultural Affairs
International Communication Agency

Susan J. Irving
Special Assistant to the Chairman
Council of Economic Advisors

Maxine Isaacs
Deputy Press Secretary to the Vice President and Special Assistant for Women's Issues
Office of the Vice President
The White House

Marilyn E. Jacox
Group Leader for Environmental Chemical Processes
Department of Commerce

Harriett Jenkins
Director of Equal Opportunity Programs
National Aeronautics and Space Administration

Issie Jenkins
Acting General Counsel
Equal Employment Opportunity Commission

Gloria C. Jiminez
Federal Insurance Administrator
Federal Emergency Management Agency

Mary K. Johrde
Head, Office for Oceanographic Facilities and Support
National Science Foundation

Anne P. Jones
Commissioner
Federal Communications Commission

Wynfred Joshua
Defense Intelligence Officer
European and Soviet Political/Military Affairs
Department of Defense

Margaret W. Kahliff
Member, Board of Directors
Export-Import Bank of the United States

Shirley Kallek
Associate Director for Economic Fields
Department of Commerce

Leslie Lazar Kanuk
Maritime Commission Commissioner
Federal Maritime Commission

Roberta Karmel
Commissioner
Securities and Exchange Commission

Audrey A. Kaslow
Commissioner
United States Parole Board

Sally Katzen
General Counsel, Council on Wage and Price Stability
The White House

Barbara Kelley
General Counsel
ACTION

Helen Kelley
Director, Older Americans Volunteer Programs
ACTION

Appendix V — Women Currently Serving in Government in Key Positions

Patricia S. Kendall
Executive Officer, Office of
  Management, Policy and Budget
General Services Administration

Joan F. Kessler
United States Attorney, Milwaukee
Department of Justice

Sylvia D. Kessler
Member, Review Board
Federal Communications
  Commission

Geraldine R. Keyes
Administrative Law Judge
Interstate Commerce Commission

Martha Keys
Special Adviser to the Secretary
Department of Health, Education
  and Welfare

Mary E. King
Deputy Director
ACTION

Susan Bennett King
Chair
Consumer Product Safety
  Commission

Nancy Kingsbury
Director, Office of Management
Peace Corps

Platonia Kirkwood
Administrative Law Judge
National Labor Relations Board

Josephine H. Klein
Administrative Law Judge
National Labor Relations Board

Marjorie Fine Knowles
Inspector General
Department of Labor

Helen S. Kupperman
Assistant General Counsel for
  General Law
National Aeronautics and Space
  Administration

Joann Langston
Associate Executive Director
Hazard Identification and Analysis
Consumer Product Safety
  Commission

Allie B. Latimer
General Counsel
General Services Administration

Esther C. Lawton
Deputy Director of Personnel
Department of the Treasury

Carolyn K. Leonard
Director, Internal Revenue Service
  Center
Department of the Treasury

Frances Lewine
Deputy Director of Public Affairs
Department of Transportation

Eleanor G. Lewis
Director of the Executive Secretariat
  for the Office of the Secretary
Department of Transportation

Jean P. Lewis
Assistant Administrator for
  Congressional and Legislative
  Affairs
Small Business Administration

Mary F. Leyland
Assistant Director for Administra-
  tion and Finance
Peace Corps

Lillian C. Liburdi
Associate Administrator for Budget
  and Program Development
Urban Mass Transportation
Department of Transportation

Appendix V — Women Currently Serving in Government in Key Positions

Diane R. Liff
Assistant General Counsel for
    Litigation
Department of Transportation

Sarajane Littlefield
AID Mission Director
Colombo, Sri Lanka
Department of State

Florence Lowe
Assistant to the Chair, Press
National Endowment for the Arts

Madeline F. MacBean
Personal Assistant to the First Lady
The White House

Virginia Dill McCarthy
United States Attorney, Indiana
Department of Justice

Adoreen McCormick
Legislative Liaison Officer
Library of Congress

Margaret E. McCormick
Deputy Counsel for the
    Vice President
Office of the Vice President
The White House

Patricia McFate
Deputy Chair
National Endowment for the
    Humanities

Patricia G. McGinnis
Deputy Associate Director for
    Human Resources Division
Office of Management and Budget

Marlene McGuirl
Chief, American British Law
    Division
Library of Congress

Barbara P. MacKenzie
Director of Congressional Relations
Commodity Futures Trading
    Commission

Ruth McLendon
Deputy Assistant Secretary for
    Overseas Citizens Services
Consular Affairs
Department of State

Martha A. McSteen
Regional Commissioner
Dallas, SSA
Department of Health, Education
    and Welfare

Margaret Maguire
Deputy Director for Planning, Heri-
    tage Conservation and Recreation
    Service
Department of Interior

Opal Mann
Assistant Administrator, Home
    Economics
Department of Agriculture

Janice Mapp
Director, Office of Community
    Youth Employment Programs
Employment and Training
    Administration

Mildred K. Marcy
Senior Advisor
Educational and Cultural Affairs
International Communication
    Agency

Ann M. Martin
Associate Commissioner for
    Occupational Planning
Department of Health, Education
    and Welfare

Patricia A. Mathis
Director, Merit Systems Review
    and Studies
Merit Systems Protection Board

Lorena Matthews
Deputy Administrator
National Credit Union
    Administration

Margot Mazeau
Assistant General Counsel
United States Arms Control and
    Disarmament Agency

Doris Meissner
Deputy Associate Attorney General
Department of Justice

Marilyn J. Melkonian
Deputy Assistant Secretary for
    Multifamily Housing Programs
Department of Housing and Urban
    Development

Janice K. Mendenhall
Assistant Administrator for Management, Policy and Budget
General Services Administration

Evelyn K. Merker
Examiner-in-Chief
Department of Commerce

Grace Mickelson
Director, Intergovernmental Affairs
Department of Health, Education
    and Welfare

Betty J. Miller
Regional Administrator, Chairperson
Federal Regional Council
Department of Housing and Urban
    Development

Holly Miller
Acting Deputy Under Secretary
Department of Interior

Kathryn Morrison
Deputy Commissioner of Aging
Department of Health, Education
    and Welfare

Azie Taylor Morton
Treasurer
Department of the Treasury

Brenda P. Murray
Administrative Law Judge
Federal Regulatory Commission

Marian Pearlman Nease
Commissioner
Federal Mine Safety and Health
    Review Commission

Marcia Sue Nelson
Director, Policy Analysis, Integration
    and Evaluation
Department of Labor

Carol A. Nemeyer
Associate Librarian for National
    Programs
Library of Congress

Joan M. Nicholson
Director, Office of Public Awareness
Environmental Protection Agency

Eleanor Holmes Norton
Chair
Equal Employment Opportunity
    Commission

Janet L. Norwood
Commissioner
Bureau of Labor Statistics
Department of Labor

Graciela Olivarez
Director
Community Services Administration

Andrea M. Ordin
United States Attorney, Los Angeles
Department of Justice

Karen Paget
Deputy Associate Director for
    Domestic and Anti-Poverty
    Operations
ACTION

Mary L. Parramore
Special Assistant to the National
    Science Board Chair
National Science Foundation

June Patron
Director of Coal Mine Workers'
    Compensation
Department of Labor

Appendix V — Women Currently Serving in Government in Key Positions / 215

Anne Perkins
Director
Intergovernmental and Congressional Affairs

Esther Peterson
Special Assistant to the President for Consumer Affairs
The White House

Betty Pickett
Deputy Director
National Institute of Child Health and Human Development
Department of Health, Education and Welfare

Ava D. Poe
Deputy Clerk of the Court
Tax Court of the United States

Barbara Pomeroy
Executive Director
United States National Commission on the International Year of the Child

Elsa Porter
Assistant Secretary for Administration
Department of Commerce

Ersa H. Poston
Vice Chair
Merit Systems Protection Board

Gretchen Poston
Social Secretary to the First Lady
The White House

Gloria Pratt
Director, Office of Foreign Economic Policy
Bureau of International Labor Affairs
Department of Labor

Ruth Prokop
Chair
Merit Systems Protection Board

Marjorie Quandt
Assistant Chief Medical Director for Administration
Veterans Administration

Elizabeth A. Rainwater
Deputy Assistant to the President for Research
The White House

Lucia J. Rather
Director for Cataloging
Library of Congress

Elizabeth Raymond
Assistant to the Secretary for Labor Relations
Office of Labor Relations
Department of Housing and Urban Development

Lillian D. Regelson
Director, Office of Policy Analysis and Management
Office of Toxic Substances
Environmental Protection Agency

Inez S. Reid
Deputy General Counsel for Regulation Review
Department of Health, Education and Welfare

Lucille Reifman
Deputy Director for Program Evaluation
Department of Commerce

Helen C. Reiner
Chief Counsel to Board Member Murphy
National Labor Relations Board

Margaret Rhoades
Acting Associate Commissioner for Public Affairs, SSA
Department of Health, Education and Welfare

Dorothy P. Rice
Director, National Center for
  Health Statistics
Department of Health, Education
  and Welfare

Barbara A. Ringer
Register of Copyrights
Copyright Office
Library of Congress

Earldean V. Robbins
Administrative Law Judge
Division of Judges
National Labor Relations Board

Dorothy Robins-Mowry
Country Affairs Officer
North African, Near Eastern Affairs
  and South Asian Affairs
International Communication
  Agency

Janice M. Rosenak
Deputy Director, Office of
  Proceedings
Section of Rates
Interstate Commerce Commission

Beatrice Rosenberg
Assistant General Counsel
Appeals Branch
Equal Employment Opportunity
  Commission

Dorothy Rosenberg
Executive Assistant to the Secretary
Smithsonian Institution

Joan R. Rosenblatt
Deputy Director, Center for Applied
  Mathematics
Department of Commerce

Mary E. Ross
Director, Division of Retirement and
  Survivors Benefits
Department of Health, Education
  and Welfare

Lois W. Roth
Field Operations Officer
International Communication
  Agency, Paris

Bertha W. Rubenstein
Executive Assistant, Directorate for
  Biological, Behavioral and Social
  Sciences
National Science Foundation

Deborah Sale
Special Assistant for Advance
Office of the Vice President

Kathleen H. Sauerbrunn
Association General Counsel for
  Regulatory Programs
Department of Housing and Urban
  Development

Janet D. Saxon
Administrative Law Judge
United States International Trade
  Commission

Gloria Schaffer
Member
Civil Aeronautics Board

Lois Schiffer
Chief of General Litigation Section
Land and Natural Resources Division
Department of Justice

Katherine P. Schirmer
Association Director for Energy and
  Natural Resources
Domestic Policy Staff

Barbara Schlei
Administrator, Agricultural Market-
  ing Service
Department of Agriculture

Robin B. Schwartzman
Deputy Director, Bureau of
  Trade Regulation
Department of Commerce

Appendix V — Women Currently Serving in Government in Key Positions

Mildred L. Seidman
Chief, Review Section, Tax Division
Department of Justice

Barbara S. Selfridge
Deputy Associate Director for Special
  Studies Division
Office of Management and Budget

Donna E. Shalala
Assistant Secretary for Policy
  Development and Research
Department of Housing and Urban
  Development

Georgiana Sheldon
Commissioner
Federal Energy Regulatory
  Commission

Nancy M. Sherman
Administrative Law Judge
Division of Judges
National Labor Relations Board

Benita A. Sidwell
Deputy Director of Administration
  and Management
National Aeronautics and Space
  Administration

Henrietta McArthur Singletary
Deputy Assistant Secretary for Rural
  Development
Department of Agriculture

Courtenay Slater
Chief Economist
Department of Commerce

Edith Barksdale Sloan
Commissioner and Vice-Chair
Consumer Product Safety
  Commission

Linda Lorraine Smith
Assistant to the Director for
  Administration
Office of Management and Budget

Helen Smits
Director, Health Standards and
  Quality Bureau
Health Care Financial Administration
Department of Health, Education
  and Welfare

Mary M. Snavely
Deputy Assistant Secretary of the
  Navy for Manpower
Department of the Navy

Diane Steed
Chief, Regulatory Policy Branch
Office of Management and Budget

Paula Stern
Commissioner
United States International Trade
  Commission

Almira Stevenson
Administrative Law Judge
National Labor Relations Board

Roma Stewart
Director
Office of Civil Rights
Department of Health, Education
  and Welfare

Lucille F. Stickel
Director, Fish and Wildlife Service
Department of Interior

Eleanor J. Stockwell
Senior Research Division Officer
Division of Research and Statistics
Federal Reserve System

Velma M. Strode
Director, Office of Equal Employ-
  ment Opportunity
Department of Labor

Brereton Sturtevant
Examiner-in-Chief
Department of Commerce

Naomi R. Sweeney
Deputy Assistant Director
Legislative Reference Division
Office of Management and Budget

Evangeline Swift
General Counsel
Merit Systems Protection Board

Patricia A. Szervo
Deputy General Counsel
Department of the Navy

Margery Tabankin
Director for VISTA and the
  ACTION Education Programs

Linda Tarr-Whelan
Deputy Assistant to the President
Office of Sarah Weddington
Women's Concerns

Nancy Hay Teeters
Governor
Federal Reserve System

Doris Thompson
Director, Office of Civil Rights
Environmental Protection Agency

Mary Ann Tighe
Deputy Chair for Programs
National Endowment for the Arts

Adrienne F. Timothy
Assistant Associate Administrator
  for Space Science
National Aeronautics and Space
  Administration

Brooke Trent
Director, Office Program
Planning and Evaluation
Equal Employment Opportunity
  Commission

Cherry Yuriko Tsutsumida
Director, Office of Congressional
  Affairs
Health Care Financing Administration
Department of Health, Education
  and Welfare

Mildred L. Tyssowski
Director of Program Operations
Department of Health, Education
  and Welfare

Ruth Van Cleve
Director, Office of Territorial Affairs
Department of Interior

Elizabeth Verville
Assistant Legal Advisor
East Asian and Pacific Affairs
Department of State

Daisy Voigt
Director of Public Affairs
Equal Employment Opportunity
  Commission

Frances M. Voorde
Deputy Appointments Secretary
The White House

Omi Gail Walden
Adviser to the Secretary
Conservation and Solar Application
Department of Energy

Joyce Walker
Deputy Associate Director for Transportation, Commerce and Housing
Office of Management and Budget

Mary L. Walker
Chief, Special Litigation Section
Department of Justice

Tamara Wall
Administrative Law Judge
National Labor Relations Board

Joan Wallace
Assistant Secretary for Administration
Department of Agriculture

Sylvia L. Waller
Scientific and Technical Advisor
Department of the Air Force

Appendix V — Women Currently Serving in Government in Key Positions

Ethel Bent Walsh
Commissioner
Equal Employment Opportunity
 Commission

Jan Watlington
Director for Legislative and Inter-
 governmental Affairs
ACTION

Barbara M. Watson
Assistant Secretary for Consular
 Affairs
Department of State

Margery Waxman
General Counsel
Office of Personnel Management

Sarah Weddington
Assistant to the President
The White House

Lorraine A. Weinberger
Member, Board of Patent
 Interferences
Department of Commerce

Mitzi M. Wertheim
Deputy Under Secretary of the Navy
Department of the Navy

Jeanne Westphal
Deputy Assistant Secretary for
 Tourism
Department of Commerce

Anne Wexler
Assistant to the President
The White House

Frances L. White
Deputy Assistant General Counsel
Department of Health, Education
 and Welfare

Joan Wieder
Administrative Law Judge
Division of Judges
National Labor Relations Board

Susan Williams
Assistant Secretary for Governmental
 and Public Affairs
Department of Transportation

Rilla Moran Woods
Deputy Commissioner of Transpor-
 tation and Public Utilities Service
General Services Administration

Charlene Woody
Deputy Assistant Director
Office of Systems Development
Library of Congress

Suzanne Woolsey
Associate Director for Human
 Resources, Veterans
Office of Management and Budget

Ellen S. Wormser
Director, Division of Health Budget
 Analysis
Department of Health, Education
 and Welfare

Patricia W. Worthy
Deputy Assistant Secretary for
 Regulatory Functions
Department of Housing and Urban
 Development

Anne Wright
Special Assistant for Constituent
 Services
Office of the Vice President

Clinton Wright
Director, Office of Training, Educa-
 tion, Consultation and Federal
 Agency Programs
Department of Labor

Gertrude Wright
Director of Legislation
Human Development Services
Department of Health, Education
 and Welfare

Mary Wright
Deputy Regional Director
Office of Surface Mining, Region V
Department of Interior

Maryann Wyrsch
Director, Budget Office
Department of Labor

Darlene Yarbrough
Central Legal Staff Director
United States Court of Military
 Appeals

Jane Hurt Yarn
Member
Council on Environmental Quality

Electra Yourke
Confidential Assistant to the Director
Equal Employment Opportunity
 Commission

Dorothy S. Yufer
Deputy Director
Strategic and Naval Warfare Systems
Department of Defense

Michele Zarubica
Special Assistant to the Assistant
 Secretary for Energy and Minerals
Department of Interior

Lynne Zusman
Special Litigation Counsel
Civil Division
Department of Justice

Index

Abortion, 2, 8, 32, 47, 56, 74, 78, 99, 105-106, 145, 154, 155
Abzug, Bella, 1-3, 40, 46, 83, 87, 98, 99, 134
Acheson, Dean, 5
Adams, Abigail, 8-9
Addams, Jane, 126
Affirmative Action, 2, 21, 53
AFL-CIO, 37, 120, 122
Africa, 6, 11, 16, 142
African Subcommittee (House), 16
Aged, legislation for, 11, 13, 19, 21, 27, 32, 51, 91
Aging, Agency on, 92
Aging, Select Committee on, 18, 26, 48, 78, 108, 118, 144
Aging, Special Committee on, 89, 115
Agnew, Spiro, 74, 84
Agricultural workers, 36, 92, 94
Agriculture, 92, 94, 141
    Committee (House), 94
    Committee (Senate), 115
    Department of, 125, 150, 154
Aid to Families with Dependent Children (AFDC), 32
Air Force (U.S.), 14
Alabama, 151-53
Albert, Carl, 84, 150
Albertus Magnus College, 66
Alioto, Joseph, 42
Amalgamated Clothing Workers of America (ACWA), 122
Americans for Democratic Action (ADA), 5
Anderson, Eugenie, 4-7
Anderson, John, 4, 5
Anthony, Susan B., 117, 157
Appropriations Committee (House), 13, 19, 60, 87, 141, 142
Arab states, 16
Armed Services Committee (House), 2, 26, 74-75, 133, 134, 135, 136, 139
Armstrong, Anne Legendre, 7-9
Armstrong, Tobin, 8
Army and Navy Nurse Corps, 15
Asian Americans, 80, 113
Atlantic Institute for International Affairs, 9
Atomic Energy Commission, 37, 104, 130
Austin, Albert, 102
Automobile Emission Standards, 21

Bailey, John, 50-51
Bakewell, Claude, 149
Banking and Currency Committee (Senate), 66, 115, 150
Banking, Currency and Housing Committee (House), 13, 57
Banking, Finance and Urban Affairs Committee (House), 45-46, 118, 146

Banking, Housing and Urban Affairs Committee (Senate), 89
Barat College, 23
Barbados, 28
Barnard College, 36
Bayh, Birch, 63
Bedford-Stuyvesant Political League (BSPL), 28, 29
Belmont, Oliver H. P. (Mrs.), 102
Benson, Ezra Taft, 94
Berea College, 95
Bicentennial Arrangements, Joint Committee on Congressional, 12
Bicentennial celebration (U.S.), 9, 12
Bilandic, Michael, 23
Black, Charles A., 10
Black, Shirley Temple, 9-12
Blacks. *See* Minorities
Blue Collar Caucus, 118
Boggs, Corinne C. (Lindy), 12-14, 18
Boggs, Hale, 12, 13
Bohen, Fred, 45
Bolton, Chester, 15
Bolton, Frances P., 15-18, 117
Bolton, Oliver P., 15, 17
Bolton Bill, 15
Boothe, William F., 102
Boschwitz, Rudy, 83
Boston University, 85, 99
Bouchles, George, 144
Bouchles, Georgia, 144
Bouquard, Marilyn Lloyd, 18-19
Brazil, 103, 105
Brewer, Albert, 153
Brigham Young University, 54, 122
Brokaw, Ann Clare, 102
Brokaw, George, 102
Brooklyn College, 28
Brown, Jerry, 42
Brown, Pat, 80
Bryn Mawr, 122
Budget Committee (House), 75, 78, 89
Bulgaria, 4, 6
Burgin, William O., 125
Burke, Yvonne Braithwaite, 19-22, 134
Burma, 104
Busing, 53, 74, 85
Butler, Donald C., 59
Byrne, Jane Burke, 22-25, 43
Byron, Beverly Butcher, 18, 25-27
Byron, Goodloe E., 25
Byron, Katharine E., 25, 26
Byron, Mary, 26
Byron, William D., 25, 26

Cadet Nurse Corps, 15
Cahill, William T., 44

221

Califano, Joseph, 62, 63
California, 10, 19, 20, 21, 36, 37, 48, 69, 80, 81, 86, 87, 88
  Court of Appeals, 80, 81
  University of, 19, 69, 87
Cambodia, 13, 32, 67, 77, 134, 146
Campaign financing, 29, 47-48, 76, 79, 116, 134-35, 139
Carey, Hugh, 98, 99, 100
Carlow College, 40
Carpenter, Liz, 40
Carswell, G. Harrold, 139
Carter, Jimmy, 4, 22, 40, 42, 48, 51, 61, 62, 63, 70, 80, 81, 82-83, 95, 116, 120, 123, 154, 155, 158, 159
Case, Clifford, 45
Cassetti, Alphonse L., 157
Celler, Emanuel, 56, 76
Central Intelligence Agency (CIA), 6, 108
Chiang Kai-shek, 104
Chicago, University of, 63, 99, 112
Child abuse, 47, 49
Children's Bureau, 37, 120
China, 11, 104, 136, 153, 154
Chinese Cultural Foundation, 43
Chisholm, Conrad, 28
Chisholm, Shirley, 2, 20, 28-31, 85
Civic affairs, 26, 117, 157
Civil Defense Agency, 94
Civil Rights, 1, 15, 39, 45, 84, 85, 104, 152, 153
  Act (1954), 1, 56
  Commission, 39
Civil Service Commission, 120
Collins, Cardiss Robertson, 18, 31-32
Colorado, 33, 34, 35, 133, 135
  College, 108
Columbia School of Social Work, 126
Columbia University, 1, 28, 44, 101, 120, 122
Commerce, Department of, 19, 95, 96, 97, 158, 159
Communism, 4, 5, 6, 103, 105, 139
Community outreach, 28, 34, 35, 98-99, 148
Community Services Administration, 32
Comprehensive Education and Training Act (CETA), 20, 32, 144
Concordia College, 94
Condé Nast, 44, 45
Congressional Black Caucus, 21, 30, 32, 85
Congressional Club, 12
Congressional Rural Caucus, 92
Congressional Senior Intern Program, 26-27
Congressional Spouses Club, 92
Congressional Wives Forum, 12
Congresswomen's Caucus, 13, 18, 20, 21, 27, 30, 32, 48, 57, 67, 74, 78, 82, 117, 118, 134, 136, 142, 145
Connecticut, 50, 51, 104
Conservation, 17, 60, 115
  See also Ecology
Consumer Advisory Committee, President's, 116

Consumer affairs, 24, 45, 46, 49, 51, 79, 115, 116, 121-22, 123, 124, 127, 149
Consumer Interests, President's Commission on, 123
Consumer Protection Act, 149
Consumers' League (New York), 119
Coolidge, Calvin, 44
Corsi, Ginny, 100
Costanza, Midge, 158
Courter, James, 108
Cox, Archibald, 69
Credit, for women, 2, 13, 66, 112, 134, 146, 154
Cuba, 153
Cuban Missile Crisis, 139
Cuomo, Mario M., 100
Cuyahoga Community College, 117

Daley, Richard, 23, 24
Daley, Richard, Jr., 24
Daniel, Dan, 135
Daughters of the American Revolution (DAR), 15, 104
Day care, 2, 28, 29, 66, 67, 82, 108, 113, 123, 141
Defense
  Department of, 77
  expenditures, 2, 20, 26, 37, 74, 76, 77-78, 85, 87, 91, 113, 133, 134, 135, 139, 144
Democratic Alternative, 1
Democratic-Farmer-Labor Party (DFL), 4-5, 6, 94
Democratic Governors Association, 51
Democratic National Committee, 5, 24, 37, 58, 110
Democratic National Convention, 12, 20, 24, 29, 37, 50, 51, 62, 100, 110, 159
Dempsey, John, 50
Denmark, 4, 5, 6
Depression, U.S. (1929), 9, 36, 118-19
Dewey, Thomas, 157
Dick, Nancy, 33-35
Disability compensation, 46
Discrimination
  race, 53, 54, 80, 104
  sex, 2, 13, 30, 51, 53, 54, 55-56, 66, 78, 118, 134, 150
Displaced homemakers, 2, 20, 34-35, 123, 154
Displaced Homemakers Assistance Act, 117
Domestic Council, 8
Domestic International Business Administration, 96
Domestic violence, 12-13, 14, 49, 110, 154
Domestic Violence Prevention and Services Act, 110
Domestic workers, 29, 85
Douglas, Helen Gahagan, 36-38
Douglas, Melvyn, 36, 37
Downs, LeRoy, 104

Draft, 2, 16, 66, 136, 157
Duke University, 95, 96

Eagleton, Thomas, 39
Eaton, Charles, 44
Ecology, 21, 43, 60, 67, 85, 108, 130
  See also Conservation
Economic Affairs, Bureau of, 96
Economic Commission for Europe, 6
Economic Committee, Joint, 57
Economic Development Administration (EDA), 96-97
Economic policy, 96-97
Education, 39, 40, 41, 53, 54, 74, 80, 81, 85, 115, 130
Education, Department of, 62, 80, 81, 138
  See also Health, Education and Welfare, Department of
Education and Labor Committee (House), 30, 53, 54, 60, 113, 141
Eisenhower, Dwight D., 5, 16, 45, 68, 71, 72, 94, 103, 104, 105, 139, 157
Election reform, 47, 48, 91
Elementary and Secondary School Amendment Act, 113
Energy
  Conservation in Buildings Act, 13
  Department of, 143, 144
  issues, 21, 27, 33, 37, 91, 130, 131, 135, 144
Equal Credit Opportunity Act, 146
Equal Employment Opportunities Commission (EEOC), 56
Equal Pay Act, 53
Equal Rights Amendment (ERA), 2, 12, 18, 33, 40-41, 45, 46, 48, 53, 55, 56, 57, 60, 66, 67, 76, 78, 89, 102, 106, 123, 134, 141, 145, 150, 154, 155

Factory inspection, 119, 149
Factory workers, 37, 119, 120
Fair Labor Standards Act, 119
Farber, Barry, 2
Farbskin, Leonard, 1
Farenthold, Frances Tarlton (Sissy), 39-41
Farenthold, George, 39
Farmer, James, 29
Farm laborers, 36, 92, 94
Farm Security Administration, 36
Fascism, 103-104
Federal Bureau of Investigation (FBI), 87
Federal Civil Defense Administration, 157
Federal Employee Flexible and Compressed Work Schedule Act, 117
Federal Employee Part-time Career Employment Act, 67, 117
Federal Energy Administration, 135
Federal Property Council, 8
Federal Security Agency, 72

Feinstein, Bertram, 42
Feinstein, Dianne, 42-43
Fenwick, Hugh, 44
Fenwick, Millicent, 13, 44-47, 144
Ferraro, Geraldine, 47-49
Fleger, Anthony, 16
Florida, University of, 74
Food and Drug Administration, 149
Food stamp program, 20, 74, 144, 150
Ford, Betty, 8-9
Ford, Gerald, 7, 8, 9, 56, 68, 69, 70, 77, 84, 150
Fordham University, 49
Foreign Affairs Committee (House), 16, 37, 44, 108
Foreign aid, 142
Foreign Intelligence Advisory Board, 105
Foreign policy, 11, 89, 104, 139
Foreign Policy, Organization of Government for the Conduct of, 8
Foreign Relations Committee, 44, 105
Freeman, Orville, 4, 5, 94
Frelinghuysen, Peter, 44, 45
Frenzel, Bill, 74
Friedan, Betty, 112
Friendship, Commerce and Navigation, Treaty of (Denmark), 5
Friends of the Earth, 43

Gahagan, Walter, 36
Gay movement, 29, 42
George Washington University, 63
Germany, 104, 127
Ghana, 11
Goldwater, Barry, 14, 103
Goranites, James, 144
Goranites, Mary, 144
Goucher College, 40
Government Operations Committee (House), 32, 57, 66, 144
Grasso, Ella, 50-52
Grasso, Thomas, 51
Great Britain, 7, 8, 9
Green, Edith Starrett, 53-55, 113
Greenland, 5
Griffiths, Hicks, 57-58
Griffiths, Martha W., 55-59, 85
Gruening, Ernest, 127

Hagen, Harold, 94
Hammond, Ogden Haggerty, 44
Hansen, Julia Butler, 59-61, 101
Harriman, Averell, 99
Harrington, Patrick J., 65
Harris, Patricia Roberts, 61-65
Hart, Gary, 92
Harvard University, 57, 77, 133, 135, 159
Hathaway, William D., 139
Havenner, Frank, 87

224 / Index

Hawaii, 105, 111, 112, 113
  University of, 112
Health and Human Resources, Department of
  See Health, Education and Welfare, Department of
Health, Education and Welfare, Department of, 46, 61, 62, 63, 71, 72, 74, 81, 92
Health issues, 32, 33, 37, 51, 57, 63, 67, 72, 76, 91, 100, 115, 141, 142, 143
Heart-break strike, 122
Hébert, F. Edward, 12, 133, 134
Heckler, John, 66
Heckler, Margaret, 13, 65-68, 78, 144
Helsinki Accords, 46
Helsinki Commission on Security and Cooperation in Europe, 46
Higher Education Act (1965, 1967), 53, 113
Higher Education Facilities Act, 53
Hills, Carla Anderson, 68-71
Hills, Roderick, 69, 70
Hispanic Americans, 8
  See also Minorities
Hitler, Adolf, 103
Hobby, Oveta Culp, 40, 68, 71-73
Hobby, William Pettus, 71, 72
Holt, Marjorie, 27, 73-75
Holt-Gramm Amendment, 144
Holtzman, Elizabeth, 13, 67, 76-80
Hood College, 26
Hoover, J. Edgar, 87
Housing, 13, 20, 35, 37, 75, 115
Housing and Community Development Act, 118
Housing and Urban Development, Department of (HUD), 19, 20, 61, 62, 68, 69, 70
Houston, University of, 39
Houston *Post*, 71, 72
Howard University, 63
Howland, Marguerite McClure, 44
Hufstedler, Seth, 80
Hufstedler, Shirley, 80-82
Hulin, Frank, 125
Hull House, 120
Humphrey, George M., 71
Humphrey, Hubert H., 4, 5, 13, 29, 82, 83
Humphrey, Muriel Buck, 82-83
Humphrey-Hawkins Full-Employment Act, 82, 118
Hyde Amendment, 78

Illinois, 22, 23, 24, 31, 32
Immigration, 78
Impeachment, 76-77, 84
India, 104
Indian Affairs
  Bureau of, 60
  Colorado Commission on, 35
Indiana, 91, 92
Indians, North American
  See Native Americans

Interdepartmental Task Force on Women, 155
Interior, Department of the, 60, 113
Interior and Insular Affairs Committee (House), 21, 60, 113, 141
International Confederation of Free Trade Unions, 122
International Ladies' Garment Workers' Union (ILGWU), 37
International Relations Committee (House), 32, 108
International Women's Year, 2, 8, 66, 78, 105, 155
  National Commission on the Observance of, 2, 66, 78
Iron Curtain, 6
Irving, Leonard, 149
Israel, 78
Italy, 104-105

Jackson, Henry "Scoop," 53
Jacobs, Andrew, 91-92
Jane Addams Peace Association, 38
Jeannette Rankin Brigade, 128
Jeffries, Jim, 92
Jewry, 1, 2, 16, 78
John Birch Society, 20
John Carroll University, 117
John F. Kennedy School of Government (Harvard), 159
Johnson, Lady Bird, 13
Johnson, Lyndon, 6, 10, 12, 13, 20, 38, 50, 56, 62, 81, 84, 113, 123
Jordan, Barbara, 40, 76, 83-86
Judiciary Committee (House), 56, 66, 76, 77, 84
Juilliard School of Music, 4, 94
Justice, Department of, 19, 69, 77

Kahn, Florence Prag, 86-88
Kahn, Julius, 87
Kansas, 88, 89, 91, 92
  State University, 91
  University of, 88
  Women's Political Caucus, 89
Kassebaum, Nancy Landon, 88-90, 91
Kean, Tom, 45
Keating, Kenneth, 157
Kennedy, Edward, 22
Kennedy, John F., 4, 6, 12, 13, 24, 50, 60, 94, 115, 122, 123
Kennedy, Robert, 53
Kennedy-Corman-Griffiths Bill, 57
Kentucky, 95
Keys, Martha, 91-93
Keys, Samuel, 91
Khrushchev, Nikita, 139
King, Martin Luther, 152
Kitchin, Paul, 125
Kjeldahl, Bill, 93-94

Knutson, Andrew, 93-94
Knutson, Coya, 93-95
Kopp, Quentin, 42
Korea, 11, 139
Koreagate, 77
Kreps, Clifton, 96
Kreps, Juanita, 58, 95-98
Krupsak, Mary Anne, 98-100
Kunin, Madeleine May, 101

Labor, Department of, 56, 104, 118, 119, 120, 122
Labor (legislation), 19, 20-21, 37, 67, 82, 85, 96, 104, 112, 119, 122-23, 127, 138, 145
See also AFL-CIO; Amalgamated Clothing Workers of America; International Confederation of Free Trade Unions; International Ladies' Garment Workers' Union
LaGuardia, Fiorello, 87
Lamm, Richard, 34
Landon, Alfred Mossman, 88, 89
Langen, Odin, 94
League of Women Voters, 4, 29, 71
Liberia, 38
Libraries (legislation), 54
Library of Congress, 105, 125
Lindsay, John, 1, 76, 77, 79
Linfield College, 54
Lloyd, Monty, 18
Louisiana, 12, 14
Lourdes Academy, 117
Luce, Clare Boothe, 7, 37, 44, 101, 102-107, 143, 156
Luce, Henry Robinson, 103, 105
Luxembourg, 61, 62
Lynch, Robert, 100
Lyndon B. Johnson School of Public Affairs, 84, 86

Macalester College, 4
McCall, Tom, 54
McCarthy, Eugene, 1, 4, 5, 37, 139, 159
McCarthy, Joseph, 139
McCarthy, Kathryn O'Loughlin, 91
McCloskey, Paul, 10
McCone Commission, 19-20
McGovern, George, 20, 29, 38, 39, 91, 92
McGrady, Edward, 120
Mack, Russell, 60
McMullen, Jay, 23
Maine, 137, 138, 139, 140, 143, 144
    University of, 144
Maraziti, Joseph, 108
Maritime Bulk Act, 14
Marshall, George, 72
Marshall Plan, 139
Martin, Joseph W., 65
Maryland, 25, 26, 27, 74, 75, 109, 110, 145, 146
    University of, 109

Massachusetts, 65, 66, 67
    University of, 101
Mass transit, 99, 100
Maui, 112
Mead, Margaret, 40
Medicaid, 2, 46, 78
Medicare, 78, 89
Mentally handicapped, 19
Merchant Marine Act, 14
Merchant Marine and Fisheries Committee (House), 150
Merritt, Paul, 85
Meyner, Helen Stevenson, 107-109
Meyner, Robert, 107, 108
Michigan, 56, 57, 58
    State University, 33
    University of, 56, 57, 88
Middle Income Housing Act, 13
Migratory workers, 36, 37
Mikulski, Barbara Ann, 12-13, 27, 40, 109-111, 117
Mikulski Commission, 110
Military Affairs Committee, 87, 104
Milk, Harvey, 42
Mills, Wilbur, 57
Mills College, 129
Mines, Bureau of, 60
Mink, Gwendolyn, 112
Mink, John, 112
Mink, Patsy, 40, 111-14, 134
Minnesota, 4, 5, 6, 82, 83, 93, 94
    University of, 133
Minorities, 1, 19, 20-21, 24, 29, 30, 31, 32, 61, 63, 80, 84, 85, 95, 97, 152, 153
Missouri, 149, 151
    University of, 57, 92
Moltkae-Hansen, Olav, 147
Mondale, Walter, 159
Montana, 126, 127
    University of, 126
Morse, Wayne, 105, 127
Moscone, George, 42
Moses, George H., 87
Moses, Robert, 119
Mt. Holyoke, 50, 119, 120
Moynihan, Daniel Patrick, 2
Murphy, George, 10
Myerson, Bess, 79

Nader, Ralph, 130
National Advisory Council on Women, 2, 40, 83
National Association for the Advancement of Colored People (NAACP), 20, 32
National Bureau of Standards, 96
National Center for Urban and Ethnic Affairs, 109
National Commission of Community Health Services, 141
National Committee on Household Employment, 123
National Council for Prevention of War, 127

National Education Defense Act, 94
National Federation of Women's Clubs, 156
National health plan, 51, 57, 72, 91
National Homestead Act, 75
National Labor Relations Board, 37, 133
National League of United Latin American Citizens Conference, 155
National League of Women Voters, 4
National Organization for Women (NOW), 56
National Parks Service, 60
National Recovery Act, 118-19
National Science Foundation, 149
National Technical Information Service, 96
National Women's Conference (Houston), 2, 99
National Women's Party, 102
National Youth Administration, 37
Native Americans, 29, 35, 60, 94, 104
    See also Minorities
Naval Affairs Committee, 138
Nazism, 4, 36, 78
Nebraska, 141-42
    University of, 141
Nehru, Prime Minister, 104
Neuberger, Maurine Brown, 114-17
Neuberger, Richard, 114-15
New Deal, 4, 36, 103, 118, 157
New Jersey, 44, 45, 107, 108
New Mexico, University of, 80
New School for Social Research, 44
New York, 1, 2, 3, 28, 29, 30, 47, 48, 49, 76, 77, 79, 98-99, 100, 119, 156
New York City Summer Food Program, 77
New York Consumers' League, 119
New York Council of Organization for War Service, 119
New York State Industrial Commission, 119
New York Stock Exchange, Board, 96
Nixon, Richard, 7, 8, 11, 37-38, 56, 66, 74, 77, 84, 115, 130, 139, 150
North Atlantic Treaty Organization (NATO), 5, 54, 105, 135, 139, 154
North Carolina, 125
North Dakota, 94
Nuclear Regulatory Commission, 131
Nursing/Nurses, 15, 16, 17, 142, 143

Oakar, Mary Rose, 117-18
Oberlin College, 108
Occupational Safety and Health Agency (OSHA), 26
Oceans and International Environmental and Scientific Affairs, Bureau of, 113, 130
Ohio, 15, 16, 17, 117, 118
Oil company profits, 78
Oregon, 53, 54, 114, 115, 116
    Dunes National Seashore Conservation Project, 115
    University of, 53, 54, 115
Oxford University, 69

Pacific Science Center, 129-30
Pacifism, 127-28
Palestine, 16
Panama Canal treaties, 82
Parent Teachers Association (PTA), 18, 54, 145
Patterson, John, 152
Paul, Alice, 102
Payne, Henry, 15
Payne, Oliver Hazard, 15
Peace Corps, 108
Pearson, James, 88
Pennsylvania, University of, 120
Pentagon, 133, 135, 144
Perkins, Frances, 40, 68, 118-21
Peterson, Esther, 116, 121-24, 159
Peterson, Oliver, 122
Pfeiffer, Jane Cahill, 95
Philanthropy, Conference on National, 41
Pick-Sloan Missouri Basin Project, 141-42
Planned Parenthood, 133
Political participation, women's, 8, 27, 40, 50, 57, 113, 135, 136, 148, 149-50, 157
Post Office and Civil Service Committee, 48, 136, 138, 145
Potsdam Conference, 104
Poverty (legislation), 16, 20-21, 29, 32, 54, 57
    See also Welfare
Pratt, Eliza Jane, 125-26
President's Task Force on Women Business Owners, 96, 158
Price, Delores, 152
Price, "Shorty," 152
Price Control Act, 37
Princeton University, 70
Prohibition, 87
Proposition 9, 43
Proposition 13, 42-43
Proxmire, William, 63, 68-69
Public Leadership Education Network (PLEN), 40
Public Works and Transportation Committee (House), 48
Public Works Committee, 18
Public works projects, 60, 87, 91, 108, 157

Racism, 19, 113
Radcliffe College, 77, 116
Rankin, Jeannette, 87, 126-29, 133
Rankin, John, 126
Rankin, Olive Pickering, 126
Rape, 19, 78
    National Center for the Prevention and Control of, 13
    Victims Privacy Act, 117
Ray, Dixy Lee, 129-32
Rayburn, Sam, 125
Reagan, Ronald, 10, 103
Red Cross, 26, 108

Refugees, 11, 13, 46
   U.S. Committee for, 105
Republican National Committee, 7
Republican National Convention, 7, 8, 16, 74, 104, 157
Republican Policy Committee, 142
Republican Study Committee, 75
Ribicoff, Abraham, 50
Rice University, 72
Richardson, Elliot, 69
Robinson, Patricia, 147
Rockefeller, Nelson, 100
Roosevelt, Eleanor, 38, 72, 120, 122
Roosevelt, Franklin, 4, 36, 37, 68, 88, 103, 118-19, 157
Roy, William, 89
Rupli, Dan, 25
Rural Development, Presidential Task Force on, 141
Russell, Bertrand, 44
Russia, 104, 133, 153
   See also Soviet Union

Salk vaccine program, 72
SALT II (Strategic Arms Limitation Treaty), 41, 89, 105
   Conference for Women on, 41
Sarasin, Ronald A., 51
Saxbe, William, 69
Schlafly, Phyllis, 46
Schroeder, Jim, 135
Schroeder, Patricia Scott, 12, 13, 26, 67, 118, 133-37, 145
Science and Aeronautics Committee (House), 157
Science and Technology Committee (House), 18
Science and Transportation Committee (Senate), 89
Scott, David, 42
Securities and Exchange Commission, 69
Segregation, 15, 53, 152, 153
Shadegg, Stephen, 102
Sheppard-Towner Bill, 127
Sierra Club, 43
Skidmore College, 159
Small Business Act, 13
Small Business Committee (House), 46, 144
Smith, Al, 119
Smith, Clyde, 138
Smith, Margaret Chase, 137-40, 149
Smith, Virginia Dodd, 141-42
Smith College, 147
Smith-Connally Bill, 138
Snowe, Olympia, 13, 48, 143-44
Snowe, Peter, 143
Snyder, Ann Clare, 102
Social, Humanitarian, and Cultural Committee, 11

Social Security, 2, 85, 92
   Act, 37, 78, 119
   benefits, 48, 56-57, 67, 72, 76, 92, 134, 138
Solid Rock League, 154
Solomon, Philip, 115
South Africa, 6
South Carolina, 147, 148
Southeast Asia, 2, 6, 67, 108, 128
Southern California, University of, 19
Soviet-American Women's Conference (Moscow), 38
Soviet Union, 5, 11, 16, 104
   See also Russia
Space exploration, 157
Spellman, Gladys Noon, 27, 145-47
Spelman College, 40
Spouses Club, 92
Stanford University, 43, 53, 69, 80, 129
State, Department of, 5, 6, 11, 19, 113, 130, 157
Status of Women, President's Commission on the, 122
Steele, Robert A., 51
Steel Worker's Caucus, 118
Steers, Newton, 14
Steinem, Gloria, 40
Stephens College, 40
Stevens, Mary, 44
Stevenson, Adlai, 108
Stevenson, Nancy, 101, 147-48
Stevenson, Norman Williams, 147
Stratton, Samuel, 99
Strauss, Lewis L., 139
Suffrage, 127, 128
Sullivan, John B., 149
Sullivan, Leonor, 148-51
Supreme Court (U.S.), 53, 55-56, 80, 112, 154
Sweden, 122

Taxation, 2, 7, 37, 46, 99, 155
Tennessee, 18
Texas, 7, 8, 39, 41, 71, 72, 84, 85, 154
   University of, 39, 71, 154
Thailand, 13
Tonkin Bay Resolution, 127
Trieste dispute, 105
Trinity College, 101
Truman, Harry, 4, 5, 37, 120
Tubman, William, 38
Tuchman, Barbara, 40
Tulane University, 13
Turner, Mary, 32
Tuskegee Institute, 153

Un-American Activities Committee (House), 37
Unesco (United Nations Educational, Scientific and Cultural Organization), 54

Index

United Democrats of Congress, 18
United Nations, 2, 6, 11, 37, 104, 105, 155
United Nations Mid-Decade Conference on Women (Copenhagen), 155
U.S. Trust Territory of the Pacific, 113
Urban Development Action Grants (UDAG), 62
Urban League, 32, 43
Ursuline College, 117
Utah, 122

Vanik, Charles, 17
Vanity Fair, 102, 103
Vassar College, 7, 39, 41
Vermont, University of, 101
Veterans Affairs Committee (House), 28, 66
Vietnam War, 1, 2, 6, 10, 60, 66, 76, 85, 113, 128, 139
Vogue, 44-45, 102
Volpe, John, 65
Voting Rights Act (1965), 1

Wage and Price Stability, Council on, 8
Wagner, Robert, 98, 119
Wallace, George, 151, 152, 153
Wallace, Henry, 5
Wallace, Lurleen, 151-53
Walsh, Thomas J., 127
War Department, 72
Waring, Joseph I., 147
Washington, 59, 60, 130, 131
    University of, 59, 129
Watergate, 69, 77, 84
Watts riots, 19, 20
WAVES (Women Accepted for Volunteer Emergency Service), 138
Ways and Means Committee, 57, 91
Weddington, Sarah, 40, 154-56, 159

Weis, Jessica, 156-58
Welfare, 57, 100, 144
    See also Poverty (legislation)
Wells College, 39, 40, 41
Western Reserve University, 17
Wexler, Anne, 158-59
White, Dan, 42
White, Wallace, 138
White House Conference on Balanced National Growth and Public Policy, 99
White House News on Women, 155
White House Preservation Committee, 105
Widow(ers), legislation for, 56-57, 136
Williams, G. Mennen, 57
Willkie, Wendell, 103, 119
Wilson, Paul Caldwell, 119
Wilzak, Adele, 109
Women and Employment Conference (Paris), 155
Women's Army Corps (WACs), 71, 72
Women's Bureau, 120, 122
Women's International League for Peace and Freedom, 38
Women's Political Caucus, 39, 91, 141
Women's Program, Office of the, 8
Women's Research and Education Institute (WREI), 57
Women Strike for Peace, 1
Works Progress Administration, 36
World Food Conference (Rome), 8
World War I, 45, 127
World War II, 5, 6, 15, 72, 127

Yale University, 69, 70
Yalta Conference, 104
Young Democrats, 26, 112, 133

Zellerbach Commission, 6